About the Authors

Marla Bonds, Psy.D., currently works as a school psychologist in the Cherry Creek School District and maintains a private practice specializing in the treatment of adolescents and their families. Marla began working with adolescents in 1984 as a Special Education Teacher of students with emotional handicaps and conduct disorders, both in day treatment settings and in the Cherry Creek Schools. She has been involved in the development and implementation of a number of innovative programs for "at-risk" and emotionally troubled youth. In 1995 she earned her doctorate in clinical psychology from the California School of Professional Psychology in Berkeley, California. Following her degree, and her heart, Marla returned to the Cherry Creek School district to continue her work with adolescents and the systems surrounding them.

Sally Stoker, M.S.W., has been a career educator for the past 25 years. Her first 20 years in education were spent as a classroom elementary teacher where she developed a special interest in teaching students prosocial skills including conflict mediation and peer counseling. After receiving her M.S.W. from the University of Denver, Sally has worked as a middle school counselor in the Cherry Creek (Colorado) School District for the past five years. She is currently a member of the steering committee that has piloted the Bully-Proofing Program in her own middle school and has firsthand knowledge of how to implement the program successfully in a large, suburban middle school. Sally has a strong belief that focusing on the potential power of the caring majority of students is the most effective way to create a safe, caring environment in our schools.

Acknowledgments

We wish to express our sincere gratitude to the entire community of Prairie Middle School who participated in the development of this middle school program from its inception. Our special thanks to the original Bully-Proofing Cadre including Paul Eppard, Becky Furhmans, Brooke Gregory, Dale Husk, Katie Plumley and Berta Trine who generously contributed their creativity, hard work, and dedication. We also want to thank Sammye Wheeler, our principal, whose consistent support made this program possible.

We acknowledge and thank the Cherry Creek School District for its encouragement of innovative program development and for creating a climate in which our project could evolve. We appreciate their support of this program.

Most importantly, we offer our gratitude to the authors of the original *Bully-Proofing Your School: A Comprehensive Approach for Elementary Schools*—Carla Garrity, Kathryn Jens, William Porter, Nancy Sager, and Cam Short-Camilli. This middle school program is an extension of their innovative, cutting-edge model for creating caring school communities. To that end, some of the material in our book has been adapted from their original work. Their generous support and guidance has been a testament to their love for children and deep desire for all students to feel safe and cared for at school.

Contents

Chapter One

Introduction and Overview

Violence

There is a form of violence in our schools today that is chronic, pervasive, and harmful to a large number of our students. It is called bullying. Not as easily identified as the overt, violent acts that make headline news, bullying is a more subtle form of violence that, if undetected and untreated, is far more damaging to a greater number of our students. In an environment where bullying has created a climate of fear and anxiety, students pay a terrible price physically, emotionally, and academically.

Bullying behaviors are prevalent in our schools today and include physical, verbal, emotional, and sexual behaviors both overt and covert, direct and indirect. Bullying occurs when "a person is exposed, repeatedly and over time, to negative actions on the part of one or more persons" (Olweus, 1991). The bullying dynamic can include boys or girls, individuals or groups, but it always involves an imbalance of power with one individual or group chronically victimizing another individual or group and exhibiting little or no remorse for the victims. And it is not only the direct victims of bullying who feel unsafe. All students who know about and witness these incidents are deeply affected as well. When students observe incidences of bullying behaviors happening daily and conclude that adults either do not notice or choose to ignore these situations, their sense of security in the school environment and in their own well-being is shaken, and their availability for learning is significantly compromised.

There have been numerous studies on the problem of bullying in the schools, both in the United States and in other parts of the world. A summary of the literature supports the alarming fact that from 15–20% of students can expect to experience some form of bullying during their school careers (Batsche & Knoff, 1994). In the United States, one study involved asking students in the rural Midwest about incidences of bullying in their own school careers. The startling results showed that 80% of high school students reported having been bullied in school while 90% of fourth through eighth graders also reported having been bullied during their school years (Hoover, Oliver, & Hazler, 1992; Hoover, Oliver, & Thompson, 1993). Students want us to know that bullying is a serious problem that can no longer be ignored.

Adults are as affected by bullying behaviors and the resulting climate of fear as are students. Adults experience incidents of bullying and harassment on the roads, in public places, and in their workplaces. And violence in teachers' workplaces—the schools—is on the increase. For example:

◆ Over 6,000 teachers are threatened annually and over 200 are physically injured by students on school grounds. (Walker & Gresham, 1997)

◆ In the 1991 school year, 28% of public school teachers were verbally abused, 15% were threatened with injury, and 3% were physically attacked. (Johnston, O'Malley, and Bachman, 1993)

◆ In a 1993 American Teacher survey one-third of teachers said that both teachers and students were more anxious about going to school because of worries about violence. (Harris & Associates, 1993)

The cases of teachers being physically attacked or threatened are dramatic and rare, but the fear of violence in general and the increase in national school place violence contribute to the perception on the part of teachers that schools are not the safe havens they were once assumed to be. And even though most teachers may not have to deal with direct physical threats to themselves or their students, they do report feeling frustrated and stressed about the increasing amount of valuable time they are required to spend dealing with students' disruptive behaviors.

The consequences of bullying are serious. We can no longer dismiss it as innocent teasing or harmless play. Victims of bullying report both physical and emotional symptoms, and demonstrate an inability to focus on schoolwork as well as lowered school attendance. Twenty-two percent of fourth through eighth graders report having academic difficulties because of peer abuse and bullying (Beane, 1999). When students are asked to describe how they have been affected by school bullying, they report such symptoms as nervousness, worrying, scared feelings in the stomach, headaches, and tiredness (Rigby, 1998). All of these complaints directly interfere with a student's ability to learn effectively. Tragically,

In schools, teachers find themselves spending increasing amounts of time attending to students' disruptive and angry outbursts, interpersonal conflicts, and off-task behavior, or worse … . Although teachers are expected to concentrate on teaching academics, they are finding that student behavior prevents them from doing so; eventually it drives many of them from the teaching profession.

(Elliott, 1998, p. 296)

in the most extreme cases, bullying has been named as the cause of both child suicide and homicide, as victims desperately search for a way to end the turmoil.

A Book Specifically Designed for Middle School

The research done on bullying in the United States shows that students report bullying is most serious in middle school and doesn't decline in severity and frequency until the high school years. The outdated belief that bullying behaviors are "just a normal part of adolescence" is both ignorant and dangerous and has resulted in adults looking the other way instead of acknowledging the problem. As a result, bullying patterns can be firmly entrenched by the time students reach middle school with bullies continuing to gain and abuse their power and victims experiencing increased hopelessness. Bullying needs to be addressed head-on in the middle school environment, where so many students are at risk.

There are many cultural reasons why bullying can become so intense during the middle school years. The average preadolescent and adolescent age child entering middle school today has already witnessed 100,000 acts of simulated violence on TV and in the movies, according to estimates by researchers in the field (Lister, 1995). This repeated witnessing of violent acts can result in a desensitization to violence in general, and a subtle acceptance of a certain mean-spiritedness toward each other that can seem—especially to vulnerable adolescents—like the "popular" way to behave. Also, in an individualistic culture such as ours that embraces the belief of survival of the fittest and rewards the risk-taker, the bully can too easily feel justified in using his or her power to dominate and intimidate others. These factors, in combination with a culture that encourages an individual to solve his own problems without asking for help from others, can combine to create a fertile ground for bullying behaviors.

Complicating these cultural issues are the very specific developmental needs and tasks of the adolescent. Bullying, a harmful dynamic at any stage, takes on even more potential for harm in the middle school environment, where students are experimenting with several important developmental tasks. The adolescent's struggle with identity, the power of the group and "group think," and the task of sorting out issues of adult authority all challenge the adolescent to learn how to use power appropriately and to maintain his or her own identity and beliefs in the context of the group. Without guidance and access to the skills to successfully accomplish these tasks, the adolescent's search for power and identity can take a negative direction and result in antisocial behaviors such as bullying.

The good news is that middle school students are up to the challenge. In fact, just as the developmental stage of adolescence can intensify bullying, it also provides the perfect context for educating students about how to make themselves and their schools safe through anti-bullying efforts. Adolescents are ready and eager to explore the more abstract concepts of power and influence and are enthusiastic about learning how to manage and direct their own power for the common good. They welcome talking with adults who are sympathetic to their needs and concerns and who understand the very real pressures facing them daily. Including middle school students in the discussion of how to make their schools safe and secure allows them to experiment with their own power in productive ways that benefit everyone.

Bully-Proofing Your School: A Comprehensive Approach for Middle Schools is a comprehensive school safety program designed specifically for middle school students. It is written for all middle school level professionals who are interested in using our greatest resource—our students—to make the changes necessary in order for our schools to be the safe and nurturing environments they are meant to be.

Basic Concepts of the Program

Bully-Proofing Your School: A Comprehensive Approach for Middle Schools is a bully prevention program based on four main concepts which are essential to its success:

- ◆ The program is designed as a systemic, comprehensive program
- ◆ The main focus is on climate change
- ◆ The program teaches skills and strategies to avoid victimization
- ◆ The emphasis is on developing the caring majority

1. The program is designed as a systemic, comprehensive program.

Researchers agree that the most effective school safety programs are programs that are comprehensive in nature and which direct attention to all systems in the school that impact the school environment. In their discussion of what makes school safety programs effective, Batsche and Knoff (1994) state: "The environment will change and the climate improve only when school systems choose to develop and implement a *comprehensive* plan designed to teach prosocial behavior, to limit aggressive behavior, and to teach skills that promote positive interactions between students." In the book *Violence in American Schools*, the establishment of a safe school plan is described as a "long-term, systematic, and comprehensive practice." (Elliott, 1998).

Bully-Proofing Your School is designed as a wraparound program which provides the framework for a school-wide safety effort. All members of the school community, adults and students, commit to a nontolerance policy about bullying and to creating a caring community. School rules and expectations are established that are understood and enforced throughout the community. All systems in the school are addressed from administration to transportation, and specific steps for implementing the school-wide program are included. Implementing the program school-wide is ideal. However, it is important for each school to assess its own needs and resources and to adapt the program accordingly, implementing only certain systems at a time as resources dictate.

2. The main focus is on climate change.

Bully-Proofing Your School is a program designed to create a positive, prosocial school climate that feels safe and secure for all members of the school community. This requires broad efforts to change the overall school culture rather than only focusing on specific skills. The commitment is to the gradual process of cultural change as members of the school community work together to create a safe school environment.

3. The program teaches skills and strategies to avoid victimization.

Included in the program are the specific skills and strategies students need both to avoid victimization and to help others. These are practical tools that are developmentally appropriate for middle school students and which emphasize the important concepts of empathy, taking a stand, and creative problem solving. A common vocabulary is emphasized throughout the curriculum to be used by all members of the school community.

4. Emphasis is on developing the caring majority.

A unique component of this program is that it focuses on the 85% of students in a school who are neither bullies nor victims, but who are in the role of bystanders and make up the silent majority. These are the students who generally have well-developed prosocial skills, but do not know how or are afraid to reclaim the power from the bullies. The *Bully-Proofing* program teaches this silent majority the skills they need to become the caring majority that holds the power and takes responsibility for making the school safe.

Overview of the Contents

Bully-Proofing Your School: A Comprehensive Approach for Middle Schools offers a complete plan for the implementation of a school-wide safety program for middle schools. The information and materials included have all been written to match the developmental needs and tasks of middle school students.

◆ **Chapter One: Introduction and Overview**

This chapter discusses bullying as a form of violence that is prevalent in schools today. It includes information about the seriousness of the problem for adolescents in middle schools. The basic concepts of the program are outlined.

◆ **Chapter Two: Developmental Issues of Adolescence**

The physical, cognitive, social, and emotional developmental issues of the adolescent years are discussed in the context of their impact on the bullying dynamic in middle school. The differences between bullying in elementary and secondary schools are described.

◆ **Chapter Three: The Basics of Bullying**

In Chapter Three the dynamic of bullying is explained and the roles and characteristics of the three main groups—bullies, victims, and bystanders—are described in detail. Specific discussions about sexual and racial harassment are included.

◆ **Chapter Four: Establishing a School-Wide Program**

This chapter outlines the information necessary to successfully implement the school-wide *Bully-Proofing* program. The basic concepts and elements of the program are described in detail with specific planning suggestions and a step-by-step plan for implementation is outlined.

◆ **Chapter Five: Faculty Training**

A detailed description of a full day faculty training workshop is included along with materials and worksheets. A section on important issues to be addressed with the staff is also included.

◆ **Chapter Six: Sixth Grade Curriculum**

This chapter includes the sixth grade curriculum for the *Bully-Proofing* program which consists of five classroom lessons and additional classwork and homework assignments. The lessons focus on the basics of bullying. Important information about the facilitation and scheduling of classroom groups is included at the beginning of the chapter.

◆ **Chapter Seven: Seventh Grade Curriculum**

The complete seventh grade curriculum is outlined and includes lessons which address the concepts of caring behaviors, empathy, inclusion, groups, taking a stand, sexual harassment, creative problem solving, and levels of risk taking. Refer to Chapter Six for information on facilitation and scheduling.

◆ **Chapter Eight: Eighth Grade Curriculum**

This chapter includes the five lessons of the eighth grade curriculum as well as additional classwork and homework assignments. The theme of the eighth grade curriculum is leadership, and the lessons focus on the characteristics and styles of positive leadership in a caring community. Refer to Chapter Six for information on facilitation and scheduling.

◆ **Chapter Nine: Interventions**

Chapter Nine provides strategies for working with bullies, victims, and parents and includes practical and workable ideas for interventions. Interventions for working with bus drivers and with new students are also included.

♦ **Chapter Ten: Maintaining the Caring Community**

This chapter summarizes the most important points about how to maintain the caring community once the rules, expectations, and skills have been taught.

♦ **Resource Guide**

Recommended resources about bullying are listed for teachers, students, and parents.

Chapter Two

Adolescent Development

Adolescence has been described as the tumultuous, stormy, roller-coaster years, as well as an identity crisis period, a time of "raging hormones," and a critical phase of life. Indeed, adolescence is a developmental period characterized by dramatic changes in physical appearance, cognitive ability, social status, and independence. In fact, the rate of physical growth that adolescents experience is surpassed only by infants during their first year of life. It is understandably a stressful period during which coping mechanisms can become frazzled and overwhelmed. It is also a sacred period, forming the bridge between childhood and adulthood. This chapter will briefly summarize the major developmental challenges of this exciting period of life and how they impact the bullying dynamics in middle school.

Physical Development

The changes of adolescence commonly begin with the onset of puberty. Dormant hormones, which were present at birth, begin to emerge; and as the levels of particular hormones increase, secondary sex characteristics evolve and body size increases. Girls generally experience puberty between the ages of 8 and 18; for boys it occurs between the ages of 9 and 19. The age of the onset of puberty, normative patterns, and speed of maturation are quite varied. However, girls usually begin and end their pubertal changes two years prior to boys. The most observable changes for girls occur over an average of four years (Offer and Boxer, 1991).

Characteristic physical changes include breast development, body and facial hair, and voice change. Some youth will experience physical growth spurts of four to six inches in a few months' time. At times growth in one area will not match the growth of other areas, leaving the young teen with disproportionate body features for a period of time. These dramatic physical transformations are likely to provoke changes in the adolescents' self-image, affect their social status, and alter the expectations held by peers and significant adults in their lives. In fact, studies have shown that early maturing boys tend to be more muscular, which leads to increased strength, athletic ability, and social status. Conversely, girls who undergo early pubescence often experience lowered self-esteem due to weight gain and societal pressure for thinness (Peterson et al, 1996).

Cognitive Growth and Moral Development

The onset of puberty ignites expanding cognitive abilities which in turn drive the adolescents toward independence from authority and greater autonomy. The primary intellectual change experienced by young teens is an increased ability to think abstractly. Jean Piaget (1965) termed this phase the Formal (abstract) Phase of development in which adolescents develop hypothetical-deductive reasoning ability. During this time, adolescents become capable of "meta" cognitions or thinking about thinking (Kuhn, 1991). Additionally, adolescents develop the capacity to consider the perspectives and viewpoints of others including views that are contrary to their own (Keating and Clark, 1980). The result is an increased ability to empathize with others, which leads to shifts in the teen's moral structures.

In the elementary school years, moral judgments are based on those of the authority figure. The concepts of right and wrong are accepted as truth, not based on any inherent understanding, and are primarily seen as rigid and unalterable. During early adolescence (approximately age ten) Piaget (1965) and Kohlberg (1981) agree that moral development becomes more flexible and the issues of right and wrong are pondered for their intrinsic moral sense. Because of this growing awareness of a more flexible world where "truth" has many meanings, teens begin to disagree with authority. They typically need time to discuss reasons for decisions and to develop their own internal decisions regarding right and wrong.

To complicate the picture, two seemingly contrasting things occur during adolescence. Young teens experience an egocentricity as well as the capacity for greater empathy. This egocentricity during the early years of adolescence leads teens toward a greater internal focus. They frequently feel like the center of attention and maintain a perspective that their feelings and thoughts are unique. The egocentricity gradually lessens through adolescence as their expanding perceptions and realities become stable and more objective. The striking contrast between the adolescent's egocentricity and empathy development can make life confusing for young teens and the adults who work with them.

Identity Development—Peer Affiliation

Adolescence is a time of increased independence from parents with increased focus on peers, friendships, group membership, and identity. As young adolescents pull away from security and dependence on their parents, more emphasis is placed on friendships that will eventually come to provide nearly the same relational intimacy they had with their parents. With this primary shift, young adolescents spend a great deal of their time and energy making friends, keeping friends, and understanding what makes friendship work. Membership in groups or cliques is common and plays an important part in the identity formation process. Teens will typically join a group of same-gender peers whom they deem similar in ideas as well as external characteristics. Membership in these groups provides teens with social integration skills as well as reassurance of their worth through social validation (Cotterell, 1996). Young adolescents become very focused on belonging, being included, and being the "same" as their identified group or clique. Worries about whether they will be invited or included in events become a central concern. To risk being "different" from the group is to risk possible rejection from the group. Membership in cliques changes occasionally and can create a great deal of stress for the "left out" group member. Importantly, many adolescents will identify with a number of groups or cliques, for instance, involvement with Boy Scouts, athletics, or music groups in addition to daily cafeteria/classroom groups. This can serve the adolescent in developing a more flexible identity as well as building resiliency against upheaval or power plays within one particular group. The prominence of group involvement begins to wane in high school and friendships often expand to include more opposite-gender peers.

Self-Esteem

The self-esteem of the adolescent is necessarily shifting and stretching to meet the continual, diverse changes of the teen experience. There are a number of studies regarding changes in self-esteem during adolescence. The majority of these studies agree that adolescents experience an increase in self-consciousness, decreased confidence in their academic ability, instability of self-image, and more frequent depressed moods (Eccles, 1991; Simmons, Rosenberg and Rosenberg, 1973). Importantly, declines in self-esteem have been related to the move from elementary to middle school rather than being age specific. For example, Simmons and her colleagues reported that girls who began junior high in seventh grade evidenced a decline in self-esteem that was not matched by seventh grade girls attending a K–8 school.

The most extreme changes in self-esteem for adolescents in the grades 5–8 occur consistently in the areas of social and physical competence and satisfaction with their bodies. As previously noted, girls who experience earlier and more advanced pubertal development are found to have poorer body image. Weight has been found to be a primary contributor to a girl's self-image. Offer and Boxer (1991), conducted a large study of secondary students and found that two-thirds of female respondents were preoccupied with weight and dieting. The rapid changes in body size and proportion, combined with cultural pressures to be tall and thin lead many young adolescent girls, and some boys, to develop eating disorders.

Racial and Cultural Identity Development

Racial and cultural identity development is another significant task for adolescents. This challenge can be particularly difficult for young teens who are a minority within their community or school and when the racial or cultural difference is a visual distinction. The intensity, magnitude, and impact of this development will be affected by a number of factors: the individual's racial and cultural background, the historical experiences of their predecessors within the given society, the racial and cultural composition and attitudes within their school and community, the individual's self-esteem, identification with parents or other role models, and the level of acculturation of their family experienced immigration. Given all these factors it is amazing we can make any generalizations about this complicated process. However, researchers have proposed various stages of ethnic identity development. A common theory presents four stages (Tse, 1999).

Stage 1—Ethnic Unawareness   Individuals are unaware of their minority status primarily due to limited contact with other ethnic groups. This stage is usually a short period before the child attends school.

Stage 2—Ethnic Ambivalence   In this stage, individuals are seemingly ambivalent or may distance themselves from their own group and adopt many of the behaviors of the dominant group. This stage usually coincides with childhood and early adolescence.

Stage 3—Ethnic Emergence   In this stage which usually begins in adolescence and continues into early adulthood, individuals realize that joining with the dominant group is not wholly possible and ineffectual in their self-esteem development. Through this realization, ethnic minority adolescents will experiment with different group associations. Frequently these associations lead adolescents to develop friendships and group membership with their own ethnic group. In middle school these groups can provide an important source of security and group identification.

Stage 4—Ethnic Identity Incorporation   The final formal stage occurs throughout adulthood and entails the resolution of many of the individual's ethnic identity conflicts. Within this stage the person joins the ethnic minority American group.

Racial and cultural identity development may best be viewed as a continually developing state which shifts and changes based on a multiplicity of individual and environmental factors. Overall, racial identity develops through racial awareness. And racial awareness is facilitated by racial socialization.

Racial socialization can be confusing or disconcerting to persons who don't understand it as a necessary part of identity formation. School personnel can become overly concerned when students align themselves with same-race peers. This can be misinterpreted as a sign of racial disharmony within the school climate. Notably, for some ethnicities, racial identity is second only to gender identity in its importance in terms of the ways in which ethnic minority persons view the world and in their self-concept (Jaret, Reitzes, 1999). In fact, in several studies, racial socialization and racial identity have been found to buffer African American adolescents against negative and stressful environmental conditions and help them overcome the stigma of pejorative social stereotypes (Miller, 1999). In this way a strong racial identity can be seen as contributing to a teen's resiliency. Given this level of impact, the racial and cultural developmental process needs to be recognized and embraced in spite of its complicated nature.

Sexual Identity Development

Sexual identity development is a strong concern for adolescents as their bodies and minds prepare for the sexual capacity and expectations of adulthood. While early adolescents may still be seeking contact with the opposite gender by hair pulling, tugging on backpacks, the casual slug in the arm, or taking pencils, the older adolescent will be asserting more direct sexual behaviors. During this explorative and often insecure time, teens will push boundaries and test limits regarding their own and others' sexuality. They will have numerous decisions to make regarding who and how to date, for how long, and the limits of physical and emotional intimacy. Many teens will attempt to defend against their own sexual identity confusion by harassing peers with derogative slurs such as, "Fag" or "Gay." This is a critical time for establishing adult codes of conduct, whereby teens are held to the same sexual boundaries and verbal expressions as adults.

The adolescent today is faced with a number of variables relating to sexual issues that are unique to the 90s and cannot be ignored. Even though the terms "Sexual Harassment," "Safe Sex," and "Date Rape" seem commonplace, for teens who frequently believe they "know it all" and are invincible, these concepts are frequently overlooked. Commodities such as the Internet and video games, as well as social catastrophes such as HIV and AIDS will have an impact on their development and social structures.

Adolescent Development and Bullying

Bullying behaviors and peer aggression reach their peak during the middle school years. In fact, the many developmental changes and needs of adolescence create numerous bully-victim dynamics which are unique to this age group. As we will discuss in Chapter Four, any factor that makes teens different from their peers will increase the likelihood that they will be targets of harassment and bullying. And because, to the young adolescent, social status means **everything**, they are extremely vulnerable to peer rejection. Additionally, this strong emphasis on social acceptance frequently leads to bullying, which includes social punishments such as shunning or spreading negative rumors. Also, young teens tend to become emotionally demonstrative when upset, which further empowers the bully.

A number of inherent differences begin to occur during adolescence, which can add to the problems of bullying in middle school. A great variation in physical stature evolves: many male students gain strength and social status while others, slower to mature, remain smaller and more vulnerable to verbal and physical harassment. Female students who begin puberty early may be considered by peers to be "overweight" and frequently can also be ostracized or left out of activities. Young teens are typically experiencing sexual identity and relational confusion that can lead some adolescents to use negative sexualized labels on others or to push physical boundaries producing sexually harassing behaviors. Racially diverse schools may have racial tensions. These tensions, in combination with the racial/cultural identity formation issues of teens, can lead to cruel racial harassment from one individual or group of students to another. Likewise, teens struggling with racial and cultural identity conflicts can become targets for harassment due to the vulnerability that accompanies anyone "different" in this age group.

One of the most damaging dynamics unique to middle school behaviors is that of group bullying. Because of the power of social acceptance and the importance of conformity, teens can be pulled into negative group behaviors that they would not engage in individually. Finally, the drive for adolescents toward autonomy and away from adult authority leads them to believe that they need to handle all of their problems by themselves. This is particularly problematic in bullying or harassing situations in which their silence may solidify their victimization. In fact, the bully is depending on their silence.

The young adolescent's self-esteem and coping resources are commonly in a fragile state due to the many changing demands of his or her body and environment. Therefore, when confronted with a harassing situation, teens can easily become overwhelmed and fail to protect themselves. Social insecurities can inhibit effective problem-solving measures that, in turn, negatively impact self-esteem. Low self-esteem has been directly linked to victimization. When young teens are unsure of themselves, they are much more likely to become prey for power-hungry peers.

Chapter Three

Bullies, Victims, and Bystanders

Section One: Bullies

Bullying is a form of interpersonal aggression which has existed for countless generations. Until recently behaviors such as teasing, hazing, sexual harassment, and physical bullying were deemed as "part of growing up" or "rites of passage." Many people assumed these behaviors would make the victim "tougher." We have learned that this is very far from the truth. The consequences experienced by the victim and bystanders are far-reaching and potentially lethal. Dan Olweus began some of the first research on bullies in Scandinavia following four teen suicides that were the result of bullying. Hoover and Oliver (1996) reported that 75–90% of students suffer harassment during their school careers. Furthermore, in a large Midwestern study conducted by Hazler, Hoover, and Oliver (1992), 15% of fourth through eighth graders reported being severely distressed by bullying.

Bullying has been defined as:

> **A person is being bullied or victimized when he or she is exposed, repeatedly and over time, to negative actions on the part of one or more persons** (Olweus, 1991).

Essentially, if the aggressor knows that his or her behaviors are disturbing to the victim and continues the act, that is bullying.

Bullying has been further delineated into direct bullying and indirect bullying.

> **Direct bullying** is face-to-face interactions which include physical attacks or any threatening or intimidating gestures.

> **Indirect bullying** requires a third party, is often more subtle, and includes social isolation, rumor spreading, and scapegoating.

Bullying, whether direct or indirect, contains several key elements. These include:

◆ **An Imbalance of Power** The imbalance can be physical, psychological, or intellectual and hinders the victim from defending him/herself.

◆ **Repeated Actions** The negative actions usually occur repetitively over a period of time.

◆ **Intentional Actions** Bullies purposefully choose actions that will hurt or intimidate the targeted victim. Bullies seldom show empathy or concern for the victim.

◆ **Unequal Levels of Affect** The victim will typically display a high level of emotional distress including yelling, crying, withdrawal, or anxiousness. The bully, however, will demonstrate very little emotion or anguish. The adolescent doing the bullying is likely to blame the victim for causing the aggressive act or believe "he/she deserved it." Bullies commonly feel justified in their actions.

Bullying behavior can include any or all of the following forms of abuse:

◆ **Physical aggression:** includes destroying property, threatening

◆ **Social aggression:** spreading rumors, racial slurs, exclusion from group

◆ **Verbal aggression:** name calling, teasing, threatening, intimidating phone calls

◆ **Intimidation:** graffiti, a dirty trick, taking possessions, coercion

◆ **Written aggression:** "slam"books, note passing, graffiti

◆ **Sexual harassment:** Any comments or actions of a sexual nature which are unwelcome and make the recipient uncomfortable

◆ **Racial and cultural (ethnic) harassment:** Any comments or actions containing racial or ethnic content (direct or indirect) which are unwelcome and make the recipient uncomfortable

---

Adapted from *Bully-Proofing Your School: A Comprehensive Approach for Elementary Schools (Second Edition)*, © Garrity et al, 2000.

Bullying behaviors often encompass demeaning, ritualistic patterns that include some form of public submission by the victim in a degrading act that clearly establishes power. For example, a physically stronger male student intentionally tips the lunch tray of a younger student, spilling food all over him, and then encourages everyone at the lunch table to laugh at the spectacle. Oftentimes these bullying "rites" include giving the victim a humiliating nickname, such as "Jiggle Butt Jalissa," which can later be used by other peers in collusion with the bully.

The Severity of Bullying

Bullying behaviors can be mild, moderate, or severe, depending on the power differences between the bully and victim, the chronicity of aggressive behaviors, the emotional stability of the victim, and environmental supports available to the victim. Significantly, it is the victim who determines if the behaviors are threatening or bullying and judges their severity. Table 3-1: Bullying Behaviors, outlines the types of bullying and attempts to categorize them by severity. Remember, any bullying behavior can be severe. Teens will always need adult help with moderate and severe bullying. Keeping these categories in mind can help adults decide when it is necessary to intervene, regardless of the desires of the teen.

TABLE 3-1   Bullying Behaviors

MILD		MODERATE			SEVERE
PHYSICAL AGGRESSION					
♦ Pushing ♦ Shoving ♦ Spitting	♦ Kicking ♦ Hitting	♦ Defacing property ♦ Stealing	♦ Physical acts that are demeaning and humiliating, but not bodily harmful (e.g., de-panting) ♦ Locking in a closed or confined space	♦ Physical violence against family or friends	♦ Threatening with a weapon ♦ Inflicting bodily harm
SOCIAL ALIENATION					
♦ Gossiping ♦ Embarrassing	♦ Setting up to look foolish ♦ Spreading rumors about	♦ Ethnic slurs ♦ Setting up to take the blame	♦ Publicly humiliating (e.g., revealing personal information) ♦ Excluding from group ♦ Social rejection	♦ Maliciously excluding ♦ Manipulating social order to achieve rejection ♦ Malicious rumor-mongering	♦ Threatening with total isolation by peer group

Adapted from *Bully-Proofing Your School: A Comprehensive Approach for Elementary Schools (Second Edition)*, © Garrity et al, 2000.

TABLE 3-1 *(continued)*			
MILD	**MODERATE**		**SEVERE**

VERBAL AGGRESSION

MILD	MODERATE				SEVERE
◆ Mocking ◆ Name calling ◆ Dirty looks ◆ Taunting	◆ Teasing about clothing or possessions	◆ Teasing about appearance	◆ Intimidating telephone calls	◆ Verbal threats of aggression against property or possessions	◆ Verbal threats of violence or of inflicting bodily harm

INTIMIDATION

MILD	MODERATE				SEVERE
◆ Threatening to reveal personal information ◆ Graffiti ◆ Publicly challenging to do something	◆ Defacing property or clothing ◆ Playing a dirty trick	◆ Taking possessions (e.g., lunch, clothing, toys)	◆ Extortion	◆ Threats of using coercion against family or friends	◆ Coercion ◆ Threatening with a weapon

RACIAL AND ETHNIC HARASSMENT

MILD	MODERATE				SEVERE
◆ Joke telling with racial or ethnic targets	◆ Exclusion due to ethnic or cultural group membership	◆ Racial or ethnic slurs, put-downs	◆ Verbal accusations, insults ◆ Public humiliation	◆ Destroying or defacing property due to ethnic or cultural group membership	◆ Physical or verbal attacks due to group membership

SEXUAL HARASSMENT

MILD	MODERATE				SEVERE
◆ Sexual or "dirty" jokes ◆ Conversations that are too personal	◆ Howling, catcalls, whistles ◆ Leers and stares	◆ "Snuggies" (pulling underwear up at the waist) ◆ Repeatedly asking someone out when he or she isn't interested	◆ Spreading sexual rumors ◆ Pressure for sexual activity ◆ De-panting ◆ Bra snapping	◆ Cornering, blocking, standing too close, following	◆ Sexual assault and attempted sexual assault ◆ Rape

These different forms of bullying usually occur together. For example, verbal abuse will accompany and follow physical intimidation. One reinforces the other. As middle school-aged teens hone their expanding cognitive abilities, their methods become more subtle and less easily detected by onlookers.

Normal Conflict and Bullying

Conflict is a normal part of interpersonal relationships and an integral part of childhood learning. It is important that young teens learn to distinguish the difference between normal conflict and bullying for several reasons. First, teens need to learn when to ask for help with a problem and when the problem is one that they can handle on their own. As youngsters progress through middle school they become increasingly reliant on themselves or ask peers for assistance. However, in bullying situations the imbalance of power can severely hinder the usual conflict resolution strategies, which further empowers the bully. Teens need to learn to recognize this pattern so that they don't continue trying ineffective strategies or think they have to solve the conflict on their own. Next, many middle school students will themselves be pulled into bullying behaviors by the bullies. This can typically be seen in a group of girls not speaking to another in the group because the bully is mad at her. It is important that students learn to recognize their own as well as their peers' bullying behaviors so they can avoid being pulled into the role of a lieutenant or become a participant in group bullying.

Normal peer conflict is characterized by the developmental level of the children involved. Middle school adolescents engage in conflicts which include angry hurtful remarks, gossip, note writing, and derogatory sexual jokes. Their presence alone does not infer that a bully-victim problem exists.

Because all youth need help when they are being bullied, it is important for adults to recognize the difference between normal conflict and bullying. See Table 3-2. Often a behavior or series of behaviors will appear to the adult as a daily hassle rather than a major stressful event. In reality, the adult needs to embrace the young teen's report of the behavior as bullying and respond from that position. The victim needs reassurance and assistance with direct coping behaviors.

TABLE 3-2 Recognizing the Difference	
Normal Conflict	**Bullying**
Equal power—friends	Imbalance of power; not friends
Happens occasionally	Repeated negative actions
Accidental	Purposeful
Not serious	Serious—threat of physical harm or emotional or psychological hurt
Equal emotional reaction	Strong emotional reaction on part of the victim
Not seeking power or attention	Seeking power, control
Not trying to get something	Trying to gain material things or power
Remorse—take responsibility	No remorse—blames victim
Effort to solve the problem	No effort to solve problem

Where Does Bullying Occur?

Studies have found that most bullying occurs in the school environment (Olweus, 1993a; Smith and Sharp, 1994). Many parents believe that bullying happens most frequently on the way to and from school. While students certainly are less supervised during the transition from home to school, the preponderance of student reports indicate bullying most often occurs at school. In secondary schools the highest incidence of bullying was reported in the hallways and classrooms (Whitney and Smith, 1993). Overall, the most important variable in the location of bullying incidents is whether there is supervision or the presence of adults who will intervene.

Gender Differences and Bullying

Studies have historically found boys to be more aggressive than girls throughout the life span. However, it is likely that bullying and aggression need to be evaluated differently for females. Boys tend to use direct forms of bullying such as physical intimidation or verbal abuse while girls use indirect, more subtle means of bullying and intimidation. These indirect means, such as social alienation and rumor starting, can be easily overlooked or not interpreted as bullying by the bullies, victims, and the adults who witness the incidents. Therefore, the prevalence of female aggression has likely been underestimated (Crick, 1995).

As we look at the key dynamics of bullying behaviors, the behavioral choices of boy bullies and girl bullies become more clear. Bullies need to establish power and dominance in areas that are important to the victim. For boys, the areas that are important are physical strength and stature, athletic ability, and achieving goals. Therefore overt, physical aggression is primarily used by boys. Girls are interested in and value interpersonal relationships. For them, friendships, social acceptance, inclusion, and feelings are paramount. Hence, girl bullies focus on relational aggression. These areas of focus are developmentally at their peak for both genders during middle school, which leaves the adolescent particularly vulnerable. It is not surprising then that bullying behaviors and the trauma they create also reach a peak during the middle school years.

Research has found the following gender differences:

◆ Boys tend to bully with direct bullying or physical or verbal aggression.

◆ Girls tend to bully with indirect bullying or social aggression.

◆ Boys who bully tend to be one or two years older than their victims. Their victims can be either boys or girls.

◆ Girl bullies tend to target other girls who are the same age as their victims.

◆ Girls are more likely to be bullied by a group.

◆ Girls are more likely to involve both boys and girls in their bullying pursuits against a victim. (See **Group Bullying**.)

◆ Physical bullying becomes less prevalent as age increases, verbal bullying becomes more prevalent with age, and indirect bullying remains nearly the same.

◆ Boys identify their behaviors as bullying more often than girls.

Group Bullying

Group bullying is a dangerous phenomenon which has puzzled people for generations. Why do people in a group act differently than they normally would if they were alone? Several factors play an important role in group bullying. Social learning theory, social contagion effect, a weakening of controls against aggressive tendencies, and normal adolescent developmental issues combine to make group bullying particularly problematic for middle school-age children.

Social learning theory explains that modeling has a central role in determining individual behaviors. Bullies frequently have a charm or magnetism that is appealing to peers. Studies have indicated that if peers or bystanders have positive attitudes toward the bully they will be more likely to imitate similar behaviors. Additionally, there is a greater chance that peers will replicate the bully's behavior if the bully is reinforced by receiving an abundance of attention or by being successful in his/her aggressive actions.

Group Bullying
Drawn by
Michael Collier

The social contagion effect has also been explained as a likely contributor to aggressive group mentality. Craig and Pepler (1995) conducted an extensive study of peer involvement in bullying episodes. They observed that peers were involved in 85% of the bullying incident in some capacity. The peers were viewed as enjoying the bullying 30% of the time and were neutral during 46% of the episodes. It appeared that observers got caught up in the arousal involved in dominance displayed within the bullying episode: much like the emotional titillation of a fight during a hockey game, basketball game, or professional wrestling. The excitement of the crowd is frequently contagious and spreads with intensity. Bystanders can experience this when watching a bullying incident and lose their sense of empathy for the victim. With little compassion for the victimized peer, bystanders can be drawn into an active role in the bullying. Bullying is in itself reinforcing to the bully as he or she experiences domination over the victim. However, when a group of bystanders watches the incident, no matter what their internal experience of the incident, it is likely that the bully will experience their attention as powerful approval that can increase the frequency of bullying. When students are repeatedly exposed to bullying behaviors, they can become desensitized; and the regulation of their aggressive impulses weakens, leaving them even more likely to get involved directly with bullying episodes.

The importance of group membership and acceptance is never stronger than during adolescence and can contribute to participation in negative group behaviors. A "group think" or "mob mentality" seems to form out of a desire to fit in and belong to the group.

Ken Rigby (1993) described one type of group bullying as "malign bullying." In malign bullying, some young teens may engage in bullying solely for group conformity. They may not have malicious goals of hurting someone, but gain pleasure in the sense of belonging to a group where the norm happens to be bullying others. In this type of group, being cruel is equal to social power. At the center of this group there will likely be a bully whose charisma and strong need for power and control are enabling him/her to establish aggressive and sinister norms for the group. The bully in the center of this group will often prey on the vulnerability of the ancillary group members and use them as **"lieutenants"** to conduct some of the cruel, dirty work. All the while, the initiating bully remains insulated from consequences.

Who Are the Bullies?

There are many common misconceptions or stereotypes of bullies. The bottom line is that there are no specific characteristics of a child who bullies. They are not just boys, not just physically large, neither failing nor top students. Bullies typically have friends who enjoy associating and aligning with the bully's power. Bullies commonly appear to have no self-esteem issues. In fact, often they have a falsely inflated self-image, which contributes to their extreme sense of entitlement and expectation of special treatment. Olweus (1987) found that children

▼ Bullies—The Facts

1. Both boys and girls bully, but their tactics are usually different. Boys usually bully with physical aggression; girls bully with social alienation or humiliation.

2. Bullies are not anxious, insecure children, but have positive (often unrealistic) self-images that reflect a strong need to dominate with power and threats.

3. Bullies are not loners, but almost always have a small network of peers who encourage, admire, and model their bullying behaviors.

4. Bullies tend to be at least average or only slightly below average academically.

5. Bullies come in all sizes and abilities and can even intimidate victims who are physically larger than they if there's an imbalance of power.

6. Bullies lack empathy for their victims and feel justified in their actions.

7. Bullies lack guilt and value the rewards they achieve from aggression, such as attention, control over someone, or material possessions.

8. Returned aggression is not usually effective, and in fact excites the bully into further attacks. Assertion, rather than aggression, is effective, however.

9. When bullies are confronted with a united front of their peers, who support the victims and believe that bullying behavior is not socially acceptable, their power is defused.

10. Bullies can separate home from school and be taught responsible school behavior, even when aggression is modeled and/or reinforced at home.

11. Bullying behavior does not usually change with traditional therapy, but requires specific intervention techniques that improve skill deficits and correct thinking errors.

12. A bully's parent(s) or other significant role model often model aggression.

13. A bully thinks in unrealistic ways, e.g., "I should always get what I want."

14. A bully commonly becomes bored easily and gets a thrill from exerting power over others.

identified as bullies by age eight were six times more likely to be convicted of a crime by the age of twenty-four. Furthermore, they were five times more likely than non-bullies to end up with serious criminal records by the age of thirty.

Bullies are easiest to identify by their **personality style** rather than by obvious characteristics such as gender, physical appearance, social status, or academic achievement.

The Lieutenants

Many times the bully's charisma, popularity, and power are intriguing and attractive to peers or bystanders. Bullies often will "befriend" one or several of these peers and use them to conduct some of the malicious behaviors. The lieutenant earns the favor of the bully or the bullying group, and the bully usually avoids the potential consequences. Lieutenants do not have the same characteristics as bullies who bully alone. They are children who, acting alone, would most likely not participate in

Once when I was in another state I saw this kid. She looked really weird. I guess she was feeling kind of sad because there were many kids looking at her in an odd way. I knew that the others were making fun of her in a silent way. Of course I was looking at her too and kind of laughing too. Afterwards I kind a felt sorry for her, and I wished I would of not laughed at her.

hurtful, malicious behaviors. They often have fragile self-esteem and are therefore easily pulled into apparent friendship with the powerful bully. Students who engage in group bullying as lieutenants are frequently unsure that the behaviors they are engaging in are deemed aggressive and hurtful. As previously stated, these students can become caught up in the need for friendship and group membership, and lose their grasp on empathy and good moral conduct. Students who act as lieutenants for the bully are one of the primary groups *Bully-Proofing Your School* is targeting. Through education about bullying behaviors, and a clearly established norm that bullying is hurtful and not tolerated, these students can learn to feel powerful as a member of the caring majority in the school rather than through alignment with the bully.

How Do Children Become Bullies?

This is a frequently asked question. There are a number of theoretical explanations that cover the gamut from genetic disposition (nature) to completely derived from societal contributions (nurture). The answer likely lies somewhere in between and is multifaceted and complex. Overall, there are three elements which have been shown to contribute to the development of children who bully others. These areas are genetic or temperament factors, family background and parenting, and environmental influences.

First, the genetic or "bad seed" theory is certainly controversial. However, children are clearly born with widely varying characteristics and dispositions. Some children, from a very early age, are prone to more aggressive and/or impulsive behaviors, and aggression is a characteristic which has been found to be stable throughout the life span (Rigby, 1996). Therefore, some children are inherently more combative, and as a result, more difficult to parent.

Second, research on child rearing practices has drawn a clear link between the development of aggression and limited parental involvement, a lack of supervision, and the use of harsh, inconsistent disciplinary practices. Parents of children who develop bullying patterns are frequently unavailable both physically and psychologically. Parents may display little care or consideration for the child's feelings which commonly results in the child having a lack of empathy for others. Children commonly feel, "If I am not cared for, why should I care for others?" (Rigby, 1996). Another parenting practice, which has been associated with bullying children, is a "power-assertive" disciplinary style that can involve vehement verbal outbursts and harsh corporal punishment applied inconsistently. Thus behaviors that may go unnoticed one day may be grounds for unbounded aggressive discipline the next day. These inconsistent and aggressive methods can lead children to model aggressive behaviors with peers and contribute to a rather paranoid world view: waiting for injustices on the one hand and on the other hand feeling justified in unjustifiable acts (Ross, 1996). The attitudes and values of some parents may also sanction aggression and dominance over others and, in effect, encourage bullying.

Importantly, children who bully are difficult to parent. Bullies can become masterful at designing excuses for their behaviors that are quite convincing. Most of the bullies' excuses are an outgrowth of their incorrect thinking patterns, which justify their behaviors and place them (the bullies) in the role of the victim. Parents of bullies may fail to correct these thinking patterns at an early age. Instead, they can too easily believe their child's clever stories or distorted ways of thinking, which further solidifies the bullying pattern.

The environment also contributes factors which may encourage bullying. Modeling is a significant behavioral influence in bullying. When children observe the bullying antics of other children or adults, they often revere the power and influence wielded by the bully and will then pattern their own behaviors after those of the aggressor. As children are further exposed to bullying incidences, they become desensitized to the suffering of the victim which makes it more likely that they will join in the bullying. Television and video and computer games are other powerful modeling influences. In the games, violence can be simulated by the teen with the goal of a high body count or enacted by an attractive hero figure whose main goal is to establish dominance over another and/or get revenge. When children watch and participate in unregulated violent media, they can become desensitized and even glamorize violence.

Finally, there is another explanation for children becoming bullies that is currently receiving attention. This category includes students who report that they are both bullies and victims. It is easiest to understand this group when the bully-victim dynamic is viewed as a continuum that includes students who chronically bully, students who report that they are both bullies and victims, and students who are continually victimized. This group of students whose members report being both a bully and a victim may increase during the middle school years because of the prevalence of group bullying and the strong need for social approval. It is important to note that many times educators can confuse bullies with provocative victims (see Section Two: Victims).

Provocative victims will have many of the same behaviors as bullies, however many of their character traits and motivations are different and therefore require different interventions. Another factor to consider is that students who chronically bully will commonly report being victimized. This can be due to their inflated self-esteem, thinking errors, or desire to avoid consequences.

Generalizations in this area are quite precarious. There are always circumstances that will defy our best attempts to understand human behavior. However, an understanding of the precipitants of bullying behaviors can be one of our best methods for developing deterrent interventions.

What Makes a School Prone to Bullying?

Bullying is not evenly divided throughout all schools, classrooms, or parts of the country. It is important to know that some schools have significantly higher incidences of bullying and intimidation. In some schools, students have a four to five times greater chance of being bullied than at other schools. Studies have found that both the size of the school and the class sizes within the school are not correlated with increased aggression. Although, socioeconomic conditions, unusually large families, and poor housing have been found to contribute some to a school's higher bullying incidence level, these factors have not been predominant. The strongest contributor to a "high-bullying" school was a school climate of opportunity for the bully.

Opportunity for the bully means ineffective or inadequate adult supervision during unstructured times such as in the hallways, during lunch hours, and on the school bus and the playground. An attitude of indifference by the teachers and other adults supervising students plays directly into the hands of the bully. In a troubling study conducted by Olweus (1984), 60% of middle school students reported that teachers tried to stop bullying "once in a while" or "almost never." Hazler, Hoover, and Oliver (1993) reported similar results from a small Midwestern community.

Teachers who bully their students can also set the tone of a school by modelling aggressive, demeaning behaviors. Teachers who use sarcasm and subtle forms of bullying can be perceived as humorous or entertaining to the bystanders who secretly plead to not be chosen as the next target.

There are some important common elements in schools where bullying and intimidation are well under control.

◆ Effective supervision is a priority.

◆ There is a strong attitude that bullying, teasing, and harassing will not be tolerated.

◆ Teachers, administrators, and all adults who supervise students intervene in both direct and indirect bullying situations.

◆ The school has well-outlined, communicated policies regarding consequences for harassment and bullying behaviors.

Specific Types of Bullying

Teasing

Teasing has been defined as: "to annoy persistently, especially in fun by goading, coaxing or tantalizing." However, teasing is a tricky phenomenon. It can be either a cruel and damaging form of bullying or it can be an engaging form of social play. Teasing, along with other forms of verbal aggression has been found to be as potentially harmful as occasional physical attacks. It is difficult for adults to observe and even more difficult to determine when and how to intervene. Teasers will commonly state, "I was just kidding" or "It was just a joke," with conviction. When adults believe the teasers, the victims can be perceived as whiners or overly sensitive. And it is often difficult to determine when the teased are enjoying the interchange or when they might really be embarrassed or hurt but are hiding it well. The very nature of teasing is ambiguous. The content is commonly open for interpretation and students are faced with whether to take it seriously or as an inclusive, affectionate interchange.

Teasing in middle school-age students is common and complex. Interpersonal communication patterns have commonly already been established, with some students who have mastered the experience of teasing and being teased and some students who can "dish it out but can't take it." Frequently students will exchange pseudo-insults by "dissing" each other in a sarcastic manner; these can be experienced as a sign of good friendship and acceptance. However, the increased cognitive and verbal skills gained during adolescence frequently lead to teasing that is more cruel than during the younger ages. Teens have the skills to pinpoint the victim's most vulnerable areas and create more subtle and punishing jabs.

Adolescent teasing often contains sexual content or innuendo. As with any teasing, this can be a positive, playful way for teens who are struggling to develop their sexual identity and relationship patterns to engage with opposite sex peers. However, sexualized teasing is often used in a cruel, defensive manner with the content referring to sexual preferences and patterns such as male homosexuality and lesbianism. This type of teasing is likely the teaser's way of defending against his/her own sexual fears by attributing them to others. These sexually harassing comments often target teens who have characteristics which are outside those of the majority of students.

Understandably, young people are confused and have conflicting ideas about teasing. While students of all ages report that teasing is the most frequent form of bullying that they experience and observe (Hoover, Oliver, and Thompson, 1993), about 90% of middle school students surveyed also reported that "most teasing I saw was done in fun—that is, not done to hurt others" (Oliver, Hoover, and Hazler, 1994). The perception of teasing involves a number of variables that lead to it being either fun or traumatizing.

Factors that influence whether teasing is experienced as fun or degrading:

◆ **Are you the teased or the teaser?** Commonly the person doing the teasing enjoys it and minimizes the effects experienced by the person being teased.

◆ **The social level of the teased and the teaser.** If a student of perceived higher social status heckles a student lower in social status, it is likely to be experienced as harassment. Whereas, two students of similar social status may exchange the same banter and experience it as playful and bonding.

Last year I got teased because I was the shortest kid and I did not have too many friends. And some kid fell down and told the teacher that I pushed him.

There was a time when my friends teased me because I liked a show and they did not. It was hurtful and friendly.

- ◆ **The self-confidence of the recipient.**
- ◆ **The content of the verbalization.**
- ◆ **The verbal and cognitive abilities of the teased.**
- ◆ **The personality of the teased.**   Serious students with little sense of humor or play may have a low tolerance for verbal bantering. Unfortunately, if their response is emotionally negative, it may make them targets for frequent taunts and bullying.

Students need to be able to discuss the numerous aspects of teasing. Some of these are listed in Table 3-3. It will be helpful if students remember to "put yourself in the other persons shoes" and think about intention before teasing others.

Teasing can be degrading
Drawn by an Eighth Grader

TABLE 3-3 Characteristics of Teasing	
Friendly Teasing	**Hurtful Teasing**
Equal power/friends	Unequal power
Neutral topic	Sensitive topic
Purpose is to be playful	Purpose is to upset
Purpose is to relate and join	Purpose is to exclude
Funny	Sarcastic

Important Reminders:
- The person being teased always gets to decide if the teasing is friendly or hurtful.
- The person doing the teasing commonly sees it as milder and with lighter consequences than the person being teased.
- Sarcasm is not a fun form of teasing. It is most often perceived as hurtful.

If the intent is to hurt, annoy or upset someone, ... it is not teasing; it is bullying.

Sexual Harassment

Sexual harassment is a form of bullying that is a very serious problem for middle school students and educators. It has been shown to affect all students regardless of age, gender, or race, in large or small schools, private or public. The American Association of University Women conducted a large study of middle schools and found that 85% of the girls and 76% of the boys had experienced sexual harassment at school. The hallways and classrooms were the most frequently cited locations for the harassment. The most frequent behaviors cited were inappropriate jokes, looks, or gestures with sexually suggestive touching, grabbing, or pinching as the second most frequent complaint (AAUW Education Foundation, 1993). Nan Stein (1995) also conducted a study of nine- to eighteen-year-old girls and found that 89% had experienced sexual torment. Alarmingly, two-thirds of the girls who reported being sexually harassed in Stein's study also reported that other people were present during the incident(s).

As with any type of bullying, sexual harassment escalates when it is ignored, tolerated, or excused. Like bullying, sexual harassment has been historically confused with normal adolescent developmental issues. Comments such as, "Boys will be boys" and "Oh that's just overflowing testosterone," are used to excuse this type of aggression. Sexual harassment has been tolerated for generations due to our society's patriarchal focus in which women have little or less power. There are many factors that have contributed to our culture's tolerance of sexual harassment. Traditional sex-role stereotyping established that men are the assertive sexual predators and women are weak and to be conquered. While

> Sexual harassment is not about sexual attraction. It is about power—more specifically the misuse and abuse of power.
>
> —Susan Strauss

many of these beliefs have recently been challenged and modified, numerous adults have had negative, demeaning experiences based on these ideals, all the while feeling that the harassment was part of growing up or just something they just had to "put up with." Television commercials, movies, and MTV have highly sexualized content which can desensitize viewers. All of these are contributing factors in the current apathy or ignorance regarding the seriousness of teen sexual harassment.

Unfortunately, when adults hesitate and do not intervene, it is perceived by the victim and bystanders as silent approval. Bystanders will commonly have one of two experiences when witnessing this harassment. Some will perceive the harassment as acceptable behavior and will use it as a model for their own behavior, particularly if the aggressor is an esteemed peer. Others will become fearful that they may be the next victim with no adult support or intervention.

Studies have also indicated that often sexual harassment occurs beyond the scope of adult supervision but in the presence of peers. For this reason, it is imperative that we teach teens that these sexual aggressions are harmful and unacceptable and that they must also intervene to assist their peers.

The *Bully-Proofing Your School* program is one of the few programs which challenges students to "Take a Stand" to help peers. By developing a "Caring Majority" of students, a school climate can be established in which both students and adults deliver the message that sexual harassment and bullying are not accepted or tolerated.

Who is sexually harassed?   Sexual harassment frequently starts during the elementary school years in the form of teasing which contains sexual content. From previously cited studies which indicate prevalence levels of 85%, 79%, and 89%, we can quickly see that the majority of students, regardless of gender, race, or ethnicity, will experience some form of sexual harassment in school. Studies reveal that early maturing, attractive females are very frequently the targets of sexual harassment during the middle school years (Shakeshaft et al, 1995). Additionally, teens, male and female, who demonstrate atypical gender-related behaviors will often become targets for harassment involving homophobic insults. This is particularly problematic during early adolescence when a teen's sexually identity is being developed. Teens, both male and female, with fragile self-esteem may fall into sexually harassing behaviors to prove to themselves and their peers that they are "normal." In fact, a teen who merely refuses to go along with harassing behavior may have his sexuality questioned. It is because of this social pressure that is it paramount for schools to have an established set of expectations and procedures regarding sexual harassment.

Students need to know:

◆ That sexual harassment is against the law

◆ What behaviors constitute sexual harassment

◆ The potential consequences for victims of sexual harassment

◆ The potential consequences for the perpetrators of sexual harassment

◆ The differences between flirting and sexual harassment

◆ Where and how to get confidential help if they are being harassed

The Law   Schools are being forced to become more overtly aware of possible sexual harassment and take action in situations involving sexual harassment. Title IX of the Education Act was initiated in 1993 and established clear guidelines protecting all students from sexual harassment in cases of school authorities exhibiting sexual pressures against a student (*quid pro quo* harassment) or in cases of persistent, unwelcome sexually harassing conduct within the school environment such that the student can't effectively participate in learning (hostile environment harassment). In fact, in a recent ruling schools have been found financially liable for student-on-student harassment when the school knows about the harassment and does nothing to stop it.

Examples of sexually harassing behaviors at middle school

◆ Graffiti of a sexual nature

◆ Sexual remarks, teasing

◆ Spreading rumors of a sexual nature about others

◆ Rating other students in terms of their physical attractiveness

◆ Sexual jokes

◆ Accusations regarding sexual orientation ("fag, lesbo, gay")

◆ Pinching, brushing against, sexually suggestive touching

◆ Explicit talk of sexual experiences

◆ Underwear exposure or torment (snuggies, de-panting, bra snapping)

◆ Verbal comments of a sexual nature about body parts

Consequences for victims of sexual harassment   The consequences for the victim of sexual harassment can be serious, pervasive, and debilitating. Adolescence is a time when young teens, particularly females, experience a lowered self-esteem due to numerous physical and social changes. Teens experiencing a compromised self-esteem often lack the resiliency and coping resources they might have at other times in their lives, leaving them especially vulnerable to the humiliating trap of sexual harassment. Common experiences of victims are:

Fear	Academic decline
Confusion	Anger
Embarrassment	Anxiety

Hopelessness

Frequent illness (headaches, nausea, ulcers)

Sleep changes (insomnia, hypersomnia)

Substance abuse

Guilt

Self-doubt

Shame

Depression

Helplessness

Truancy

Appetite changes

Sexual Harassment and Flirting

Young adolescents are embarking on a long journey of sexual identity development which will move them from prepubescence to full adulthood. They will have many challenges as they strive to understand their own sexuality and their interpersonal relations. As teens begin to "go out" and/or date, they will inevitably experience confusion regarding their own and others' physical and emotional boundaries. Youth will need help in determining the difference between flirting and getting to know someone and intimidating or embarrassing them with sexualized comments. Likewise, it can be difficult for the recipient of sexual attention to determine if the behaviors constitute sexual harassment. Importantly, teens need to be told directly that it is the receiver of the action who determines whether the action is desirable or harassment. Body language, voice tone, physical space, and power differences can evoke very different meanings for the same phrases. It is important for teens to understand that male and female perceptions may differ regarding sexual behaviors. Actions that may seem trivial to a young man can be perceived as frightening and threatening to a young woman. Nan Stein has developed the following list which accompanies an excellent video titled, "Flirting or Hurting" (WGBY-TV, 1997), to assist teens in exploring this difficult area. (See Resource Guide.) See Table 3-4 for a brief comparison of sexual harassment and flirting.

What Can Schools Do to Prevent Sexual Harassment?   The best deterrent to sexual harassment in schools has been through school-wide education of staff and students. Equally important is the establishment of a school climate in which it is widely known and demonstrated that sexual harassing behaviors are acknowledged and consequented.

Schools need to take an active role in investigating reports of sexual harassment. Victims need to have support, privacy, respect, and sensitivity when they report abuses. If "blaming the victim" occurs, victims will potentially become retraumatized and perpetrators will maintain the power in the school climate. Additionally, schools need to take reasonable measures to ensure the privacy of all of the parties involved in the sexual harassment incident. Due process should be carefully followed for all involved parties during the investigation and possible grievance process. Lastly, and most importantly, school professionals should take great care to see that no retaliation measures are enacted toward students who report sexual harassment. Should any retaliation occur, it should be dealt with swiftly using legal regulations and guidelines.

TABLE 3-4 Sexual Harassment vs. Flirting	
Sexual Harassment makes the receiver feel:	**Flirting makes the receiver feel:**
Bad	Good
Angry/sad	Happy
Demeaned	Flattered
Ugly	Pretty/attractive
Powerless	In control
Sexual Harassment results in:	**Flirting results in:**
Negative self-esteem	Positive self-esteem
Sexual Harassment is perceived as:	**Flirting is perceived as:**
One-sided	Reciprocal
Demeaning	Flattering
Invading	Open
Degrading	A compliment
Sexual Harassment is:	**Flirting is:**
Unwanted	Wanted
Power-motivated	Equality-motivated
Illegal	Legal

Adapted with permission from S. Strauss and P. Espeland (1992). *Sexual harassment and teens.* Minneapolis, MN: Free Spirit Publishing Inc.

The following list of school interventions is recommended by the Office of Civil Rights (OCR). Further information can be obtained in their pamphlet, *Sexual Harassment: It's Not Academic.* (See Resource Guide.)

◆ Develop and publicize a sexual harassment policy that clearly states sexual harassment will not be tolerated and explains what types of conduct will be considered sexual harassment.

◆ Develop and publicize a specific grievance procedure for resolving complaints of sexual harassment.

◆ Develop methods to inform new administrators, teachers, guidance counselors, staff, and students of the school's sexual harassment policy and grievance procedure.

◆ Conduct periodic sexual harassment awareness training for all school staff, including administrators, teachers, and guidance counselors.

◆ Conduct periodic age-appropriate sexual harassment awareness training for students.

◆ Establish discussion groups for both male and female students where students can talk about what sexual harassment is and how to respond in the school setting.

◆ Survey students to find out whether any sexual harassment is occurring at the school.

◆ Conduct periodic sexual harassment awareness training for parents of elementary and secondary students.

◆ Work together with parents and students to develop and implement age-appropriate, effective measures for addressing sexual harassment.

Racial and Cultural Harassment

Racial and cultural prejudice most often manifests itself in the form of bullying. Verbal harassment has been reported to be the most prevalent type of racial harassment (Ross, 1996). However, social exclusion is also a prominent type of racial and cultural bullying which occurs in middle school.

When I was 8 years old, I saw a friend being picked on. The kid that was being picked on was Korean. The bully was making fun of the kid's religion and color and said she was ugly and nasty. He made fun of her grades. After the bully was done, I told the principal and that made my friend happy.

Adolescents have reported that the most common reason young people are harassed is for, "Not fitting in" (Oliver, Hoover, and Hazler, 1994). Interestingly, the students being studied actually added this vague response to the questionnaires, which further emphasizes the importance of group identity and acceptance. What does this mean for young teens of minority racial or cultural backgrounds? Obviously, being members of minority status will make them potential targets for bullying. However, racial and ethnic harassment is laden with numerous factors that leave adolescent victims particularly vulnerable.

Racial and cultural heritage is most often a sensitive and prideful, self-esteem issue and bullies know it. Students who experience racial or cultural name-calling or slurs, experience an insult not only to themselves but also to their entire race or family (Ross, 1996). Additionally, adolescence is a time when racial and cultural identity is being recognized and integrated into the teen's overall self-image. This is compounded by the strong developmental need to "fit in" and belong. Teens commonly form groups with peers of similar backgrounds, race, or ethnicity to meet developmental needs surrounding security and group identity. When these groups are not available or are ostracized by others, anger, isolation, and self-esteem issues can evolve.

It can be helpful to remember that **all** students will likely experience bullying behaviors at sometime during their school career. However, it is the student's response to bullying that will further provoke the bully and hook the targeted student into a bully-victim interactional pattern. Additionally, a student's awareness of racial/cultural issues waxes and wanes through participation in various groups. Some affiliations may be with people of similar backgrounds, such as in religious groups or family gatherings. Others may be with teens of varied backgrounds through participation in school sports, choir, or clubs. By establishing a variety of group memberships, teens of all races and cultures can gain resiliency through development of a more robust and flexible individual and group identity.

Section Two: Victims

Bullying is a dynamic that has captured the attention of educators as they focus attention on creating safe schools where teachers can teach and students can master the academic and developmental tasks required of them to become successful adults. Unfortunately, because of our heightened concerns about violence, the majority of attention to this problem has focused on the bullies rather than the victims. This neglect of the study of victims has led researchers to label victims as "the largest and also the most neglected group of special needs children in both the United States (Greenbaum, 1989) and the United Kingdom" (P.K. Smith, 1991).

According to the report, "Student Victimization at School," the National Center for Education Statistics reports that one-half of the 6,504 students surveyed in grades six through twelve witnessed some type of crime or victimization at school. The largest percentage of these students, 56%, reported that bullying had occurred in their schools, with statistics bearing out that bullying takes place more in middle or junior high school than at any other level. (National Center for Education Statistics, "Student Victimization at School," October, 1995). Other studies bear out these statistics, which means that for every incidence of bullying that is taking place in our schools there is a victim who is suffering.

The fact is: bullying wouldn't exist without children who are available as victims. Bullies and victims are both integral parts of the same dynamic, and we need to focus equal attention on the victims of this pattern of peer aggression in order to understand it fully. Who are these victims? What are the characteristics that distinguish them as victims? What are the short- and long-term effects of bullying on victims? And perhaps most importantly, what are some of the behaviors that keep bullying in place and make it resistant to our attempts to eliminate it? It is important for us to answer some of these questions if we are to understand and effectively address the bullying dynamic in our schools.

Though serious and damaging at any age, victimization can become particularly serious during the adolescent years. There are several factors that come into play in the middle school years which make bullying resistant to intervention. First, bully-victim patterns that are not addressed remain stable over time. Patterns that are not eliminated during the elementary years are firmly entrenched and repeated when students enter middle school, with the same bullies terrorizing the same victims in a well-established pattern. Secondly, as children grow older, they become both wiser about not getting caught and more adept at indirect forms of bullying that are more difficult for adults to identify and target. Bullying can easily go "underground" in a middle school culture that includes both a "code of silence" and an unspoken policy of non-reporting to adults. Finally, the importance of both social status and fitting in that characterize middle school culture further complicates the issue. Bullies are sometimes viewed as the "popular" students and therefore may seem desirable associates to their peers. In contrast, victims can be seen as "unpopular" and a social risk to their peers, assuring their continued social isolation and victim status.

Types of Victims

The definition of a victim is someone who is "exposed, usually repeatedly and over time, to negative actions on the part of one or more bullies" (Olweus, 1991; Perry et al, 1990). Unfortunately, victimization is stable over the years. A child who is targeted by bullies one year will continue to be a target the next year unless there is adult intervention. This poses a serious problem for middle school students who have been consistently targeted by bullies during their elementary years.

Victims tend to have certain characteristics in common, although it is difficult to determine which traits exist before the bullying or develop as a result of the bullying. Although looking different may be one reason children are victimized, victims are more likely to be targeted by a bully because of a passive and anxious personality type and because they are socially isolated. Students who are anxious and insecure, cry easily, and are lacking appropriate social skills are prime targets for bullies.

Students with special education needs may also be at greater risk of being bullied. This can be due more to their lack of social skills or incorrect interpretation of a social situation than it is to their disability.

Although victims share some common characteristics, they can be categorized into three different types based on their responses to bullying behaviors.

Passive Victims

The most typical and recognizable type of victim is the **Passive Victim.** They are the most common type of victim and are referred to as "passive" because they do not fight back.

A passive victim is a child who:*

- ◆ Is nonassertive and submissive
- ◆ Is cautious and quiet
- ◆ Cries easily and collapses quickly when bullied

- Has few friends and is not connected to a social network

- Is anxious and insecure

- Lacks humor and prosocial skills

- Is physically weak—boys especially

Provocative Victims

The second type of victim is the **Provocative Victim.** Provocative victims are fewer in number and are more difficult to identify. They can often be misidentified or mistakenly seen as bullies because they do engage with the bully and try to fight back. However, because of their poor social skills and misreading of social cues, they are ineffective with bullies and always lose the battle.

A provocative victim is a child who:*

- Is aggressive and argumentative

- Displays disruptive and irritating behaviors

- Is easily emotionally aroused

- Prolongs the conflict even when losing

- May be diagnosed with Attention Deficit Hyperactivity Disorder (ADHD)

Vicarious Victims

There is a third category of victims, recently identified, that is crucial to understanding the dynamic of bullying, especially in the middle school setting. This group is made up of **Vicarious Victims**, also called the surrogate victims. Vicarious victims are children who either witness or hear about incidents of bullying in their school and are affected by the climate of fear that bullying generates in the environment (Ross, 1996).

A vicarious victim is a child who:

- Feels vulnerable as a potential target

- Has a moderate to high degree of empathy and sensitivity

- Does not take a stand against bullying because of fear

- Experiences guilt about his or her failure to act

Although vicarious victims may be less identifiable than other, more obviously victimized students, they also suffer from the physical and emotional consequences of bullying. Fortunately, when taught the skills included in the *Bully-Proofing* program, this group of students can be mobilized as members of the caring majority of students who take a stand against bullying in order to make their schools safe.

---

*Adapted from *Bully-Proofing Your School: A Comprehensive Approach for Elementary Schools*, Copyright © Garrity et al, 2000.

The above characteristics are the ones commonly identified by adults researching the bully-victim problem. It is also important to make note of the factors identified by adolescents as the characteristics that put certain children at risk for being harassed and bullied. In *The Bullying Prevention Handbook* Hoover and Hazler report on the reasons middle and high school students give for why certain students are targeted for bullying or harassment (Hoover and Oliver, 1996). Table 3-5 shows the results of their findings.

TABLE 3-5 Highest Ranked Reasons for Being Bullied		
Eighth through twelfth grade[1]		
Rank	**Males**	**Females**
1	Didn't fit in	Didn't fit in
2	Physical weakness	Facial appearance
3	Short tempered	Cried/emotional
4	Who friends were	Overweight
5	Clothing	Good grades
Fourth through eighth grade[2]		
Rank	**Males**	**Females**
1	Didn't fit in	Didn't fit in
2	Who friends were	Who friends were
3	Physical weakness	Clothes worn
4	Short tempered	Facial appearance
5	Clothing	Overweight

[1] Hoover, Oliver, and Hazler (1992)
[2] Hoover, Oliver, and Thomson (1993; data slightly reworked)

We can see from the chart that "not fitting in" is the most common reason listed for being bullied. Though this term is subjective and perhaps difficult to define, the important thing to note is how important "fitting in" is to adolescents. Those students who don't fit in, as judged by their peers, are at much higher risk for bullying.

Dynamics Affecting Victims in Middle School

Victims who have been subjected to bullying for long periods of time find themselves in a no-win situation. Their responses are ineffective, the bullying continues and intensifies, and their self-esteem and confidence continue to deteriorate, solidifying their victim status. There are

Not "Fitting In"
Drawn by
Heather Michaels

four important dynamics that particularly influence the bully-victim pattern in middle school. These dynamics can influence the victims' responses in ways that keep the bullying in place.

1. Code of Silence

Bullying has been described as "the silent nightmare" (P.K. Smith, 1991, p. 243). Victims find themselves trapped in a "code of silence" that prevents them from getting the help they need. One reason they are silent is because they have given up hope that others will help them. They have been told by parents that bullying is "part of growing up," by teachers to "figure it out yourself," and by unfriendly and silent peers that they are alone and unworthy of support. All this is complicated by the very strong ethic of middle school culture: to inform is the ultimate disgrace, and handling problems oneself is the ideal and mature solution. Asking others for help with problems is "uncool," and for the victim who has been suffering in silence this leads to a strong sense of embarrassment and self-blame that compounds the problem. This code of silence is the bully's greatest source of protection (Ross, 1996).

2. Downward Spiral

Victims who are caught in the web of bullying get trapped in a downward spiral of lowered self-worth and confidence. The more they get bullied, the worse they feel; and the worse they feel about themselves and respond ineffectively, the more they are bullied. This in turn leads to increased disapproval and avoidance by peers who, the older they get, offer less support. Gradually, victims begin to blame themselves and believe that they deserve the bullying; in some cases they even seek out a familiar bullying interaction. Without interventions to correct this cycle, victims give up (because none of their strategies have worked) and enter a downward spiral into hopelessness and despair.

3. Indirect or Relational Victimization

Until recently, most studies of the bully-victim interaction focused on the aggressive or physical form of bullying most commonly perpetrated by boys. There have been few studies on the experiences of girls as bullying victims. As all adults who work in middle schools know, peer aggression among girls is just as common as among boys; and the female victims of these bullying episodes suffer serious consequences.

The most common form of bullying among girls is called relational aggression and involves harmful interference in others' social relationships and friendships (Crick and Bigbee, 1998). This bullying takes various forms of social alienation, from gossiping and embarrassing to malicious exclusion, rejection, rumormongering, and in extreme cases, total isolation by the peer group. Because of the extreme importance of social relationships and social networks to adolescent girls, interference in these relationships can be very harmful and the victims can suffer serious emotional upset and despair that distracts them from the day-to-day business of learning.

It is also important to note that girls respond to bullying differently than boys. Whereas male victims tend to get mad and act out aggressively when victimized, female victims report being sad, rather than mad. Their feelings of sadness, especially about interference in their very important social relationships, can overwhelm and immobilize them, making them even more vulnerable to further victimization. It is important that we work with girls to teach them it's okay to be appropriately angry when they are victimized, and to avoid the self-blaming behavior patterns that all victims are at risk for.

4. Peers Response to Bullying

Unfortunately, as children approach adolescence and experience the strong developmental needs for peer acceptance and belonging, they become less sympathetic to their peers who are seen as victims. Adolescents report that they view bullying as a natural part of growing up; and by the time they reach middle school, they begin expressing beliefs that blame the victims for "bringing it upon themselves."

This lack of sympathy for the victims may be a result of the strong need of adolescents for social status and acceptance. In middle school, peers become hesitant to associate with victims for fear that they will lose status if seen befriending them. For children who themselves are searching for their own sense of belonging, associating with known victims may seem too big a risk to take.

For the victims, this is catastrophic. Already isolated and socially disconnected, this unsympathetic and blaming attitude by their peers not only feeds into the victim's cycle of self-blame, but also encourages the bully to continue bullying—safe in the knowledge that peers will not intervene.

Consequences of Bullying to Victims

Victims of bullying can suffer severe, long-lasting consequences. Bullying is not a harmless, adolescent rite of passage; it can be a harmful, damaging set of behaviors that leaves its victims suffering both short- and long-term effects.

Academic Effects

The negative effects of bullying on academic success include a dislike and avoidance of school as well as poor academic performance. We cannot expect children to learn when they do not feel safe and when their energy for learning is being drained by worry and anxiety. Victims of bullying often avoid school and show high rates of absenteeism. For example, as many as 7% of America's eighth graders stay home at least once a month because of bullies (Banks, 1997). Even if victims do attend school, they are often too distracted and worried to attend to their academic tasks. In fact, a study done by Hazler et al (1993) of victims of bullying showed a serious drop in grades for 90% of the victims. As Ross states in her book *Childhood Bullying and Teasing*, "The damaged feeling of self-worth that results from bullying makes it impossible for the victims to reach their academic and social potential." (Ross, 1996, p. 91).

Health Problems

It is generally accepted that mental stress and emotional turmoil have a direct bearing on physical health and well-being. In the past we have focused primarily on the effects of stress on adults, but we now know that in our fast-paced, high-achieving society, children also experience debilitating stress. This is particularly true for the victims of bullying for whom school ". . . is a place of continual and sometimes unbearable stress that produces health consequences that we cannot ignore." (Rigby, 1998, p. 35).

Children in Australia answered questions anonymously about how school bullying has affected them (Rigby, 1998). Here are some of their statements:

◆ Not feeling well; not wanting to eat or do anything

◆ Nervousness, worrying, loss of sleep, sick and scared feeling in the stomach

◆ I've felt dizzy like I was going to faint or something

◆ Getting very depressed, staying home, vomiting, attempting suicide

◆ Headaches, hay fever, vomiting

◆ Stomachaches, feeling sick every morning about going to school because of bullying

◆ Tense, headaches, nausea, all that crap

There can be no doubt that there is a connection between victimization and health problems that also contributes to higher rates of absenteeism among victims. Interestingly, it is often the school nurse who is the most informed about those students in our schools who are victims. They are often the students who spend time in the nurse's office with either real or imagined physical complaints as a way to escape the bully. Paying attention to our students' physical complaints can help us both identify and intervene with victims appropriately.

Adjustment Problems

Studies of bullying also document serious adjustment problems for the victims of bullying. These include emotional distress, depression, loneliness, anxiety, and lowered self-esteem. The daily stress victims face can be overwhelming. When coupled with the typical anxiety experienced by middle schoolers in their normal development, the effects can be paralyzing. Both Rigby and Olweus have researched the long-term effects of bullying and found that victims of bullying suffer more depression than nonvictims. Olweus (1992) specifically states that victimization during the middle school years predicts depressions and low self-esteem ten years later, even after the actual external bullying has ended.

In more serious cases, students who are repeatedly victimized and who do not learn effective coping responses tend to have higher levels of suicidal ideation and are, therefore, more prone to suicide. Faced with seemingly unending harassment and intimidation, some victims see no way out other than ending their own lives. And, in some extreme cases, the effects of constant bullying can turn a victim into the aggressor, as witnessed in recent tragedies involving school homicides. With an increased number of students who report taking weapons to school to protect themselves, we need to be especially alert to the socially isolated victim who may resort to desperate means to end the bullying behavior. A study by the Pittsburgh Youth Study showed that victimization was more likely to predict adolescents' gun-carrying than the reverse (Van Kammen and Loeber, 1995). Though extreme, it is important for us to understand that serious, prolonged bullying can result in horribly destructive behaviors, including both suicide and homicide.

Section Three: **Bystanders**

Bystanders, the 85% of students in a school who are not actively involved in the bullying dynamic, have the most potential for solving this very serious problem. And yet, this silent majority of students is the most ignored and underused resource in our schools. In fact, most bullying prevention programs neglect this group entirely, forgetting that bullying is an activity that involves many more people than the identified bullies and victims. When bullying is understood as an interpersonal activity that takes place in a broad social context (Craig and Pepler, 1996), it is easy to recognize the important role played by bystanders. In any typical middle school environment, bystanders far outnumber both bullies and victims, yet their value as a majority group is often unrecognized and their potential for power is wasted.

Bystanders are crucial to the success of the *Bully-Proofing Your School* program. The foundation of the *Bully-Proofing* program is the development of this silent majority of bystanders into the caring majority who take responsibility for creating safe and bully-free schools. By mobilizing this very important group, schools can become the caring communities both students and teachers expect and deserve.

Who Are the Bystanders?

Bystanders are the students in the school who are not actively involved in the bullying dynamic and are not officially identified as bullies or victims. They account for a large percentage (up to 85%) of the school population, affording them majority status. But for various reasons, bystanders do not take advantage of this potential strength in numbers. Instead, they remain silent and inactive, aware of the bullying, but unable or unwilling to take action against it.

The most common characteristic of bystanders is not the way they look or a particular personality pattern. Instead, what they have in common is their inaction in bullying situations. The label "bystander" means just that—the student who "stands by" when he or she sees bullying or harassing behaviors taking place. And although bystanders may not be seriously traumatized by the bullying they observe, they do pay a price for choosing not to act. Bystanders can experience anxiety and guilt for not taking action which can eventually lead to a lowered sense of both self-respect and self-confidence (Hazler, 1996). Over time, a sense of personal powerlessness can develop, resulting in a pattern of avoidance and inaction.

The most serious consequence of these avoiding behaviors for bystanders is that they can become desensitized to negative behaviors around them, resulting in a diminished capacity for empathy. As they become

On the bus there were some kids who were sitting down. A boy came in and sat by them. He started cussing at them and hitting them for no reason. I wanted to tell him to stop but he was a lot bigger than me so I didn't. The next day the girls' arms were sore and I felt bad I didn't tell him to stop.

**Letter from
bystander**

A time when I regret that I wished I took a stand is when I was at the park. A kid was being picked on because he was a nerd. The other three kids didn't care that everyone was watching. They were pushing him and teasing him. The other nerdy kid just kept walking away.

No one helped him, and I knew how he felt because people made fun of me about my size. I wanted to help him, but I was one and they were many. I really wanted to say something, but didn't. So I walked away.

The next day I went to the park to rollerblade and I saw the kid digging in the sand. I went up to him and he had a fat lip. I really felt bad that I didn't help him. I was mad.

less sensitive to other students' pain, they become more susceptible to aligning with the bullies. If bystanders join the bullies, then the caring majority loses power and the social environment suffers.

Middle school students who are in the role of bystanders are not cold and heartless individuals, but they are often confused about both their responsibilities and their roles. They commonly give three basic reasons for why they do not get involved (Hazler, 1996):

1. They don't know what to do;

2. They are afraid of retaliation;

3. They are afraid they might do the wrong thing, which would make the situation worse.

Complicating the issue even further, middle school students are also extremely conscious of social status issues, which often results in them not reaching out to help a victim because of their worries about losing status. For example, if a student watches another student who is not in his social group being bullied, not only might he be afraid of being the bully's next victim, but he also might be afraid to take action out of fear that his own group will reject him for reaching out to an outsider. These concerns are very real for middle school students, and it is the responsibility of adults to teach students about the responsibilities of members in a caring community as well as the skills to deal effectively with bullying situations.

How Do We Mobilize the Bystanders?

The *Bully-Proofing Your School* program is the primary intervention for mobilizing the bystanders. It is a comprehensive bully prevention program designed to create a positive, prosocial school climate that feels safe and secure for all members of the school community. The skills and strategies included in the program are primarily designed to mobilize the silent majority of students to take responsibility for creating a safe school climate. The lessons in the curriculum include basic information about the bullying dynamic itself, strategies to avoid victimization of self and others, and the skills needed to develop the concepts of empathy: taking a stand for what is right, creative problem solving, positive leadership, and building community.

The classroom lessons provide students the forum to discuss openly with their peers their concerns and feelings about school safety issues. This format allows them the opportunity to learn that they are not alone in their fears and worries, and they begin to experience that there truly is strength in numbers. Through class discussions, students learn that everyone has at some time been victimized or watched someone else being hurt and not known what to do. By listening to each other they discover that others, like them, know bullying is wrong but are afraid to do anything about it for fear of upsetting the status quo. Just hearing that they are not alone and that others share their concerns can give bystanders the confidence to speak up and take a stand for what they know is right. Giving them the opportunity to talk about and share their concerns is one of the first steps in mobilizing the silent majority toward a common goal of safe schools.

It is also important to make clear to the bystanders that standing by and doing nothing during bullying episodes can reinforce the bullies' behaviors. In fact, if bystanders observe bullying taking place and do nothing to assist the victim, bullies can interpret this as approval of their behaviors (Craig and Pepler, 1996). It is crucial for the bystanders to understand that their inaction can encourage the bullies' behaviors, and taking some kind of action is better than doing nothing at all. The *Bully-Proofing* lessons teach that being members of the caring community involves taking responsibility for helping the victims.

By encouraging and teaching the silent majority of students that they have a responsibility to take a stand against bullying, we can harness their tremendous potential and expand on their natural desire to be in a school where they feel safe and taken care of by each other. Their reward is not only the self-satisfaction they receive by acting responsibly, but also the positive attention from the school and community that they earn by being members of the caring majority.

Chapter Four

Establishing a School-Wide Program

Philosophical Basis

In a culture such as ours, where more and more children are separated from their extended families and isolated in their own neighborhoods, it is crucial that they feel connected to their schools and experience school as a community where they are responsible for their own and each other's well-being and safety. The focus of the *Bully-Proofing Your School* program is on creating safe and caring school communities where children do feel connected and the power is in the hands of the caring majority. This caring majority is made up of all members of the school community—students, teachers, administrators, support staff, parents—working together to create an environment that feels supportive to everyone.

The article "The Classroom as Community" includes results from a study conducted by the staff of the Child Development Project that show there are many benefits to students experiencing school as community (Kohn, *Beyond Discipline*, p.1). The more often students experienced their school as a community, the more they reported the following benefits:

- ◆ Liked school
- ◆ Saw learning as valuable on its own
- ◆ Felt safe and willing to take academic risks

◆ Felt comfortable enough to participate without the fear of being judged

◆ Were more concerned about others

◆ Handled conflict effectively

The *Bully-Proofing* program is based on this model of school as community and involves a process of climate change that takes from three to five years to be solidly in place as part of the school-wide culture. The initial commitment to begin this project should be made in the context of this understanding, which encourages careful, long-term planning rather than "quick fix" solutions to the problems of bullying.

Gaining school-wide staff support and enthusiasm for the *Bully-Proofing* program can seem like a daunting task. But the task is made easier when the school staff understands that sharing the responsibility for creating a safe school with the students will ultimately make the their jobs easier. When students begin taking a stand **against** bullying and **for** treating each other with kindness and respect, teachers are again free to spend their time doing what they love—inspiring and teaching students. The *Bully-Proofing* program makes it possible for teachers to teach, students to learn, and parents to trust that their children are safe in their school environment.

This chapter outlines the information necessary to successfully implement the school-wide *Bully-Proofing* program. The basic concepts and elements of the program are described in detail with specific planning suggestions. A step-by-step plan for implementation is offered and particular challenges and their solutions are discussed. Keep in mind that it is important for each school to assess its own needs and resources carefully and to adapt the program accordingly. The success of any school-wide safety effort depends on a realistic assessment of resources available before the program is undertaken.

Basic Concepts

There are four basic concepts that form the basis of the *Bully-Proofing Your School: A Comprehensive Approach for Middle School* program. These were discussed in detail in Chapter One, but a brief review is provided below as a summary. See Handout/Transparency 5D.

It is important for the school staff to understand these basic concepts before they commit to implementing the program. For some adults, the concept of sharing responsibility for the school climate with the students can be threatening because it involves shifting from a vertical power structure to a horizontal power structure. But if the staff can be helped to understand the value and benefit of including students in this powerful process, the program will have a much greater chance for success, and implementation will be easier.

Handout/Transparency 5D

HANDOUT/TRANSPARENCY 5D
Four Basic Concepts of the
Bully-Proofing Your School **Program**

The program is designed as a systemic, comprehensive program.

♦ School-wide commitment to nontolerance for bullying

♦ Development of school-wide rules and expectations

♦ School-wide commitment to creating a caring community

♦ All systems are involved (administration, teachers, students, support staff, transportation, community liaisons)

The main focus is on climate change.

♦ Designed to create a positive, prosocial school climate

♦ Commitment is to broad cultural change

♦ Program is viewed as a process of gradual change

The program teaches skills and strategies to avoid victimization.

♦ Introduces a common vocabulary to be used system-wide

♦ Skills include how to take a stand for self and others

♦ Emphasizes concept of taking responsibility for each other

♦ Develops skills of problem solving and community building

Emphasis is on developing the caring majority.

♦ Goal is to shift power away from the bullies to the silent majority members

♦ Focus is on empowering and mobilizing the silent majority to become the caring majority

♦ The caring majority is the foundation of the caring school environment

Basic Elements of School-Wide Implementation

There are ten basic elements that a school needs to have in place in order for the *Bully-Proofing* program to be optimally successful. Taking the time to assess and plan for each of these elements is an important step in school-wide implementation. See Handout/Transparency 4A.

Handout/Transparency 4A

1. Staff acknowledgment of the problem of bullying and their commitment to the creation of a safe school

As it has become more and more clear that school safety is an educational priority, school districts have issued policies and directives which address safety issues. In the book *Violence in American Schools* Stephens states that "School safety must be placed at the top of the educational agenda. Without safe schools, teachers cannot teach and students cannot learn." (p. 253). However, administrative policy and directives alone will not ensure that students feels safe. Instead, it is the acknowledgment by all school staff members that bullying and harassing

Handout/Transparency 4A

H A N D O U T / T R A N S P A R E N C Y 4 A
Ten Basic Elements

The ten basic elements a school needs to have in place for the program to be successful are as follows:

1. Staff acknowledgment of the problem of bullying and their commitment to the creation of a safe school

2. Administrative support for the program

3. School-wide discipline plan in place

4. Bully-Proofing Cadre formed to design and guide implementation of the program

5. Assessment of current school climate and safety issues

6. Training of staff

7. Training of students—classroom curriculum

8. Support from the parent community

9. Strategies for ongoing development of the caring community

10. Evaluation of the program

behaviors occur and are damaging to students and the school climate that is the first crucial step toward solving the problem. When adult staff members are helped to understand—on an emotional level—that students cannot learn in a climate of fear, they find it easier to commit to being part of the solution. In their bullying intervention model, Hoover and Oliver (1996) refer to the "empathetic" school as a place where all members of the school community, adults and students alike, understand that they are responsible for each other feeling safe and respected. When this understanding is in place and staff members take both individual and group responsibility for making schools safe, the success of the *Bully-Proofing Your School* program has a much higher potential for success.

During this initial phase of implementation, it is important to allow time for staff members to ask questions and voice concerns about the program, as well as to brainstorm both the barriers and contributors to its potential success. Schools frequently make the mistake of rushing through this initial stage without allowing time for the discussion and examination of these important issues up front. By deliberately taking the time to discuss these issues, facilitators can be proactive in diffusing future resistance and concerns.

2. Administrative support for the program

It is especially important that administrators appreciate that policy change alone will not make a difference in school culture or climate. Administrators, along with all staff members, need to educate themselves about the true nature of effective change as a process, instead of as a "quick fix." Their respect for the philosophy and the comprehensive nature of the *Bully-Proofing Your School* program is crucial, as is their agreement to commit the necessary resources to the project, ideally as a three-year plan. Administrators who make available both the time and money to staff members who are willing to design and implement the program for the school are invaluable to the success of the program. Most importantly, the administrator's personal belief in the value of the program as well as his or her public commitment to it can make or break its success.

3. School-wide discipline plan in place

If the *Bully-Proofing Your School* program is to be effective, there must be a school-wide discipline plan already in place in the school. This discipline plan provides a code of conduct for the school that must include a "no tolerance, no nonsense" approach toward bullying. The *Bully-Proofing* program then operates inside this broad discipline plan with the clear understanding by all members of the school community that bullying will not be tolerated. It is recommended that information about the *Bully-Proofing* program, and specifically its nontolerance position on bullying, be publicized in the discipline sections of the student and parent handbooks and reviewed periodically. It is also effective to write the school rules in bully-proofing language so that the vocabulary of the program is incorporated into the behavioral expectations and procedures of the school.

4. Bully-Proofing Cadre formed to design and guide implementation of the program

An effective way to coordinate all the various efforts involved in planning this school-wide program is to form a committee of members of the school community who are interested in and committed to successfully implementing the program. This committee or cadre acts as the driving force behind the program and works to keep the school's focus on the important work of school safety. In the process, committee members become the "culture carriers" of the climate change for the school. The size of the committee can be determined by the needs of the school, but an optimum number for both efficiency and effectiveness is eight to twelve members. Ideally, committee members should represent a cross section of the school community including an administrator, student, parent, counselor, dean, teacher from each grade level, mental health team representative, and a member of the school security team. It is also necessary to select a member of the committee to serve as committee chairperson. The chairperson should have strong organizational skills, the ability to facilitate effective group processes, and the respect of the majority of the school community.

The main task of the committee is to design the *Bully-Proofing* program to fit the special needs and resources of the school. Specific tasks of the planning committee are varied and include goal setting, problem solving, scheduling, designing staff presentations, curriculum development and implementation, teacher training, and publicity. Though many skills are required by committee members, it is most important to gather together a group of positive-thinking, creative people who have the respect of their fellow staff members and who, in turn, respect and understand the complex process of cultural change. Selecting committee members who are themselves models of caring community members goes a long way toward inspiring the staff to become committed to the *Bully-Proofing Your School* program.

5. Assessment of current school climate and safety issues

Assessment is a vital step in the implementation of any comprehensive school safety program. Sometimes, in their enthusiastic rush to start new programs, educators neglect this very important step, which can result in programs that seem directionless and unfocused. Before implementing the *Bully-Proofing* program it is important to assess the present school climate in order to determine what problems exist and how to address them. The assessment can consist of three different parts:

Part I: Assessment of relationships

>   A.   How do students treat each other?
>
>   B.   How do staff members treat each other?
>
>   C.   How do students and staff members treat each other?

Handout/Transparency 4B

Part II: Assessment of systems. What strategies are currently being used in the following areas to create a positive school climate?

>   A.   Administration/Discipline
>
>   B.   Staff
>
>   C.   Classroom
>
>   D.   Counseling/Mental Health
>
>   E.   Special Education
>
>   F.   Parents
>
>   G.   Athletics and Activities
>
>   H.   Supervision and Security
>
>   I.   To and From School/Bus

J. Community

K. Physical Plant

L. Unstructured Time

Part III: Assessment of bullying behaviors. Colorado School Climate Survey (Handout 4C)

Parts I and II of the assessment process include topics to address in faculty meetings as the staff begins to take an honest look at the present climate in the school, beginning with the very important issue of the relationships between people in the school. With a carefully planned and sensitive facilitation of the discussion of these important questions, the adults in the school can begin to examine the present school climate. Following this discussion, they can begin to focus on the type of climate and learning environment they want to create for their students and themselves.

Part III, the Colorado School Climate Survey, is an instrument that provides valuable information about school climate as perceived by students, parents, and school staff. The survey provides information in the following four main areas:

1. Incidences personally experienced by the respondent including verbal, physical, and exclusionary forms of bullying as well as experiences of sexual and ethnic/racial harassment

2. Incidences of bullying behaviors observed by the respondent

3. Feelings of safety across locations in the school

4. Perceptions of the overall school climate including the areas of adult and student helping behaviors, sense of inclusion, and enjoyment of school

Survey results provide the school with information in each of the above areas which is helpful both in establishing a baseline measure of the current school climate and in designing effective interventions to achieve the desired school climate. Different forms of the survey exist for students, parents, and staff and for elementary and secondary schools.

This survey can be used as a presurvey before the *Bully-Proofing* program has been implemented to determine the present level of bullying in the school and as a postsurvey approximately one year later to document the success of the program. The presurvey provides excellent data to the staff about their students' perceptions of the bullying problem. It can also be used to motivate staff members who have difficulty acknowledging that bullying problems exist or who underestimate the extent of the problem. Surveys filled out by the staff and the parents can be used to compare the perceptions between different members of the school community as well as to examine discrepancies between the perceptions of these different groups.

6. Training of staff

Once the staff members of the school have acknowledged that bullying problems exist and have committed to working together to solve the problem, it is imperative that they be trained in the basic concepts of the *Bully-Proofing Your School* program. The program, to be successful, depends on each and every adult staff member in the school taking personal responsibility for dealing with bullying behaviors on a day-to-day basis. To do this effectively, teachers need to understand the dynamics of bullying as well as techniques to combat it.

The ideal staff training would include the entire school staff representing all the systems in the school participating in a one-day bully-proofing workshop. A suggested outline for this type of training is included in Chapter Five and can be facilitated by members of the Bully-Proofing Cadre who have already been trained. If a full day is not available for staff training, making a training workshop available for interested staff members outside of school time, possibly for teacher recertification credit through the state department of education, is an efficient way of creating an informed, confident cluster of staff members committed to working together to implement the program.

At the very least, the entire school staff representing all systems in the school should receive an initial training that includes the philosophy and basic elements of the program and specific information about the dynamics of bullying and victimization. This information could be shared with the faculty during staff meetings and inservice days, with the Bully-Proofing Committee planning the presentations and facilitating the discussions. The more adults in the building who have a thorough background in the *Bully-Proofing* program, the easier it is to implement the program successfully.

Depending on the model used to present the classroom curriculum to the students, the teachers can learn the specific skills and strategies of the curriculum along with the students during the classroom lessons. One recommendation for the first year of the program is to have trained facilitators go into the classrooms to teach the lessons, with the requirement that the teachers be present during the lessons and participate along with the students. With this model, teachers are not required to plan or teach the lessons, but are expected to participate and learn the same skills and strategies as the students. This allows for students and teachers to participate in the learning process together and helps to assure that the concepts and skills become a part of the daily culture of the classroom. Teachers are also asked to facilitate certain homework and classwork assignments between weekly visits by the facilitators in order to further develop the program concepts.

During the second year of program implementation, a suggested delivery model is to have one trained facilitator join the classroom teacher in teaching the curriculum. Pairing a support facilitator with the classroom teacher requires that they spend time planning the lessons together, with the goal being that the classroom teacher becomes more comfortable with and responsible for the classroom curriculum. By the third year of implementation, the teacher can pair again with a support facilitator or, if necessary, be solely responsible for teaching the bully-proofing curriculum.

It is also important and valuable to spend time with the staff addressing the issues related to the relationships among adults in the school and the climate of caring among staff members. Teaching middle school students is a challenging and stressful job that is made even more difficult in an unfriendly or nonsupportive environment. It is imperative that educational professionals take the time to explore the characteristics of healthy staff relationships and work environments. Chapter Five addresses these topics and includes ideas for exploring these kinds of issues.

7. Training of students—classroom curriculum

Chapters Six, Seven, and Eight of this manual contain the complete classroom curriculum of the *Bully-Proofing Your School* program, with lessons designed specifically for sixth, seventh, and eighth grade students. Each grade level curriculum includes seven specific lessons unique to the grade level and designed to be taught over a five-week period. Each set of lessons builds on the concepts taught the previous year. The main concepts taught at each grade level are shown in Handout/Transparency 5R.

HANDOUT/TRANSPARENCY 5R
Curriculum Overview

CURRICULUM OVERVIEW		
Sixth Grade: The Basics About Bullying		
Bullies	Bystanders	Empathy
Definition and Types of Bullying	Teasing	Taking a Stand
Normal Conflict vs. Bullying	Sexual Harassment	Inclusion
Victims	HA HA SO Strategies	
Seventh Grade: Creating the Caring Community		
Review of the Basics	Cliques	Flirting
Empathy	Taking a Stand	Levels of Risk-Taking
Inclusion	Sexual Harassment	Creative Problem Solving
Eighth Grade: Leadership		
Review of the Basics	Groups and Cliques	Empathy
Sexual Harassment	Characteristics and Styles of Positive Leadership	Taking a Stand
Flirting	Intention	Creative Problem Solving
Inclusion		
New Students: Establish a Connection with Their School		
New Students—Shared Experiences	Normal Conflict vs. Bullying	Empathy
Definition and Types of Bullying	Victims	Taking a Stand
No-bullying Expectations Stressed	Bystanders	Inclusion
Bullies	HA HA SO Strategies	Sexual Harassment

Planning how to deliver the curriculum to every classroom in the school is an important task of the Bully-Proofing Committee. Deciding who the facilitators will be and how to schedule them into the classrooms throughout the year can be challenging and depends on a realistic assessment of the resources available in the school.

The classroom lessons are designed as forums for students to discuss with peers their concerns about school safety issues. It is the intention of the program that these classroom sessions inspire open discussions and provide opportunities for students to examine their own beliefs and behaviors that affect their relationships with others. Because of this, it is important that the facilitators understand how to create a trusting, learning environment in which students feel safe in expressing their opinions and concerns. Specific tips on how to do this effectively are included as a preface to the curriculum in Chapter Six.

8. Support from the parent community

Support from the school's parent community is an important factor in the success of the *Bully-Proofing* program. Parents appreciate being officially informed of new school programs and being given the opportunity to participate in the development and implementation of these programs. Including them in the beginning stages of the plan to implement the *Bully-Proofing* program can help to assure the success of the school-wide effort and is an important factor in developing the cooperation and support of the community at large.

Listed below are some suggested steps for successfully involving parents in the program:

Handout 4D

◆ Write an introductory letter to parents which announces the school's formal adoption of the *Bully-Proofing* program and explains the key elements of the program. This letter should also include very clear information about the school's "no tolerance, no nonsense" policy around bullying. See Handout 4D (at the end of this chapter) for an example of a parent letter.

◆ Invite a parent or parents to be members of the school's Bully-Proofing Committee. These parent members can play a crucial role in the committee's task of developing a plan for working and communicating with parents as the program develops. Parent members can also play a role in developing positive public relations with the school's parent community.

◆ Invite the parent community to a program orientation meeting that includes the basic information about the program and an overview of the classroom curriculum. This meeting should allow adequate time for parents to ask questions and express any concerns they may have about the implementation of the program and how it will affect their children. For example, if parents express concern about students being singled out or labeled, it would be appropriate during this meeting to let parents know that individual students are never identified as bullies or victims during classroom lessons, and that during classroom discussions, students are not permitted to use people's names. Depending on the size of the school, one or several orientation sessions for parents can be scheduled with the goal being that of trying to reach as many parents as possible.

◆ Develop a plan for consistent ongoing communication with parents about the program through community meetings, PTCO meetings, school newsletters, and other publicity tools. Include parents in any school-wide bully-proofing projects or programs by asking them to help with the planning or implementation. Keep the parent community informed throughout the school year of the progress and success of the program.

9. Strategies for ongoing development of the caring community

As we have learned, the *Bully-Proofing Your School* program is about much more than just dealing with bullies. The foundation of the entire program is centered on the concept of community—of working together to create a caring school community characterized by a climate that makes all its members feel respected and safe. The requirement, beyond teaching the classroom curriculum and specific interventions with bullies and victims, is the careful and creative planning of ongoing activities, projects, programs, and publicity that encourage and motivate the members of the school community in their continuous efforts to improve the school. Designing ways to promote the concepts of the program so that they become integral parts of the school culture is a challenging task, but one that is required if the program is to sustain itself over time.

One of the most important strategies for mobilizing the silent majority into the caring community is to design a way to continue caring community discussions with the students after the classroom curriculum is completed. Ideally, each classroom in the school would have one identified time during the week, such as a homeroom or advisory period, when safe school issues are discussed. During this time, students and adults can talk together about their successes, challenges, and concerns. They can practice skills such as taking a stand or levels of risk-taking. Most importantly, this time can be used to reinforce positive and caring student behaviors and to acknowledge students' efforts to be members of the caring community. This goal is to be inclusionary, not competitive, and to encourage all members of the class to be successful in making choices that contribute to a safe school environment.

Designing school-wide strategies is one of the major tasks of the school's Bully-Proofing Committee. Though many of the initial tasks of the committee are concrete and immediate, such as putting together the schedule for classroom presentations, the task of designing the ongoing strategies to spread the message of the program throughout the culture of the entire school takes creative energy and long-term planning.

Listed below are just some of the ideas schools have used in their efforts to promote the development of the caring community. It is important for each individual school implementing the program to design projects that are both workable and appropriate for their school.

Ideas for Development of the Caring Community

◆ Incorporate the bully-proofing vocabulary into the school rules that are posted throughout the school. Work with staff members, including deans and counselors, to use the vocabulary in their interventions with students.

◆ Regularly publicize bully-proofing news in school newsletters and publications.

◆ Invite the local media to feature the program in newspapers and on television.

◆ Begin the school year with a bully-proofing assembly including activities designed around program concepts.

◆ Conduct a school logo contest and ask students to design the school's caring community logo to be used on charts, in publications, and on school t-shirts, sweatshirts, pencils, supplies, book covers, and so forth.

◆ Organize a school poster contest or project.

◆ Introduce an "I caught you caring" campaign. Make "I caught you caring" slips available for people to fill out when they observe someone doing a caring act. Slips can be posted on hallway walls. Slips can also be turned in to the main office for weekly random drawings and acknowledgments.

◆ Put "I caught you caring" boxes in classrooms.

◆ Incorporate concepts into daily classroom curriculums. Identify bullying dynamics in literature, politics, history, the arts, etc. Create writing assignments organized around bullying concepts.

◆ Sponsor caring community dances.

◆ Create a photographic collage of students "caught" doing caring things. Hand out disposable cameras to adults throughout the building and ask them to take photos of students. Display the collage in a public place.

◆ Award students who act as caring community members.

◆ Produce videos about caring community concepts by and for students to be shown to the school community.

◆ Invite teachers to present ideas that they have developed to the staff.

◆ Decorate classroom doors with bully-proofing concepts and themes.

◆ Provide teachers with ideas and strategies about fostering a sense of community in the classroom.

10. Evaluation of the program

Evaluation of the program's effectiveness is very important to its success. All members of the school community need periodic feedback about the program's progress in order to stay motivated and focused. Too often school programs are undertaken but never evaluated to document their success, which can contribute to both a loss of interest and commitment by the school staff.

The *Bully-Proofing Your School* program can be evaluated both formally and informally. Both types of evaluation provide valuable information about successful parts of the program and the parts that need more focus.

Formal Evaluation Measures

◆ *The Colorado School Climate Survey* (Handout 4C) Recommended as both a pre- and postsurvey, it can be administered to students before program implementation and approximately one year later to document program effectiveness. Comparing percentages from both the pre- and postsurvey results is an effective way of providing feedback to the school community about which parts of the *Bully-Proofing* program have been effective and which areas need adjustment and added focus.

| Handout 4C |

◆ *Other school surveys* Many schools have accountability committees that are required to survey students and parents about their perceptions of school safety. These surveys can also be used to evaluate the success of the *Bully-Proofing* program. Though not as specific as the Colorado School Climate Survey, these more generic surveys can certainly point to the program's success if perceptions of school safety increase after the *Bully-Proofing* program has been in place.

◆ *Behavior referrals/Suspension rates* Some schools have the capability to track the number of behavior referrals and school suspensions from year to year. If schools can classify these according to bully-related issues, it is possible to use the rates as a means of evaluating the success of the program. It is important to note that it is common for reports and complaints of bullying behaviors to increase after the initial implementation of the program because of the program's strong anti-bullying message. However, after approximately one year of program implementation, these numbers should decrease.

Informal Evaluation Measures

◆ *Student interviews* Interviewing students about their perceptions of the program and how it is or isn't working provides valuable information that cannot be accessed through a formal survey. The interviewing process also reinforces the message to students that they are valued members of the caring community and that their opinions are respected.

◆ *Written evaluations* Asking both students and staff members to give written evaluations of the program allows them to include more detailed information about the program than the formal survey permits. These can be filled out anonymously, if appropriate, and are useful in identifying particular issues that are not being identified by other means.

◆ *Discussion groups* It is important to make time for staff, students, and parents to periodically discuss the status of the *Bully-Proofing* program. This can be done at faculty meetings, on staff training days, at PTCO meetings, in classrooms, and at student meetings. Since the school community has made a commitment to the program as a school-wide effort, it makes sense for time to be set aside to discuss how the program is progressing. Consistently putting bully-proofing on the school's agenda serves to keep it at the forefront of people's efforts and energies.

Challenges to Success

It is realistic to anticipate the challenges that typically arise for staff members when planning a school-wide program such as *Bully-Proofing*. Acknowledging and strategizing ways to overcome these in the beginning stages of planning can help to minimize their impact once the program is underway. Listed below are some of the typical challenges that may arise with comments and suggestions for each.

Time Constraints

There is no way to discount the very real concerns teachers have about adding "another new program" to their already full plates. Acknowledging up-front that this program will take time to design and implement is important and should be discussed with the staff. But what helps to alleviate this fear are consistent reminders that, though the program will take time and effort, the rewards are great and will ultimately **save adults time** as everyone shares the responsibility for creating a safe school. It is a rewarding process to shift the focus of the school's attention onto students' caring behaviors. The program benefits adults and students alike, as a caring community is developed in which teachers can teach and students can learn.

Denial of Problem

Some of the staff may remain unconvinced that it is necessary to intervene in bullying situations and may continue to ignore the problem. This can become particularly pronounced in middle schools where adults can mistakenly cling to the incorrect belief that adolescents need less supervision as they grow older and that it is best to let them solve their own problems. Educating staff about the seriousness of bullying and its damaging effects on students helps to correct some of these outdated beliefs. Teachers and other staff members need reminders not to underestimate the incredible influence they have on their students, despite adolescent protests to the contrary. Using research data on students' concerns about school safety, as well as the data from the school's own presurvey results, is very helpful in awakening reluctant staff members to the very real problems of bullying.

Leadership and Resources

When considering a new school-wide program, one of the staff members' first questions is "Who is going to do the work?" Even though it is necessary for each individual staff member to take responsibility for dealing with bullying issues, it is both effective and reassuring for a middle school to create a Bully-Proofing Committee with a chairperson who will supervise the efforts. Forming a committee gives credence to the importance and scope of the program, assures the staff that the effort is organized and well-managed, and makes its general implementation more manageable for everyone. Furthermore, reimbursing committee members for their extra time and effort by giving them release time, curriculum pay, or recertification credit serves to make this dedicated group feel valued, appreciated, and motivated.

Discomfort With Issues

Another challenge to the success of a program such as *Bully-Proofing* can be staff members' discomfort with the issues surrounding bullying as well as a lack of confidence in their abilities to deal with bullying successfully. Teaching staff members the basic information about the dynamics of bullying is a first step toward increasing both their comfort level and their confidence in dealing with bullying issues. Most importantly, these issues need to be addressed in a safe and caring environment in which everyone is respected for their beliefs and concerns, and no one is judged or criticized. Included in the recommended staff training in Chapter Five are various exercises that encourage staff members to share their own experiences with bullying and to talk with teammates about their individual styles of dealing with conflict. Teamwork and cooperation are emphasized as the staff works together to build a caring community for themselves as well as for their students.

Overwhelmed

The idea of implementing a school-wide climate program in a large middle school can seem like an overwhelming project to many staff members. Some adults initially feel this sense of being overwhelmed, and they disconnect both emotionally and mentally from the concept. To prevent this from happening, it is important to carefully plan the initial presentation and early discussions about the *Bully-Proofing* program so that the staff feels emotionally connected to the concepts and hopeful about their ability to make a difference in the school environment. A disorganized and haphazard introduction to the program will not inspire confidence, but will instead increase apathy or outright resistance.

Steps for School-Wide Implementation

Listed below are the suggested steps for implementing the *Bully-Proofing Your School* program in middle school. The steps begin with the assumption that the school has already decided to use the program and that administrative support and a strong disciplinary plan are already in place. It is preferable that the adoption of the program by the school be a democratic decision by the entire staff, rather than a top-down directive from administration. However, it is realistic to acknowledge that schools choose to implement the program under a variety of mandates and for many different reasons. The important steps for successful implementation are listed below. Please note that it is important to adapt the steps to fit your school and to do them in the order that works best for your situation.

Handouts 5D and 4A
Handout/Transparency 5R

Step 1   The program orientation is presented to the entire staff. It includes the philosophical basis, the four basic concepts, and the ten basic elements of the program (Handouts 5D and 4A), and an overview of the classroom curriculums (Handout/Transparency 5R).

Step 2   A complete bully-proofing workshop is offered to all interested staff members. (See Chapter Five.) If possible this is offered for Department of Education credit or for credit toward advancement on the salary schedule.

Step 3   A Bully-Proofing Cadre is formed and a chairperson is selected. (See Chapter Four.)

Handout 4D

Step 4   A letter is sent home to the parents to explain the basics of the program and to invite them to an orientation session. (See Handout 4D.)

Handout 4C

Step 5   The Colorado School Climate Survey or a comparable climate survey is conducted with the students, staff, and parents to assess the current school climate and to inform the program design. (See Handout 4C.)

Step 6   The cadre designs the schedule and facilitation model for the classroom curriculums. (See Chapters Four and Six.)

Step 7   Facilitators conduct classroom sessions throughout the school.

Step 8   Strategies are developed for school-wide programs to expand the concepts beyond the classroom sessions into the school culture. (See Chapter Four.)

Step 9   Plans are made for continued consultation, staff development, and parent orientation throughout the school year.

Step 10   Formal and informal evaluations are conducted to determine the progress of the program. (See Chapter Four.)

Implementing the school-wide *Bully-Proofing Your School* program is a major undertaking which requires commitment, time, and effort on the part of all members of the school community. Throughout its implementation, it is important to remember that this program represents a process of climate change and therefore requires both determination and patience on the part of the school community as the new concepts take hold. Keeping the end goal in mind—creating a safe and caring school environment where the power is in the hands of the caring majority, not the bullies—will inspire the staff to stay involved and focused as the program develops and gradually becomes part of the school culture.

HANDOUT/TRANSPARENCY 4A
Ten Basic Elements

The ten basic elements a school needs to have in place for the program to be successful are as follows:

1. Staff acknowledgment of the problem of bullying and their commitment to the creation of a safe school

2. Administrative support for the program

3. School-wide discipline plan in place

4. Bully-Proofing Cadre formed to design and guide implementation of the program

5. Assessment of current school climate and safety issues

6. Training of staff

7. Training of students—classroom curriculum

8. Support from the parent community

9. Strategies for ongoing development of the caring community

10. Evaluation of the program

HANDOUT/TRANSPARENCY 4B
Climate Chart

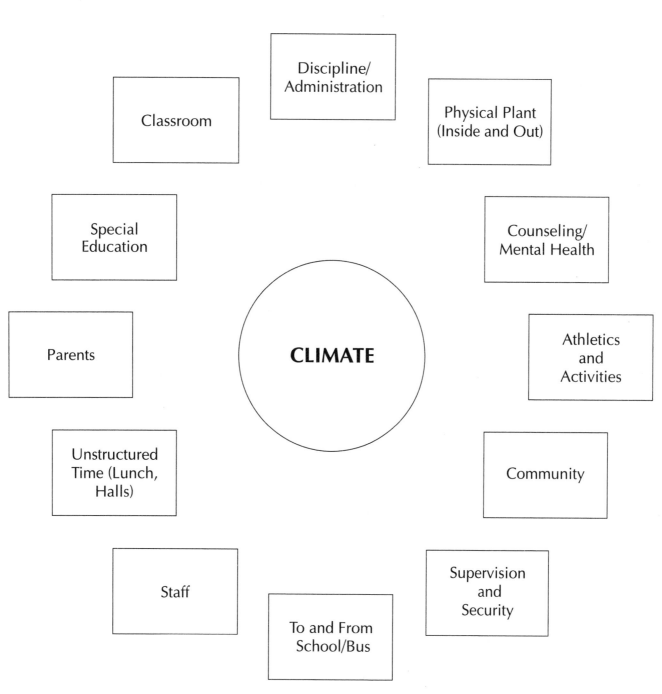

Draw a solid line to areas of significant impact on climate and a dotted line to what the school is doing well.

HANDOUT 4C
Colorado School Climate Survey

Secondary Schools

Description

Bullying and harassment in the schools can present students and school staff with significant and far-reaching problems. In order to intervene effectively with these problems, it is important to thoroughly assess the extent and nature of bullying within the school. The **Colorado School Climate Survey (CSCS)** is an instrument that provides comprehensive information about bullying and school climate as perceived by students, parents, and school staff. Separate versions are available for elementary and secondary schools. The **CSCS** provides information across four important domains:

Has This Happened to You?

The **first domain** asks about incidences of bullying personally experienced by the respondent. At the elementary level, this domain assesses verbal, physical, and exclusionary forms of bullying, as well as stealing and threatening. The secondary school version of the **CSCS** includes questions about sexual and ethnic/racial harassment as well.

Have You Seen This Happen?

The **second domain** asks about incidences of bullying observed by the respondent. Respondents answer questions about each of the types of bullying listed in the first domain. Together, these two domains provide a comprehensive evaluation of bullying behaviors in the school.

For each of these first two domains, follow-up questions are asked about perpetrators and locations of the bullying behaviors as well as what students did in response to the incidences (both experienced and observed).

How Safe Do You Feel?

The **third domain** includes questions about how safe respondents believe that students are across several locations in the school.

What Is Your School Like?

The **fourth domain** asks questions about respondents' perceptions of the overall school climate. School climate encompasses the general areas of adult and student helping behavior, sense of inclusion, and enjoyment of school.

Survey results provide each school with a profile that includes information from each of the above domains. This information is helpful both in establishing a baseline measure of the current school climate and in designing effective interventions to achieve the desired school climate. The **CSCS** can also be used to document the progress of identified interventions.

HANDOUT 4C (*continued*)

Group Administration Instructions for Students

Please read this completely before administering the CSCS.

1. Read through the questions before you read them out loud to the students.

2. You may define words that are not familiar to the students. However, if you are asked to clarify what is meant by a particular item, let the students know that they should answer it as best they can according to whether or not they think the behavior has occurred or the item is true.

3. FYI: for the section that asks about frequency of bullying behaviors, "Less than one time per week" refers to an event that has happened on one or more occasions, but has not occurred on a weekly basis.

4. Hand out the questionnaire.

Say: **This set of questions asks you to tell about your school and things that may or may not have happened to you at school. There are no right or wrong answers. Please answer the questions to show what you think about your school. Please do not write your name anywhere on the questionnaire. This way, your answers will remain private.**

5. Read each question and pause briefly to allow time to respond. Remember to read any instructions (e.g., **check only one box, check all that apply**) that go along with the question. Finally, read the response choices (e.g., never, less than one time per week, one time per week, two to four times per week, five or more times per week) after you have read the first two questions of each of the four domains (Has This Happened to You?, Have You Seen This Happen?, How Safe Do You Feel?, and What Is Your School Like?)

6. Collect questionnaires and return them to the designated person. As you collect the questionnaires, please be sure to check that the students have completed the form properly.

Note: It is important that the questionnaires are read to the students. This is to help ensure that the students, regardless of reading level, understand all the questions. The questionnaire can be administered over multiple sessions. Please administer at least one of the four domains (Has This Happened to You?, Have You Seen This Happen?, How Safe Do You Feel?, and What Is Your School Like?) at a time.

Suggested time for completion is approximately 30 minutes.

HANDOUT 4C (*continued*)

School _____   Code _____

Date _____

Secondary School Student Report

This set of questions asks you to tell about your school and things that may or may not have happened to you at school. There are no right or wrong answers. Please answer the questions to show what you think about your school.

Has This Happened to You?

For the following, check only **ONE** box for each item.

During the *past month* other students:	never	less than 1 time per week	1 time per week	2–4 times per week	5 or more times per week
Hit, pushed, or kicked me on purpose					
Said mean things, teased me, or called me names					
Told stories about me that were not true					
Did not include me in what they were doing					
Took things that belong to me					
Threatened to hurt me or take things					
Touched, grabbed, or pinched me in a sexual way that was unwanted					
Made negative comments of a sexual nature about me					
Said mean things, teased me, or called me names because of my race or ethnicity					
Wrote notes, spread rumors, or wrote graffiti of a sexual nature about me					

If any of these happened to you (**check all that apply**):

What did you do?				
I got help from an adult at school		I got help from my parents	
I got help from another student		I ignored it or walked away	
I hit, kicked, or pushed back		I told them to stop	
I said mean things, teased, or called them names		I tried to stop them by saying or doing something funny	
I told the person I agreed with what he or she said about me		I said things to myself to help me feel better	
I avoided the person so I would not get hurt or teased again		I did nothing	

HANDOUT 4C (*continued*)

Who was it done by?

a girl	
a boy	
a group	

Where did it happen?

classroom	
school grounds	
hallways/lunchroom	
going to and from school	
bathroom/locker room	
before or after school activity	

Who did you tell?

no one	
a friend	
an adult at school	
a parent	
bus driver	
other	

Have You Seen This Happen?

For the following, check only **ONE** box for each item.

(Check the box **ONLY** if the item happened to someone else (not to you)).

During the *past month:*	never	less than 1 time per week	1 time per week	2–4 times per week	5 or more times per week
I saw someone get hit, pushed, or kicked on purpose by other students					
I heard students say mean things, tease, or call someone names					
I heard students tell stories about someone that were not true					
I saw students not let someone join in what they were doing					
I saw or heard that students took things that belong to someone else					
I heard students threaten to hurt someone or take their things					
I saw someone get touched, grabbed, or pinched in a sexual way that was unwanted					
I heard students make negative comments of a sexual nature about somebody					
I heard students say mean things, tease, or call someone names because of their race or ethnicity					
I saw notes, heard rumors, or saw graffiti of a sexual nature about someone					

HANDOUT 4C (*continued*)

If you heard or saw any of these things happen (**check all that apply**):

What did you do?

I did nothing	
I asked the person who was hurt/teased/left out to join me	
I helped the person who was hurt/teased/left out to get away	
I helped the person come up with ideas about how to handle the problem	

I got help from an adult at school	
I stood up to the person who was teasing	
I talked to the person who was hurt/teased/left out about how he/she felt	

Who was it done by?

a girl	
a boy	
a group	

Who did you tell?

no one	
a friend	
an adult at school	
a parent	
bus driver	
other	

Where did it happen?

classroom	
school grounds	
hallways/lunchroom	
going to and from school	
bathroom/locker room	
before or after school activity	

How Safe Do You Feel?

During the **past month**, this is how safe I felt in each of these places (check only **ONE** box for each):

	very unsafe & scared	unsafe & scared	kind of unsafe	kind of safe	safe	very safe
In the classroom						
On the school grounds						
In the hallways and lunchroom						
Going to and from school						
In the bathroom/locker room						
At before or after school activities						

HANDOUT 4C (*continued*)

What Is Your School Like?

Check the **ONE** box that best describes you/your school:

	never/ hardly ever true	sometimes true	often true	almost always/ always true
The other students help if they see someone being bullied or harassed				
Students tell adults at school when other students are being bullied or harassed				
If someone is alone during free time, others will include them				
Students at this school encourage other students to do the best they can at their schoolwork				
There are clear rules at our school				
The teachers and staff help if they see someone being bullied or harassed				
Students who misbehave take a lot of my teacher's time				
Adults at this school care that the students do the best school work they can				
My school tries to make everyone feel included				
I usually can find someone to hang out with during free time				
When I'm upset, other students try to comfort me or cheer me up				
I like going to school				
I am afraid to go to school				

Grade: _____ **I am a:** Boy ☐ Girl ☐

I usually go to and from school by:

(check only one)

walking	
bike	
car	
bus	

I am:

Asian	
African American	
Hispanic	
Native American	
White	

(check all that apply)

Other: _____

HANDOUT 4C (*continued*)

School _____   Code _____

Date _____

Secondary School Staff Report

This set of questions asks you to tell about your school and things that may or may not have happened at this school. There are no right or wrong answers. Please answer the questions to show what you think about your school.

Has This Happened to Your Students?

For the following, check only **ONE** box for each item.

During the *past month* students at this school:	never	less than 1 time per week	1 time per week	2–4 times per week	5 or more times per week
Hit, pushed, or kicked other students on purpose					
Said mean things, teased, or called other students names					
Told stories about other students that were not true					
Did not include other students in what they were doing					
Took things that belong to other students					
Threatened to hurt other students or take things					
Touched, grabbed, or pinched other students in a sexual way that was unwanted					
Made negative comments of a sexual nature about other students					
Said mean things, teased, or called other students names because of their race or ethnicity					
Wrote notes, spread rumors, or wrote graffiti of a sexual nature about other students					

If any of these happened (**check all that apply**):

Who was it done by?

a girl	
a boy	
a group	

Where did it happen?

classroom	
school grounds	
hallways/lunchroom	
going to and from school	
bathroom/locker room	
before or after school activity	

Who did the child(ren) tell?

no one	
a friend	
an adult at school	
a parent	
bus driver	
other	

HANDOUT 4C (*continued*)

How Safe Are Your Students?

During the **past month**, this is how safe I felt students were in each of these places (check only **ONE** box for each):

	very unsafe & scared	unsafe & scared	kind of unsafe	kind of safe	safe	very safe
In the classroom						
On the school grounds						
In the hallways and lunchroom						
Going to and from school						
In the bathroom/locker room						
At before or after school activities						

What Is Your School Like?

Check the **ONE** box that best describes this school:

	never/hardly ever true	sometimes true	often true	almost always/ always true
The other students help if they see someone being bullied or harassed				
Students tell adults at school when other students are being bullied or harassed				
If someone is alone during free time, others will include them				
Students at this school encourage other students to do the best they can at their school work				
This school tries to make everyone feel included				
There is a consistent disciplinary policy at this school				
The teachers and staff help if they see someone being bullied or harassed				
Students who misbehave take a lot of my time				
The administrators help me in dealing with students				
Teachers respect each other and try to work together				
Adults at this school care that the students do the best school work they can				
Most people at this school are kind				
I like working at this school				
I feel safe at this school				

HANDOUT 4C (*continued*)

School _____   Code _____

Date _____

Secondary School Parent Report

This set of questions asks you to tell about your child's school and things that may or may not have happened to him or her at school. There are no right or wrong answers. Please answer the questions to show what you think about your child's school.

Has This Happened to Your Child?

For the following, check only **ONE** box for each item.

During the *past month* other students:	never	less than 1 time per week	1 time per week	2–4 times per week	5 or more times per week
Hit, pushed, or kicked my child on purpose					
Said mean things, teased, or called my child names					
Told stories about my child that were not true					
Did not include my child in what they were doing					
Took things that belong to my child					
Threatened to hurt my child or take things					
Touched, grabbed, or pinched my child in a sexual way that was unwanted					
Made negative comments of a sexual nature about my child					
Said mean things, teased my child, or called my child names because of his or her race or ethnicity					
Wrote notes, spread rumors, or wrote graffiti of a sexual nature about my child					

If any of these happened to your child (**check all that apply**):

Who was it done by?

a girl	
a boy	
a group	

Who did your child tell?

no one	
a friend	
an adult at school	
a parent	
bus driver	
other	

Where did it happen?

classroom	
school grounds	
hallways/lunchroom	
going to and from school	
bathroom/locker room	
before or after school activity	

HANDOUT 4C (*continued*)

How Safe Is Your Child?

During the **past month**, this is how safe I felt my child was in each of these places (check only **ONE** box for each):

	very unsafe & scared	unsafe & scared	kind of unsafe	kind of safe	safe	very safe
In the classroom						
On the school grounds						
In the hallways and lunchroom						
Going to and from school						
In the bathroom/locker room						
At before or after school activities						

What Is Your Child's School Like?

Check the **ONE** box that best describes your child's school experience:

	never/hardly ever true	sometimes true	often true	almost always/ always true
The other students help if they see someone being bullied or harassed				
Students tell adults at school when other students are being bullied or harassed				
If someone is alone during free time, others will include them				
Students at this school encourage other students to do the best they can at their school work				
There is a consistent disciplinary policy at this school				
The teachers and staff help if they see someone being bullied or harassed				
Students who misbehave take a lot of the teacher's time				
The administrators support teachers in dealing with students				
Adults at this school care that the students do the best school work they can				
Parental involvement is valued by this school				
I like having my child at this school				
Most people at this school are kind				

HANDOUT 4C (*continued*)

Grade: _____   **My child is a:** Boy ☐   Girl ☐

He/she usually goes to and from school by:

(check only one)

walking	
bike	
car	
bus	

I am:

Asian	
African American	
Hispanic	
Native American	
White	

(check all that apply)

Other: _____

HANDOUT 4D
Sample Letter to Parents

_____
(Date)

Dear Parents(s)/Guardian(s):

_____ School invites you to join with us in
(Name of School)
developing a theme of kindness and respect within our entire community.

We strongly believe that school can be a safe and nurturing environment
for all. One of our goals for this year is to create a caring community at our school
where everyone feels safe and has a sense of belonging. To facilitate this effort, we
are implementing a school-wide safety program called *Bully-Proofing Your School.*

This program will be most effective when the parental community, the administration,
the staff, and the students all have a shared belief that kindness and respect for
each other is of great value in our school and contributes to a positive environment
for better academic performance. With the *Bully-Proofing* program, bullying and
aggressive behaviors do not have a place at our school and will not be tolerated. On
the other hand, acts of kindness will be recognized and rewarded.

A committee of staff members has attended training workshops and is working to
adapt the *Bully-Proofing* program to our school's specific needs. The entire school
will be trained in the program throughout the school year. We ask that as parents in
the _____ Community you discuss the
program with your child since your support is crucial to its success.

Please join us at the (PTCO, staff, community) meeting on _____
(Date)
at _____ in the _____ to
(Time)   (Place)
learn more about our program. Your input is not only welcomed, but necessary to the
success of the program.

Sincerely,

_____
(Name)
Principal

Chapter Five

Faculty and Staff

Section One: **Faculty Training**

The faculty training portion of this program encompasses approximately one day, or seven hours of educational sessions. The training information is presented in a daylong format. However, approximate times are given for each section so that the facilitator can divide the information into blocks of time that suit the needs of the school. Half-day and full-day training sessions have an advantage because the training can be conducted more quickly, attendance is more likely to be consistent, and program implementations can begin sooner. Importantly, the facilitator should have a clear understanding of the specific needs of the school and tailor the training to match those requirements.

The facilitator should also have a strong grasp of the concepts of developing a school-wide program (Chapter Four) so that questions regarding program needs and philosophy can be answered and discussed. An outline of the training is presented first with the approximate times for delivery of the material.

The material outlined in this chapter for presentation to the faculty is in summary form and intended to complement the more in-depth explanations in the other chapters.

▼ Middle School Faculty Training Presentation

Session One

I. **Introduction**
   A. Why Bully-Proof?
   B. Outcomes-Systems Impacting the Climate of the School
   C. Four Basic Concepts of the Program

II. **Visualization**

III. **Myths and Facts**

IV. **Bullying**
   A. Define Bullying
   B. Types of Bullying
   C. Levels of Severity in Bullying
   D. Gender Differences
   E. Normal Conflict vs. Bullying

V. **Bullies**
   A. Characteristics
   B. Motivations
   C. Group Bullying and Lieutenants

VI. **Victims**
   A. Characteristics of Three Types of Victims
   B. Dynamics Affecting Middle School Victims
   C. Effects of Bullying

VII. **Bystanders**

VIII. **Answer Myths and Facts**

IX. **Conflict Resolution Questionnaire**

X. **Strategies With Bullies**

XI. **Strategies With Victims**

XII. **Strategies With Bystanders**

Session Two

XIII. **Program Implementation**
   A. Cadre—makeup, leadership, tasks

XIV. **System Interventions**
   A. Administration
   B. Discipline
   C. Student Community (Training)
      1. Overview of curriculum
      2. Structure of curriculum delivery
      3. Activities:
         ◆ *Activity 1:* HA HA SO
         ◆ *Activity 2:* Sexual Harassment vs. Flirting
         ◆ *Activity 3:* Creative Problem Solving—Lounge Scenario
         ◆ *Activity 4:* Creative Problem Solving—Movie Scenario
   D. Staff Community (Training and Support)
   E. Parent Community
   F. Athletics and Activities
   G. Transportation/To and From School
   H. Community

XV. **Creating the Caring Community**
   A. Activities: Logo contest, posters, t-shirts, "I Caught You Caring" campaign, newsletter, classroom postings, bus acknowledgments and rewards, photo collage, dances, Olympics, etc.

XVI. **Developing a Plan**

Faculty Training

Session One

I. Introduction

A. Why should you Bully-Proof your school?

Introduce the program by discussing the prevalence and long-term effects of bullying. The following studies illustrate the seriousness of bullying as well as establish the most effective method of intervention as systemic, wraparound programs such as the *Bully-Proofing Your School* program.

Add your own school's safety data if available. It can be helpful to present specific information from safety surveys, accountability surveys, or antidotal information regarding the feelings of safety within your own school's climate. The purpose of presenting this data at the beginning of the presentation is to

> For every conflict that slips by the staff unnoticed, for every time the adults look the other way, the greater the likelihood the students will feel unprotected and a climate of fear will prevail. This climate of fear fosters bullying.

Handout/Transparency 5A

HANDOUT/TRANSPARENCY 5A
What Research Says About Bullying

♦ A large Midwestern study found that 15% of fourth through eighth graders were severely distressed by bullying.

(Hazler, Hoover, and Oliver, 1992)

♦ In a study of Midwestern middle and high school students, 60% of those who reported being victimized relayed that school personnel responded poorly.

(Hoover, Oliver, and Hazler, 1992)

♦ The highest rates of bullying and the most often reported trauma were reported during grades 5–8.

(Hoover, Hazler, 1996)

♦ A school-wide, systemic program has been found to be the most effective method for dealing with the problem of bullying.

(Elliott, Hamberg, and Williams, 1998)

emotionally engage the faculty with the reality that bullying happens at your school and it has serious consequences.

Review the purpose of the program. Use the points in Handout/Transparency 5B to describe the overall purpose of the *Bully-Proofing Your School* program.

B. Present and discuss the various systems that make up the climate of the school.

Briefly discuss each of the systems impacting the overall school climate using Handout/Transparency 5C. Emphasize the need for, and positive outcome of, each of the systems having common expectations, language, and interventions. See Figure 5-1 on page 97.

C. Review the four basic concepts of the *Bully-Proofing* program. See both Chapter Four and Handout/Transparency 5D (page 98) for further details.

Handout/Transparency 5B
Handout/Transparency 5C
Handout/Transparency 5D

Handout/Transparency 5B

H A N D O U T / T R A N S P A R E N C Y   5 B
The Purpose of Bully-Proofing

◆ Safe, respectful, cooperative schools

◆ Higher incidence of academic/social learning and teaching

◆ Improve teacher morale, sense of effectiveness and empowerment

◆ System-wide message about intolerance for bullying

◆ Change the balance of power so silent majority becomes an empowered caring majority

◆ All students have an opportunity to experience power, control, attention, popularity, value, and influence in ways that enhance academic/social learning and teaching.

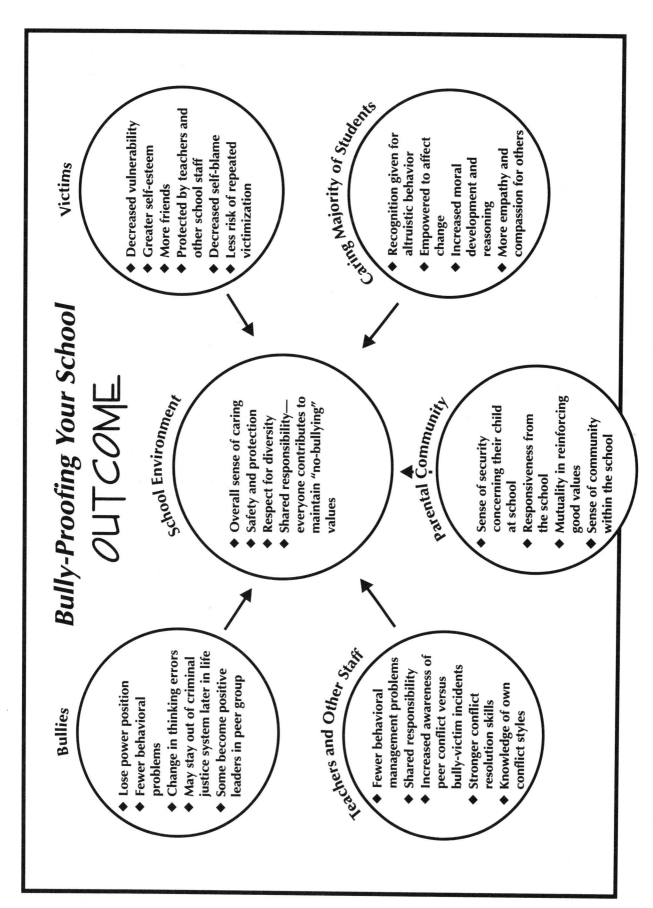

Bully-Proofing Your School
OUTCOME

Victims
- Decreased vulnerability
- Greater self-esteem
- More friends
- Protected by teachers and other school staff
- Decreased self-blame
- Less risk of repeated victimization

Caring Majority of Students
- Recognition given for altruistic behavior
- Empowered to affect change
- Increased moral development and reasoning
- More empathy and compassion for others

School Environment
- Overall sense of caring
- Safety and protection
- Respect for diversity
- Shared responsibility—everyone contributes to maintain "no-bullying" values

Parental Community
- Sense of security concerning their child at school
- Responsiveness from the school
- Mutuality in reinforcing good values
- Sense of community within the school

Bullies
- Lose power position
- Fewer behavioral problems
- Change in thinking errors
- May stay out of criminal justice system later in life
- Some become positive leaders in peer group

Teachers and Other Staff
- Fewer behavioral management problems
- Shared responsibility
- Increased awareness of peer conflict versus bully-victim incidents
- Stronger conflict resolution skills
- Knowledge of own conflict styles

Figure 5-1

HANDOUT/TRANSPARENCY 5D
Four Basic Concepts of the
***Bully-Proofing Your School* Program**

The program is designed as a systemic, comprehensive program.

- ◆ School-wide commitment to nontolerance for bullying
- ◆ Development of school-wide rules and expectations
- ◆ School-wide commitment to creating a caring community
- ◆ All systems are involved (administration, teachers, students, support staff, transportation, community liaisons)

The main focus is on climate change.

- ◆ Designed to create a positive, prosocial school climate
- ◆ Commitment is to broad cultural change
- ◆ Program is viewed as a process of gradual change

The program teaches skills and strategies to avoid victimization.

- ◆ Introduces a common vocabulary to be used system-wide
- ◆ Skills include how to take a stand for self and others
- ◆ Emphasizes concept of taking responsibility for each other
- ◆ Develops skills of problem solving and community building

Emphasis is on developing the caring majority.

- ◆ Goal is to shift power away from the bullies to the silent majority members
- ◆ Focus is on empowering and mobilizing the silent majority to become the caring majority
- ◆ The caring majority is the foundation of the caring school environment

II. Conduct a Visualization

A. Emotional Hook

It is important that staff become emotionally aware of the need for this program. An emotional hook is often very effective to assist staff in remembering or realizing that this is a pervasive problem with long lasting emotional effects. An effective strategy can be to invoke a visualization of the staffs' experiences with bullying within their own lives. Other helpful emotional hooks can be students' stories of bullying incidences and the effects on them, stories from books such as *Chicken Soup for the Teenage Soul* (Canfield, J., Hansen, M.V., and Kirberger, K., 1997), newspaper articles, safety survey results from your school or district, or one of your own experiences. A visualization of a past experience of bullying is presented here as an example.

B. Visualization and Discussion

1. Ask participants to get comfortable in their chairs and prepare themselves for a visualization activity. Invite

people to close their eyes if that feels comfortable to them. Guide participants through the following instructions. (Allow waiting time between each of the instructions.)

"Remember a time either recently or when you were in school, when you were bullied, . . . or bullied someone, . . . or saw someone bullied.　(Wait)

- ♦ Where were you?

- ♦ Who was around?

- ♦ What role were you playing? Bully? Victim? Observer or Bystander?

- ♦ How were you feeling?

- ♦ What did you do?

- ♦ What do you wish you would have done, or could have done?

- ♦ What do you wish someone else would have done?

2. Invite participants to slowly bring their consciousness back to the room. Ask for volunteers to share their experiences. Relate stories to the seriousness of bullying. Adults who were bullied as children can often remember every detail years later including the name of the bully, names of friends who helped or participated, and so forth. This experience is similar to PTSD (Post-Traumatic Stress Disorder) experiences. Remind participants that their past experiences will influence how they deal with students and bullying.

III. Myths and Facts

Hand out the worksheet "Myths and Facts" (Handout/ Transparency 5E, page 135). Ask participants to complete the questions using their current knowledge. The answers will be given and discussed later. Used in this way the quiz functions as a provocative pretest.

Handout/Transparency 5E

Facilitator Note:　Another way to use "Myths and Facts" is to display the questions on the overhead projector. Ask for a show of hands from the faculty regarding each of the answers. Then teach them the answers from the questionnaire. It is important to allow for discussion because many of the answers may be unexpected or need further explanation. The answers and brief explanations are on pages 107–111.

IV. Bullying

A. Define bullying.

Handout/Transparency 5F

1. Bullying has been defined as:

A person is being bullied or victimized when he or she is exposed, repeatedly and over time, to negative actions on the part of one or more persons.　(Olweus, 1991)

Handout/Transparency 5E

HANDOUT/TRANSPARENCY 5E
Myth or Fact?

Directions:

Determine whether each of the following statements is a "Myth" (M) or a "Fact" (F).

1. Bullies are boys. _____

2. Bullies are insecure and have low self-esteem. _____

3. Bullies don't have friends. _____

4. Bullies are usually failing in school. _____

5. Bullies are physically larger than their victims. _____

6. Bullies don't really mean to hurt their victims. _____

7. Bullies usually feel badly about their actions, but they just can't help themselves. _____

8. Looking different is the main reason children get bullied. _____

9. If the victim fights back, the bully will back down. _____

10. Telling on a bully will only make the situation worse for the victim. _____

11. Other children should stay away from the bully-victim situations or they'll get bullied as well. _____

12. All teachers can learn to handle a bully. _____

13. Unless you change the bully's home life, nothing will help. _____

14. Bullies need therapy to stop bullying. _____

15. Bringing the parents of the victim and of the bully together for discussion is a good idea. _____

16. Once a victim always a victim. _____

17. Victims have usually brought the trouble upon themselves. _____

18. Learning disabled students are at higher risk of being victimized. _____

_____
Adapted with permission of authors. *Bully-Proofing Your School: A Comprehensive Approach for Elementary Schools (Second Edition)* Copyright, 2000.

2. Differentiate between the two types of bullying behaviors:

Direct bullying: Face-to-face interactions that include physical attacks or any threatening or intimidating gestures.

Indirect bullying: Requires a third party, is often more subtle, and includes social isolation, rumor-spreading, and scapegoating.

3. Describe the key elements of bullying.

Key Elements of Bullying

Imbalance of power: The imbalance can be physical, psychological or intellectual, and hinders the victim from defending himself or herself.

Repeated: The negative actions usually (not always) occur repeatedly over a period of time.

Intentional: Bullies purposefully chose actions that will hurt or intimidate the targeted victim.

Unequal levels of affect: The victim will typically display a high level of emotional distress including yelling, crying, withdrawal or anxiousness. The bully, however, will demonstrate very little emotion or anguish. The adolescent doing the bullying is likely to blame the victim for the aggressive act or state that, "he/she deserved it." Bullies commonly feel justified in their actions.

B. Explain the different types of bullying.

Emphasize that frequently these behaviors happen together or the bully may use verbal aggression to reinforce physical intimidation. As teens become more intelligent, their bullying tactics become more subtle and increasingly difficult for onlookers to detect. See Chapter Three for more detailed information.

Types of Bullying

♦ **Physical Aggression:** Includes destroying property, threatening

♦ **Social Aggression:** Spreading rumors, racial slurs, excluding from group

♦ **Verbal Aggression:** Name calling, teasing, threatening, intimidating phone calls

♦ **Intimidation:** Graffiti, a dirty trick, taking possessions, coercion

♦ **Written Aggression:** Slam books, note passing, graffiti

♦ **Sexual Harassment:** Any comments or actions of a sexual nature that are unwelcome and make the recipient uncomfortable.

♦ **Racial and Cultural (Ethnic) Harassment:** Any comments or actions containing racial or ethnic content (direct or indirect) that are unwelcome and make the recipient uncomfortable.

C. Explain the different levels of severity in bullying behaviors (see the Bullying Behaviors Chart on pages 102 and 103).

Stress that adolescents will **always** need help with moderate to severe bullying incidences. Because teens frequently feel that they are, or must be, independent and "grown up," they may rebuff offers of help from adults. In cases of severe bullying, it will be necessary for adults to intervene anyway. Remind staff that the bullying dynamic contains a power differential that can significantly hinder coping strategies of the average teenager. When teens feel that they have to "handle it" themselves, they may resort to unrealistic or dangerous retaliation.

Handout/Transparency 5G

Bullying Behaviors Chart		
MILD	**MODERATE**	**SEVERE**

PHYSICAL AGGRESSION

MILD		MODERATE		SEVERE	
◆ Pushing ◆ Shoving ◆ Spitting	◆ Kicking ◆ Hitting	◆ Defacing property ◆ Stealing	◆ Physical acts that are demeaning and humiliating, but not bodily harmful (e.g., de-panting) ◆ Locking in a closed or confined space	◆ Physical violence against family or friends	◆ Threatening with a weapon ◆ Inflicting bodily harm

SOCIAL ALIENATION

MILD		MODERATE		SEVERE	
◆ Gossiping ◆ Embarrassing	◆ Setting up to look foolish ◆ Spreading rumors about	◆ Ethnic slurs ◆ Setting up to take the blame	◆ Publicly humiliating (e.g., revealing personal information) ◆ Excluding from group ◆ Social rejection	◆ Maliciously excluding ◆ Manipulating social order to achieve rejection ◆ Malicious rumormongering	◆ Threatening with total isolation by peer group

VERBAL AGGRESSION

MILD		MODERATE		SEVERE	
◆ Mocking ◆ Name calling ◆ Dirty looks ◆ Taunting	◆ Teasing about clothing or possessions	◆ Teasing about appearance	◆ Intimidating telephone calls	◆ Verbal threats of aggression against property or possessions	◆ Verbal threats of violence or of inflicting bodily harm

INTIMIDATION

MILD		MODERATE		SEVERE	
◆ Threatening to reveal personal information ◆ Graffiti ◆ Publicly challenging to do something	◆ Defacing property or clothing ◆ Playing a dirty trick	◆ Taking possessions (e.g., lunch, clothing, toys)	◆ Extortion	◆ Threats of using coercion against family or friends	◆ Coercion ◆ Threatening with a weapon

RACIAL AND ETHNIC HARASSMENT

MILD		MODERATE		SEVERE	
◆ Joke telling with racial or ethnic targets	◆ Exclusion due to ethnic or cultural group membership	◆ Racial or ethnic slurs	◆ Verbal accusations, putdowns ◆ Public humiliation	◆ Destroying or defacing property due to ethnic or cultural group membership	◆ Physical or verbal attacks due to group membership

(continued)

Bullying Behaviors Chart *(continued)*					
MILD		**MODERATE**		**SEVERE**	
SEXUAL HARASSMENT					
◆ Sexual or "dirty" jokes ◆ Conversations that are too personal	◆ Howling, cat calls, whistles ◆ Leers and stares	◆ "Snuggies" (pulling underwear up at the waist) ◆ Repeatedly asking someone out when he or she isn't interested	◆ Spreading sexual rumors ◆ Pressure for sexual activity ◆ De-panting	◆ Cornering, blocking, standing too close, following	◆ Sexual assault and attempted sexual assault ◆ Rape

Adapted with permission of authors. *Bully-Proofing Your School: A Comprehensive Approach for Elementary Schools (Second Edition)*, Copyright, 2000.

D. Describe and discuss the gender differences in bullying behaviors. See Handout/Transparency 5H.

Handout/Transparency 5H

HANDOUT/TRANSPARENCY 5H
Gender Differences and Bullying

◆ Boys tend to bully with direct bullying or physical or verbal aggression.

◆ Girls tend to bully with indirect means such as social aggression.

◆ Boys who bully tend to be 1 to 2 years older than their victims. Their victims can be either boys or girls.

◆ Girl bullies tend to target other girls who are the same age to be their victims.

◆ Girls are more likely to be bullied by a group.

◆ Girls are more likely to involve both boys and girls in their bullying pursuits against a victim.

◆ Boys identify their behaviors as bullying more often than girls.

E. Explain the difference between normal conflict and bullying.

Introduce the difference by explaining that interpersonal conflict is a normal part of growing up. Children and teens need to learn how to handle normal conflict. Often they need adult support to direct them back to the situation so they can learn to work through the conflict without direct adult intervention. However, in situations of bullying, young teens need direct adult help. Oftentimes educators and parents are confused about when a conflict is in the "normal" range and when it may constitute bullying and need adult intervention. Learning the difference between normal conflict and bullying can help school staff and parents decide when to intervene. See Handout/Transparency 51.

V. Bullies

A. Describe the characteristics of bullies.

It is helpful to point out that bullies cannot be accurately described by particular physical characteristics or as belonging to any social or intellectual group. They are best described as

Handout/Transparency 51

HANDOUT/TRANSPARENCY 51
Normal Conflict vs. Bullying

NORMAL CONFLICT VS. BULLYING

Normal Conflict	Bullying
Equal power—friends	Imbalance of power; not friends
Happens occasionally	Repeated negative actions
Accidental	Purposeful
Not serious	Serious—threat of physical harm or emotional or psychological hurt
Equal emotional reaction	Strong emotional reaction on part of the victim
Not seeking power or attention	Seeking power, control
Not trying to get something	Trying to gain material things or power
Remorse—take responsibility	No remorse—blames victim
Effort to solve the problem	No effort to solve problem

having a particular **personality style**. That style is described below.

- ◆ A bully is a child who values the rewards that aggression can bring.

- ◆ A bully is a child who lacks empathy for his or her victim and has difficulty feeling compassion.

- ◆ A bully tends to lack guilt. He or she fully believes that the victim provoked the attack and deserved the consequences.

- ◆ A bully likes to be in charge, to dominate, and to assert with power. A bully likes to win in all situations.

- ◆ A bully's parent(s) (or other significant role model) often model aggression.

- ◆ A bully thinks in unrealistic ways (e.g., "I should always get what I want.").

- ◆ A bully commonly becomes bored easily and gets a thrill from exerting power over others.[1]

B. Explain the common motivations to bully.

- ◆ Gain power

- ◆ Gain popularity and attention

- ◆ Act out problems from home

- ◆ Copy what someone else does whom they admire

- ◆ Perceive it as fun

- ◆ Inflated self-esteem

C. Summarize group bullying and lieutenants.

See Chapter Three for more information. Stress that group bullying is a dangerous phenomenon that can become particularly powerful during adolescence. Review several of the factors that play a role in teens' engagement in group bullying. They are summarized below:

- ◆ Social learning theory asserts that modeling is a primary de-terminant of human behavior. Bullies frequently have cha-risma and social power that is appealing to peers. If peers or bystanders have a positive attitude toward the bully, they are more likely to imitate his or her behavior.

- ◆ If the bully is given a great deal of attention, or his/her aggressive behaviors are not admonished, there is greater likelihood that peers will pattern their behaviors after those of the bully.

---

[1] Adapted with permission of authors. *Bully-Proofing Your School: A Comprehensive Approach for Elementary Schools (Second Edition)*, Copyright, 2000.

♦ Peers have been found to be involved in 85% of all bullying episodes in one way or another (Craig and Pepler, 1995). Observers can be caught up in the emotional arousal of the aggressive incident much like the excitement at a hockey game when a fight breaks out. Peers caught up in the excitement can lose their sense of empathy for the victim and be pulled into bullying behaviors.

♦ No matter what the internal experiences of the bystander are, the bully will experience their attention as a powerful approval that can increase the incidences of bullying.

♦ When students are repeatedly exposed to bullying behaviors, they can become desensitized and the regulation of their aggressive impulses weakens, leaving them even more likely to get involved directly with bullying episodes.

♦ Bullies are commonly surrounded by peers or "friends" who are attracted to the bullies' social power. These peers do not have the same malicious goals as the bully, but are driven to them by their desire for acceptance and group membership. Bullies will often use these ancillary group members as "lieutenants" to do some of their cruel, dirty work, leaving the bully insulated from consequences.

VI. Victims

Handout/Transparency 5J

A. Review and discuss the characteristics of three types of victims. Refer to Chapter Three for more detailed information. See Handout/Transparency 5J, page 107.

Handout/Transparency 5K

B. Describe the problem dynamics for middle school age victims. More specific information can be found in Chapter Three. See Handout/Transparency 5K, page 108.

The dynamics affecting victims in middle school are as follows:

1. A code of silence

2. A downward spiral

3. Indirect or relational victimization

4. Peer response to bullying

Handout/Transparency 5L

C. Review the consequences of short- and long-term bullying on middle school victims. See Handout/Transparency 5L, page 109.

VII. Bystanders

Handout/Transparency 5M

Review the characteristics of bystanders by using Handout/Transparency 5M, page 110.

VIII. Answer "Myths and Facts" See Handout/Transparency 5E.

Handout/Transparency 5E

Encourage discussion of the different answers and or concerns.

HANDOUT/TRANSPARENCY 5J
Three Types of Victims

A Passive Victim:

- Is nonassertive and submissive
- Is cautious and quiet
- Cries easily and collapses quickly when bullied
- Has few friends and is not connected to a social network
- Is anxious and insecure
- Lacks humor and prosocial skills
- Is physically weak—boys especially

A Provocative Victim:

- Is aggressive and argumentative
- Displays disruptive and irritating behaviors
- Is easily emotionally aroused
- Prolongs the conflict even when losing
- May be diagnosed with Attention Deficit Hyperactivity Disorder (ADHD)

A Vicarious Victim:

- Feels vulnerable as a potential target
- Has a moderate to high degree of empathy and sensitivity
- Does not take a stand against bullying because of fear
- Experiences guilt about his/her failure to act

Myths and Facts: The Answers

1. Both boys and girls bully, but their tactics are usually different. Boys usually bully with physical aggression, girls with social alienation or humiliation.

2. Bullies are not anxious, insecure children, but have positive (often unrealistic) self-images that reflect a strong need to dominate with power and threats.

3. Bullies are not loners, but almost always have a small network of peers who encourage, admire, and model their bullying behaviors.

4. Bullies tend to be at least average or only slightly below average academically.

5. Bullies come in all sizes and abilities. They can even intimidate victims who are physically larger than they if there's an imbalance of power.

6. Bullies lack compassion for their victims and feel justified in their actions.

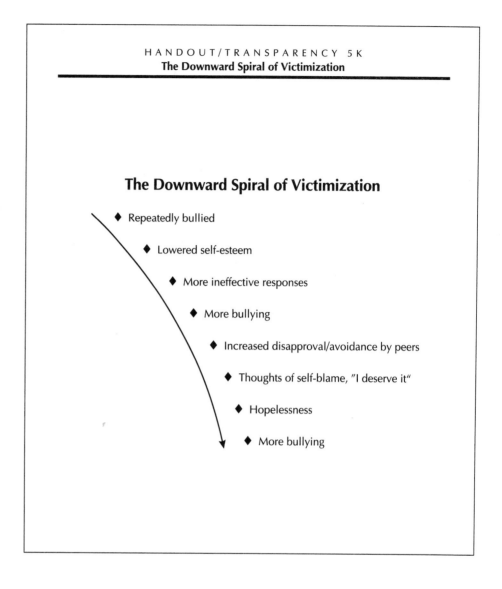

7. Bullies value the rewards they achieve from aggression, such as attention, control over someone, or material possessions.

8. Looking different is one reason children are victimized, but not the main reason. Isolation and personality type are more often determining factors.

9. Returned aggression is not usually effective and, in fact, excites the bully into further attacks. Assertion, rather than aggression, is effective, however.

10. If all the adults within a school are committed to preventing bullying behavior, requiring adult intervention will help equalize the power imbalance between the bully and victim.

11. When bullies are confronted with a united front of their peers who support the victims and believe that bullying behavior is not socially acceptable, their power is defused.

HANDOUT/TRANSPARENCY 5L
Effects of Bullying on Victims

Academic

School avoidance, truancy

Lowered grades and reduced learning

Lowered self-esteem

Diminished academic risk taking

Health Problems

Loss of appetite	Stomachaches, vomiting	Headaches
Nervousness	Depression	Loss of sleep
Frequent trips to the school nurse		

Adjustment Problems

Emotional distress	Lowered self-esteem	Loneliness
Anxiety	Homicidal ideation and attempts	
Depression	Suicidal ideation and attempts	

12. Some teachers are threatened by conflict-ridden situations and aggressive children. In this program, teachers identify their predominant conflict resolutions styles and identify other staff members with complementary styles they can turn to for support with difficult situations.

13. Bullies can separate home from school and be taught responsible school behavior even when aggression is modeled and/or reinforced at home.

14. Bullying behavior does not usually change with traditional therapy, but requires specific intervention techniques that increase skill deficits and correct thinking errors. There are some simple, proven intervention tactics, which will be taught in conjunction with this program, that prevent bullying behavior.

15. It is often not a good strategy to bring the parent(s) of a bully and the parents(s) of the victim together; it should be avoided at all costs. It is essential to meet with each

HANDOUT/TRANSPARENCY 5M
Bystanders

Bystanders

♦ Most ignored and underused resource in our schools

♦ 85% of a school population—the "silent majority"

♦ Become desensitized over time—diminished empathy

Why Don't They Get Involved?

1. Fear of retaliation

2. Don't know what to do

3. Afraid they'll make things worse

4. Worry about losing social status

5. Don't believe that adults will help

Silent Majority ♦ Caring Majority ♦ Caring Community

set of parents individually to provide them the specific assistance they need to help their child. However, there are a number of victim-offender mediation programs that can be used effectively to bring the bully and the victim together.

16. The cycle of victimization can be broken by working at the school and classroom levels, and by working with an individual child who is victimized.

17. The responsibility for the aggression is the bully's. However the victims of bullying are not randomly targeted. They are victimized because of characteristics and behaviors which make them easier targets for a bully. These include being physically weak, crying easily, being anxious and insecure, and lacking age-appropriate social skills.

18. Students with special education needs may be at greater risk of being bullied by others due to factors such as a

disability or the fact that they may be less well integrated socially. If they have behavioral problems and act out aggressively, they can become provocative victims. If they have trouble processing social cues, they may act shy and inhibited and become passive victims. However, having a disability is not the main reason children get bullied.[2]

IX. Conflict Resolution Questionnaire

Handout 5N

Rationale:

When establishing a school-wide policy regarding bullying, it is important to recognize that staff will have different abilities, levels of comfort, and strategies for dealing with aggressive students. It is very important to establish time to explore these different styles and develop some strategies and support for staff who will be essential in facilitating the school climate change. The Conflict Resolution Questionnaire can be used as an effective method for facilitating this discussion. The five types of conflict resolution styles: No-Nonsense, Problem Solving, Compromising, Smoothing, and Ignoring—can be discussed as each comprising valuable strengths in different situations. Some staff will have management styles that naturally support the victim. Some may have predominantly no-nonsense styles which can be extremely effective in dealing with bullies. It is important that these styles be discussed in a manner that honors each of them. It is equally important to establish that staff need to work collaboratively, capitalizing on each other's strengths when dealing with difficult conflicts. An atmosphere of trust and mutual support in dealing with difficult behavioral situations is vital to establishing a positive school climate. If staff look the other way, regularly engage in power struggles with bullying students (further empowering them), or are fearful of students, a climate change will founder.

A. Have the faculty answer the conflict resolution styles questions and score their responses.

B. Facilitate a small group discussion regarding the different styles commonly used to deal with conflict between staff and students.

   It can be helpful to arrange the faculty into small groups or teams who have similar duties or share the same group of students. After completing the questionnaire, the small group can discuss their specific styles and strategize about supporting each other using their specific strengths. Again, the facilitator should emphasize that no one style is better than another. They are all important and complement each other among team members. Stress that the adults need to use each other collaboratively to avoid being snared in the bully's trap.

---

[2] Adapted with permission of authors. *Bully-Proofing Your School: A Comprehensive Approach for Elementary Schools*, Copyright 2000.

HANDOUT 5N
The Conflict Resolution Questionnaire

Teaching children to solve their own problems with peers is a difficult task. Some children seem to naturally do this better than others. We do know that those children who are not good at this skill can be taught strategies which assist them. There are no absolute right or wrong ways to solve problems, but there are techniques that work better at different ages and developmental levels.

The following questions will identify your primary approach to solving problems within your area of the school.

Directions:

Read the statements below. If a statement describes a response you typically make to conflict, write "3" in the space next to the question. If it is a response you occasionally make, write "2" in the space, and if you rarely or never make that response, write "1."

When there is a conflict, I:

1. Tell the children to stop it. _____
2. Try to make everyone feel at ease. _____
3. Help the children understand each others' point of view. _____
4. Separate the children and keep them away from each other. _____
5. Let the principal handle it. _____
6. Decide who started it. _____
7. Try to find out what the real problem is. _____
8. Try to work out a compromise. _____
9. Turn it into a joke. _____
10. Tell the children to stop making such a fuss. _____
11. Encourage one child to give in and apologize. _____
12. Encourage the children to find an alternative solution. _____
13. Help the children decide what they can compromise on. _____
14. Try to divert attention away from the conflict. _____
15. Let the children solve it, as long as no one is hurt. _____
16. Threaten to send the children to the principal. _____
17. Present some alternatives from which the children can choose. _____
18. Help all the children to feel comfortable. _____
19. Get all the children busy doing something else. _____
20. Tell the children to try to settle it on their own. _____

_____

Adapted from *Creative Conflict Resolution* © 1984 by William J. Kriedler. Published by Good Year Books. Used by permission of Pearson Learning.

C. Facilitate a large group discussion.

Bring the discussion back to the entire faculty. It can be helpful to have staff raise their hands to identify which members have particular styles and strengths. Encourage the use of individuals with a no-nonsense approach for support with students who bully. Victims also need support and other styles such as the "Problem Solver" may better assist them. Reinforce the need for the entire faculty to realize that bullying, aggressive students have developed sophisticated, tricky techniques. Staff need to use each other for awareness and support.

X. Strategies With Bullies

A. Review with staff the strategies for dealing with students who bully. (See Chapter Four.) Summarize the concepts using Handout/Transparency 5O.

HANDOUT/TRANSPARENCY 5O
Strategies With Bullies

Strategies With Bullies

♦ A no-nonsense style

♦ Use prosocial consequences

♦ Give brief, clear descriptions of unacceptable behavior and consequences

♦ Do not have a long discussion of the situation

♦ Correct the bully's thinking errors

♦ Identify the victim's emotions

♦ Build empathy for the victim

♦ Re-channel power—do not try to suppress

♦ Set the culture for your school through the caring majority

Adapted with permission of authors. *Bully-Proofing Your School: A Comprehensive Approach for Elementary Schools (Second Edition)*, Copyright, 2000.

XI. Strategies With Victims

A. Summarize the recommended strategies and resources for supporting victims. See Chapter Nine for more specific interventions and resources. (Handout/Transparency 5P, page 114.)

Handout/Transparency 5P

XII. Strategies With Bystanders

A. Summarize the recommended strategies and resources for supporting bystanders. (See Chapter Four.) Summarize the concepts using Handout/Transparency 5Q, page 115.

Session Two

XIII. Program Implementation

A. Explain the model of forming a Bully-Proofing Cadre (committee) to design and guide implementation of the

HANDOUT/TRANSPARENCY 5P
Strategies With Victims

Strategies With Victims

♦ Use a supportive, fear-reducing style

♦ Reduce self-blame by clear identification of cruel behavior

♦ Demonstrate compassion and empathy

♦ Connect victim to helpful peers

♦ Mobilize caring majority in the classroom

♦ Remind of HA HA SO strategies

♦ Consider individual help with friendship skills

Adapted with permission of authors. *Bully-Proofing Your School: A Comprehensive Approach for Elementary Schools (Second Edition)*, Copyright, 2000.

program. Summarize the different aspects of the cadre's role within the school.

The cadre:

♦ Ideally includes a representative from each area of the school: administrator, student, parent, counselor, dean, teacher from each grade level, mental health advisor, security representative.

♦ Provides a broad source for creative ideas as well as spreads the responsibility so that one or two people don't get over burdened.

♦ Becomes the "culture carriers" of the climate change for the school.

♦ Helps facilitate communication of the program's activities and goals.

♦ Uses creativity to shape the *Bully-Proofing* program to fit the unique needs and resources of your school.

HANDOUT/TRANSPARENCY 5Q
Strategies for Bystanders

Strategies for Bystanders

♦ Normalize fears and worries

♦ Emphasize strength in numbers

♦ Communicate the expectation to take action

♦ Teach skills and strategies to take a stand

♦ Acknowledge and reward caring behaviors

♦ Directs specific activities that might include scheduling curriculum facilitation, designing student recognition campaigns, making parent presentations, leading teacher training, or coordinating publicity.

Refer participants to Handout/Transparency 4B.

Handout/Transparency 4B

XIV. Review the specific systems affecting the school climate

Refer participants to Handout/Transparency 4B. Stress that the strengths and concerns in each of the systems will vary greatly from school to school. For example, some schools will have few students riding buses while others have large numbers of students riding buses. Challenge staff members to think about each of these individual systems and consider the following questions:

♦ What programs are already in place in each of these areas?

♦ What are the particularly challenging areas for your school?

◆ Which of these areas impact the overall school climate more than the others?

◆ Are there other areas, not listed here, that you will need to add for your school (i.e., English as a Second Language Students)?

Discuss the key points in the following areas:

A. Administrative Support

Emphasize the crucial need for administrative support. Administrators, as leaders, need to embrace this culture change as a process and not as a "quick fix" program. This will require patience, diligence, and a strong commitment to provide the necessary resources for the project as a long-term plan. The administrator's personal belief in the value of the program and his or her public commitment to its success and modeling can make or break its success.

B. School-Wide Discipline Plan

Stress the following points:

◆ The discipline plan must be school-wide.

◆ Consequences should be well-defined, non-emotionally communicated, and consistently carried out.

◆ Must include a "no tolerance, no nonsense" approach towards bullying.

◆ The message concerning zero tolerance of bullying needs to be communicated throughout the school (within the school rules, discipline policies, etc.) as well as communicated clearly through the expectations of all of the adults in the school.

◆ Behavior that is counterproductive to the caring school community, whether against any school rule or not, needs to be confronted by all of the school members who observe it. While many students' bullying actions may not be against any school "rule" or constitute a referral to the dean, they are against the ethics of a positive, caring school community. These behaviors need to be confronted and a clear message given that bullying, intimidation, and disrespectful behaviors are not tolerated.

Periodically throughout the multi-year climate change process, the school staff need time to come together, in small groups or as a whole, to discuss difficulties, problem areas, or concerns regarding school behavioral policies. Depending on the format of your presentation, it may be helpful to include time for an in-depth discussion of your school's current discipline system, its strengths, and its weak areas. Teachers and all staff need to feel heard and contribute to overall school policies regarding discipline and interventions with aggressive students. This participation will increase the likelihood that staff will enforce the policies, and keep administration aware of potential problems areas.

C. Student Community

Training of students—classroom curriculum

1. **Give an overview of the curriculum to staff.** The outline of the curriculums that follows is a brief overview. In the interest of time each lesson usually cannot be reviewed with the staff. Depending on the model of delivery chosen for implementation in your school, classroom teachers will either have the opportunity to learn the material in the classroom as their students learn the material or as they co-facilitate the lessons. If the classroom teachers are going to participate in co-facilitating the lessons, it would be helpful to review with them the "Facilitator Notes" that precede the curriculum in Chapter Six. The section explaining the difference between structured classroom instruction and process-oriented classroom groups can be particularly helpful for teachers.

Each set of lessons builds on the concepts taught the previous year. The main concepts taught at each grade level are listed in Handout/Transparency 5R, page 118.

Handout/Transparency 5R

2. **Briefly explain the overall structure for the curriculum group delivery.** The classroom curriculum of the *Bully-Proofing Your School: A Comprehensive Approach for Middle Schools* program contains lessons designed specifically for 6th, 7th, and 8th grade students. Each grade level curriculum includes five lessons unique to the grade level and two additional lessons intended to be taught by the classroom teacher as follow-up instruction prior to the next bully-proofing session. The sessions are written to fit into 45 minute class periods. Notably, they may take longer when the facilitator is new to the material or your school may have a model of delivery that allows for more student discussion time or expansion of the concepts. The most effective delivery would entail that the sessions be taught over a five-week period.

3. **Conduct several of the following activities throughout the faculty training.** The activities are very useful to assist the faculty and/or parent groups in understanding the bully-proofing concepts. Additionally, faculty can experience a "group session" as the facilitators model group facilitation skills.

Handout/Transparency 5R

HANDOUT/TRANSPARENCY 5R
Curriculum Overview

CURRICULUM OVERVIEW		
Sixth Grade: The Basics About Bullying		
Bullies	Bystanders	Empathy
Definition and Types of Bullying	Teasing	Taking a Stand
Normal Conflict vs. Bullying	Sexual Harassment	Inclusion
Victims	HA HA SO Strategies	
Seventh Grade: Creating the Caring Community		
Review of the Basics	Cliques	Flirting
Empathy	Taking a Stand	Levels of Risk-Taking
Inclusion	Sexual Harassment	Creative Problem Solving
Eighth Grade: Leadership		
Review of the Basics	Groups and Cliques	Empathy
Sexual Harassment	Characteristics and Styles of Positive Leadership	Taking a Stand
Flirting	Intention	Creative Problem Solving
Inclusion		
New Students: Establish a Connection with Their School		
New Students—Shared Experiences	Normal Conflict vs. Bullying	Empathy
Definition and Types of Bullying	Victims	Taking a Stand
No-bullying Expectations Stressed	Bystanders	Inclusion
Bullies	HA HA SO Strategies	Sexual Harassment

Activity 1: HA HA SO

HA HA SO instruction and activity

Handout/Transparency 5S

A. Teach the HA HA SO strategies to the staff. See Handout/ Transparency 5S and 5T on page 119 and 120.

B. HA HA SO Activity

1. Divide staff into six groups.

Handout/Transparency 5T

2. Distribute Handout/Transparency 5T to each group. Assign one of the HA HA SO strategies to each group.

3. Ask each group to develop a skit using the strategy assigned to their group. Instruct them to have a bully, victim, by-standers and one narrator if they choose. Give the staff from 5–10 minutes to practice their skits.

HANDOUT/TRANSPARENCY 5S
HA HA SO Strategies

Ha Ha So Strategies

	STRATEGIES	TIPS
H Help:	Seek assistance from an adult, friend, or peer when a potentially threatening situation arises. Seek help also if other strategies aren't working.	1. Brainstorm all of the sources of help at your school—deans, counselors, teachers, nurse. 2. Stress the different ways to get help—anonymously, in a group, dean's hotline.
A Assert Yourself:	Make assertive statements to the bully addressing your feelings about the bully's *behavior*.	1. Should not be used with severe bullying. 2. Not as effective with group bullying. 3. Victim should look bully straight in the eye. 4. Use "I" statements. *Example:* "I don't like it when you pull on my backpack." 5. Make assertive statement and walk away. *Example:* "Stop talking about me behind my back."
H Humor:	Use humor to de-escalate a situation.	1. Use humor in a positive way. 2. Make the joke about what the bully said, not about the bully. 3. Make humorous statement and then leave the situation. 4. *Example:* When insulted about hairstyle, say "Gee, I didn't know you cared enough to notice."
A Avoid:	Walk away or avoid certain places in order to avoid a bullying situation.	1. Best for situations when victim is alone. 2. Avoid places where the bully hangs out. 3. Join with others rather than be alone.
S Self-Talk:	Use positive self-talk to maintain positive self-esteem during a bullying situation.	1. Use as a means to keep feeling good about self. 2. Think positive statements about self and accomplishments. 3. Rehearse mental statements to avoid being hooked by the bully. *Examples:* "It's his problem," "She doesn't know what she's talking about," "I know I'm smart." 4. Use positive self-talk when practicing all strategies.
O Own It:	"Own" the put-down or belittling comment in order to diffuse it.	1. Agree with the bully and leave the situation. 2. Combine with humor strategies such as, "Yeah, this **IS** a bad haircut. The lawn mower got out of control this weekend." 3. Combine with assertive strategies such as, "Yes, I did fail the test and I don't appreciate you looking at my paper."
Important Reminders:	1. Practice these strategies in any order, in any combination, or numerous times. 2. The Caring Community can remind each other of the strategies. 3. The Caring Community can help support the victim in using the strategies. 4. If the strategies aren't working, leave or disengage from the situation.	

4. Remind staff of the rules of role play:

   ♦ No physical contact. Acting is acting.

   ♦ No inappropriate language.

   ♦ Once the skit is over, the role is ended.

   Tip to facilitators: When matching students with roles, don't allow a bully to play the role of a bully.

5. Ask each of the groups to perform their skit for the large group.

6. Discuss the pros and cons for using particular strategies in this and other circumstances.

   Scenario: You are on the bus. As usual, the same kid is sitting behind you. He/She is kicking your seat, pulling your hair, and making rude comments about you. This has been happening every day for the past week.

HANDOUT/TRANSPARENCY 5T
HA HA SO STRATEGIES

Scenario: You are on the bus. As usual, the same kid is sitting behind you. He/She is kicking your seat, pulling your hair, and making rude comments about you. This has been happening every day for the past week.

Directions: Give an example of how you could use each of the strategies below to solve this problem.

Help _____

_____

Assert Yourself _____

_____

Humor _____

_____

Avoid _____

_____

Self-Talk _____

_____

Own It _____

_____

Activity 2: Sexual Harassment vs. Flirting

This activity is a good way for the faculty to get a feel for the lessons as well as explore some of the difficult questions and issues that may arise during the lessons on sexual harassment. You will need Handout/Transparency 5U and copies of the Handout/Transparency 5V: Sexual Harassment or Not—That Is the Question activity sheet.

A. Review the differences between sexual harassment and flirting.

B. Divide the faculty into groups of five or six persons. Distribute Handout 5V to each group. Ask them to answer the questions regarding the behaviors that could indicate sexual harassment and the behaviors that could indicate flirting in each of the scenarios.

C. Review the sexual harassment facilitator notes with the faculty. Reviewing these ideas can help alleviate some of the faculty discomfort with the topic. See Chapter 7, Lesson 4.

Activity 3: Creative Problem Solving—The Faculty Lounge

Handout/Transparency 5W

The following activity is very effective for staff education. It can be conducted as part of the initial training or later during a short staff training period.

A. Teach or review the concepts of low, medium, and high levels of risk involved in taking a stand to assist someone.

1. **Low Risk:** Relating behaviors that don't upset anyone such as saying, "I'm sorry that happened," or "He shouldn't be saying that. It's rude and it's not O.K."

   Examples: Ignoring gossip or throwing a note away.

2. **Medium Risk:** Joining or other caring gestures that may pull some attention to the helper.

   Example: Asking others to join you if they are not included in an activity.

3. **High Risk:** Confronting behaviors. Assertive stances that may go against the group or the bully such as saying, "Stop that. We don't do that at our school," or "No, I won't give Margaret the silent treatment. I'm not angry with her. You are."

B. Divide the faculty into groups of four or five people per group.

C. Distribute Handout 5W. Ask each group to read the scenario and creatively think of a low, medium, and high risk solution to the adult situation.

   Scenario: You're in the faculty lounge eating lunch. You overhear a staff member at another table making negative and sarcastic statements about a colleague who is not in the room. This has been happening periodically since the first of the year. You're worried that the statements he/she is making are starting to circulate throughout the building, and you have noticed that this kind of negative talk is spreading.

   Ask groups to report their answers. Discuss the variables that affect whether people experience behaviors as low, medium, or high. Stress the importance of embracing individual differences and guard against judgments as long as the behaviors are caring.

Activity 4: Creative Problem Solving—The Movie Theater

Handout/Transparency 5X

The following activity is very effective with staff education. It can be conducted as part of the initial training or later during a short staff training period.

A. Teach or review the concepts of low, medium and high levels of risk involved in taking a stand to assist someone. (See low, medium and high levels of risk-taking above.)

B. Divide the faculty, parents, or students into groups of four or five people per group.

C. Distribute Handout 5X. Ask each group to read the scenario and creatively think of a low, medium, and high risk solution to the situation.

Scenario: You are sitting in the movie theater before the show begins. It is very crowded and almost all of the seats are taken. You are behind an elderly woman who is sitting next to an empty seat that has a sweater draped over it. You watch as a large man sits in the empty seat with the sweater. The woman says, "This seat is saved;" and the man replies in a very angry, intimidating manner, "What do you mean. There are **no saved seats.**" The man settles into the seat and makes no effort to move even when the woman makes repeated requests. The woman looks very distressed. What could you do as a caring community member?

Ask groups to report their answers. Discuss the variables that affect whether people experience behaviors as low, medium, or high. Stress the importance of embracing individual differences.

D. Staff Community

Establishing a staff community where staff members feel respected and safe is essential for this program. Depending on your particular circumstances, fostering open, respectful, accepting relationships among staff can be a process that parallels the one with students. It can take time and several interventions and training with a large faculty to listen to concerns, develop ideas, train new staff, and continually integrate the concepts. Impress upon the faculty that they are a very important key to the modeling, and upholding the caring community expectations on a daily and hourly basis. See Chapter Five, Section Two: Staff Issues for intervention ideas. Additionally, Activity #3 can be an effective introduction and exploration of the faculty roles in taking a stand for each other.

E. The Parent Community

Familiarize the faculty with the importance of having parental communication and involvement in the *Bully-Proofing* program. (See Chapter Four.)

Oftentimes schools will have unique challenges regarding the involvement of their parent community. Some of these challenges might include many non-English speaking parents, a mobile population or long-established patterns of disharmony between parents and the school. If this is the case with your school, emphasize the need to think creatively, work with patience, and hope to establish a plan for change. Review with the staff the suggested steps for involving parents. Ask them to think about ways to involve parents specifically in their school.

F. Athletics and Activities

These two areas have the potential for very positive or negative climate development. Athletics and activities can provide numerous opportunities for developing and building assets such as self-esteem, one-on-one connections with admired adults, leadership, responsibility, team work, and/or creativity. These areas, however, if not guided and monitored within the same caring community framework as the rest of the school can breed powerful negative leadership.

Emphasize the importance of these areas with the faculty. Ask them to consider your own school situation and begin thinking of your school's strengths and weaknesses regarding development of positive leadership within the athletic and activity areas.

G. Transportation

Summarize with the faculty some of the concerns regarding student trips to and from school, whether they walk or ride the bus. (See Chapter Nine.) Administrators, deans, and counselors are frequently well informed of the common problems during this mostly unsupervised time of the day. However teachers may not realize the number of students and the multitude of obstacles that make it such a precarious part of every day for many students. Review the ideas presented in Chapter Four.

H. Community

Recent and past school violence incidences have made it particularly important to inform and involve the community in the efforts of our schools. Additionally, the community can be an excellent source for mentoring, grant moneys, rewards or incentives, presentations, publicity, and so on. Impress upon the faculty that thinking of ways to involve the community can significantly accelerate the progress of the program. For example, when the media covers stories of students taking a stand to help others, students, parents, and community members learnd that being a caring community member is the way to become recognized at your school.

XV. Strategies for ongoing development of the caring community

Listed below are just some of the ideas schools have used in their efforts to promote the development of a caring community. It is important for each individual school implementing the program to design projects that are both workable and appropriate. Present some of the following ideas to the faculty. Challenge them to think of some creative strategies for your own school.

Ideas for Development of the Caring Community

1. Incorporate the bully-proofing vocabulary into the school rules that are posted throughout the school. Work with staff members, including deans and counselors, to use the vocabulary in their interventions with students.

2. Regularly publicize bully-proofing news in school newsletters and publications.

3. Invite the local media to feature the program in newspapers and on television.

4. Begin the school year with a bully-proofing assembly with activities designed around program concepts.

5. Conduct a school logo contest and ask students to design the school's bully-proofing logo to be used on charts, in publications, and on school T-shirts, sweatshirts, pencils, supplies, and/or book covers.

6. Organize a school poster contest or project.

7. Introduce an "I caught you caring" campaign. Make "I caught you caring" slips available for people to fill out when they observe someone doing a caring act. Slips can be posted on hallway walls; they can also be turned in to central office for weekly random drawings and acknowledgments.

8. Put "I caught you caring" boxes in classrooms.

9. Incorporate concepts into curriculums by identifying bullying dynamics in novels, politics, history, etc. Create writing assignments organized around bullying concepts.

10. Sponsor caring community dances.

11. Create a photographic collage of students "caught" doing caring things. Hand out disposable cameras to adults throughout the building and ask them to take photos of students. Display the collage in a public place.

12. Present awards to students who act as caring community members.

13. Produce videos around caring community concepts by and for students to be shown on Channel 1 or in classrooms.

14. Invite individual teachers and teacher teams to present ideas that they have developed to the staff.

15. Decorate classroom doors with bully-proofing concepts and themes.

XVI. Developing a plan for the school

A. Divide the faculty into groups by teams or departments. Instruct them to complete the planning sheet.

B. Reconvene as a whole faculty and ask groups to share their ideas, goals and concerns.

HANDOUT/TRANSPARENCY 5Y
Bully-Proofing Action Plan

Bully-Proofing Action Plan

Three things I learned which are most applicable to my school:

1. _____

2. _____

3. _____

Three action steps for utilization in my school:

1. _____

2. _____

3. _____

Barriers that may/do exist to carrying out these steps:

_____

_____

_____

_____

_____

_____

Solutions/strategies for dealing with barriers:

_____

_____

_____

_____

_____

_____

Optional Activity

Review and discuss the following points with your faculty. (See Handout/ Transparency 5Z.) Use the statements to generate discussion regarding staff concerns and questions.

HANDOUT/TRANSPARENCY 5Z
What is Necessary for Bully-Proofing to Work

What is Necessary for Bully-Proofing to Work

1. The majority of teachers buy into it.

2. There is support from the administration.

3. There is an available facilitator to get the program started, to educate, to consult, and to handle logistics.

4. Patience. The greatest benefits will be seen starting in the middle of the second year.

5. Believe that ultimately your jobs as teachers and administrators will be easier. The children will keep the momentum going. Observe a tape of this or visit a school to see for yourself.

6. Not every child will change. Approximately 5% of the bullies and/or provocative victims will not benefit. Your job is not to change them; your job is to not allow them to disrupt.

7. Give up the notion that a power struggle with the bully is the only means of changing behavior.

8. "No" will mean "no" and consequences will happen.

9. The greatest control comes from the children themselves who eventually get tired of not having friends, and feeling left out. They will have the ultimate choice to join the caring majority or continue to be left out. You cannot change that choice. You can only show them the right way to get power.

10. Thinking of the big picture and where you want the climate of the school to be is more important than the day-to-day brush fires.

11. Think like the children do. They like the tools, the phrases, and the power of making and keeping their school safe.

12. Think about what you already have in place to enhance the climate of your school.

13. The broader the spectrum of character traits you can list, the better off things will be. Give every child value. Think of traits that enhance the classroom, playground, and school (i.e., a smile, a sense of humor, being tidy, being ready to work, being a good sport, sharing).

14. The caring majority is a positive peer culture group that most children will elect to join if given the means and opportunity. Those who elect not to may have that option; but they may not disrupt the rest of the group.

15. The most effective teacher, administrator, or dean combines two attributes: limit setting with relationship building.

16. The school is a community and, once that community is built into a safe and caring one, the children will work to keep it that way.

HANDOUT/TRANSPARENCY 5A
What Research Says About Bullying

◆ A large Midwestern study found that 15% of fourth through eighth graders were severely distressed by bullying.

(Hazler, Hoover, and Oliver, 1992)

◆ In a study of Midwestern middle and high school students, 60% of those who reported being victimized relayed that school personnel responded poorly.

(Hoover, Oliver, and Hazler, 1992)

◆ The highest rates of bullying and the most often reported trauma were reported during grades 5–8.

(Hoover, Hazler, 1996)

◆ A school-wide, systemic program has been found to be the most effective method for dealing with the problem of bullying.

(Elliott, Hamberg, and Williams, 1998)

HANDOUT/TRANSPARENCY 5B
The Purpose of Bully-Proofing

◆ Safe, respectful, cooperative schools

◆ Higher incidence of academic/social learning and teaching

◆ Improve teacher morale, sense of effectiveness and empowerment

◆ System-wide message about intolerance for bullying

◆ Change the balance of power so silent majority becomes an empowered caring majority

◆ All students have an opportunity to experience power, control, attention, popularity, value, and influence in ways that enhance academic/social learning and teaching.

HANDOUT/TRANSPARENCY 5C
Bully-Proofing Your School

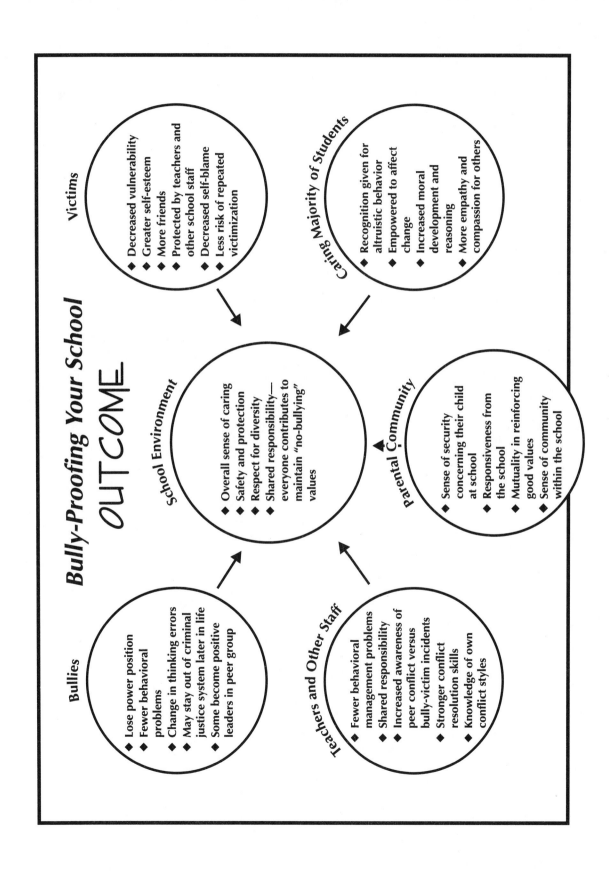

Bully-Proofing Your School
OUTCOME

Victims
- Decreased vulnerability
- Greater self-esteem
- More friends
- Protected by teachers and other school staff
- Decreased self-blame
- Less risk of repeated victimization

Caring Majority of Students
- Recognition given for altruistic behavior
- Empowered to affect change
- Increased moral development and reasoning
- More empathy and compassion for others

School Environment
- Overall sense of caring
- Safety and protection
- Respect for diversity
- Shared responsibility—everyone contributes to maintain "no-bullying" values

Parental Community
- Sense of security concerning their child at school
- Responsiveness from the school
- Mutuality in reinforcing good values
- Sense of community within the school

Bullies
- Lose power position
- Fewer behavioral problems
- Change in thinking errors
- May stay out of criminal justice system later in life
- Some become positive leaders in peer group

Teachers and Other Staff
- Fewer behavioral management problems
- Shared responsibility
- Increased awareness of peer conflict versus bully-victim incidents
- Stronger conflict resolution skills
- Knowledge of own conflict styles

HANDOUT/TRANSPARENCY 5D
Four Basic Concepts of the
Bully-Proofing Your School Program

The program is designed as a systemic, comprehensive program.

◆ School-wide commitment to nontolerance for bullying

◆ Development of school-wide rules and expectations

◆ School-wide commitment to creating a caring community

◆ All systems are involved (administration, teachers, students, support staff, transportation, community liaisons)

The main focus is on climate change.

◆ Designed to create a positive, prosocial school climate

◆ Commitment is to broad cultural change

◆ Program is viewed as a process of gradual change

The program teaches skills and strategies to avoid victimization.

◆ Introduces a common vocabulary to be used system-wide

◆ Skills include how to take a stand for self and others

◆ Emphasizes concept of taking responsibility for each other

◆ Develops skills of problem solving and community building

Emphasis is on developing the caring majority.

◆ Goal is to shift power away from the bullies to the silent majority members

◆ Focus is on empowering and mobilizing the silent majority to become the caring majority

◆ The caring majority is the foundation of the caring school environment

HANDOUT/TRANSPARENCY 5E
Myth or Fact?

Directions:

Determine whether each of the following statements is a "Myth" (M) or a "Fact" (F).

1. Bullies are boys. _____

2. Bullies are insecure and have low self-esteem. _____

3. Bullies don't have friends. _____

4. Bullies are usually failing in school. _____

5. Bullies are physically larger than their victims. _____

6. Bullies don't really mean to hurt their victims. _____

7. Bullies usually feel badly about their actions, but they just can't help themselves. _____

8. Looking different is the main reason children get bullied. _____

9. If the victim fights back, the bully will back down. _____

10. Telling on a bully will only make the situation worse for the victim. _____

11. Other children should stay away from the bully-victim situations or they'll get bullied as well. _____

12. All teachers can learn to handle a bully. _____

13. Unless you change the bully's home life, nothing will help. _____

14. Bullies need therapy to stop bullying. _____

15. Bringing the parents of the victim and of the bully together for discussion is a good idea. _____

16. Once a victim always a victim. _____

17. Victims have usually brought the trouble upon themselves. _____

18. Learning disabled students are at higher risk of being victimized. _____

Adapted with permission of authors. *Bully-Proofing Your School: A Comprehensive Approach for Elementary Schools (Second Edition)* Copyright, 2000.

HANDOUT/TRANSPARENCY 5F
What is Bullying?

Definition of Bullying:

A person is being bullied or victimized when he or she is exposed, repeatedly and over time, to negative actions on the part of one or more persons.

(Olweus, 1991)

Key Elements of Bullying

Imbalance of power: The imbalance can be physical, psychological or intellectual, and hinders the victim from defending himself or herself.

Repeated: The negative actions usually (not always) occur repeatedly over a period of time.

Intentional: Bullies purposefully choose actions that will hurt or intimidate the targeted victim.

Unequal levels of affect: The victim will typically display a high level of emotional distress including yelling, crying, withdrawal or anxiousness. The bully, however, will demonstrate very little emotion or anguish. The adolescent doing the bullying is likely to blame the victim for the aggressive act or state that, "he/she deserved it." Bullies commonly feel justified in their actions.

Types of Bullying

Physical Aggression: Includes destroying property, threatening

Social Aggression: Spreading rumors, racial slurs, excluding from group

Verbal Aggression: Name calling, teasing, threatening, intimidating phone calls

Intimidation: Graffiti, a dirty trick, taking possessions, coercion

Written Aggression: Slam books, note passing, graffiti

Sexual Harassment: Any comments or actions of a sexual nature that are unwelcome and make the recipient uncomfortable.

Racial and Cultural (Ethnic) Harassment: Any comments or actions containing racial or ethnic content (direct or indirect) that are unwelcome and make the recipient uncomfortable.

HANDOUT 5G
Bullying Behaviors Chart

MILD		MODERATE		SEVERE	
PHYSICAL AGGRESSION					
◆ Pushing ◆ Shoving ◆ Spitting	◆ Kicking ◆ Hitting	◆ Defacing property ◆ Stealing	◆ Physical acts that are demeaning and humiliating, but not bodily harmful (e.g., de-panting) ◆ Locking in a closed or confined space	◆ Physical violence against family or friends	◆ Threatening with a weapon ◆ Inflicting bodily harm
SOCIAL ALIENATION					
◆ Gossiping ◆ Embarrassing	◆ Setting up to look foolish ◆ Spreading rumors about	◆ Ethnic slurs ◆ Setting up to take the blame	◆ Publicly humiliating (e.g., revealing personal information) ◆ Excluding from group ◆ Social rejection	◆ Maliciously excluding ◆ Manipulating social order to achieve rejection ◆ Malicious rumormongering	◆ Threatening with total isolation by peer group
VERBAL AGGRESSION					
◆ Mocking ◆ Name calling ◆ Dirty looks ◆ Taunting	◆ Teasing about clothing or possessions	◆ Teasing about appearance	◆ Intimidating telephone calls	◆ Verbal threats of aggression against property or possessions	◆ Verbal threats of violence or of inflicting bodily harm
INTIMIDATION					
◆ Threatening to reveal personal information ◆ Graffiti ◆ Publicly challenging to do something	◆ Defacing property or clothing ◆ Playing a dirty trick	◆ Taking possessions (e.g., lunch, clothing, toys)	◆ Extortion	◆ Threats of using coercion against family or friends	◆ Coercion ◆ Threatening with a weapon
RACIAL AND ETHNIC HARASSMENT					
◆ Joke telling with racial or ethnic targets	◆ Exclusion due to ethnic or cultural group membership	◆ Racial or ethnic slurs	◆ Verbal accusations, putdowns ◆ Public humiliation	◆ Destroying or defacing property due to ethnic or cultural group membership	◆ Physical or verbal attacks due to group membership
SEXUAL HARASSMENT					
◆ Sexual or "dirty" jokes ◆ Conversations that are too personal	◆ Howling, cat calls, whistles ◆ Leers and stares	◆ "Snuggies" (pulling underwear up at the waist) ◆ Repeatedly asking someone out when he or she isn't interested	◆ Spreading sexual rumors ◆ Pressure for sexual activity ◆ De-panting	◆ Cornering, blocking, standing too close, following	◆ Sexual assault and attempted sexual assault ◆ Rape

Adapted with permission of authors. *Bully-Proofing Your School: A Comprehensive Approach for Elementary Schools (Second Edition)*, Copyright, 2000.

HANDOUT/TRANSPARENCY 5H
Gender Differences and Bullying

◆ Boys tend to bully with direct bullying or physical or verbal aggression.

◆ Girls tend to bully with indirect means such as social aggression.

◆ Boys who bully tend to be 1 to 2 years older than their victims. Their victims can be either boys or girls.

◆ Girl bullies tend to target other girls who are the same age to be their victims.

◆ Girls are more likely to be bullied by a group.

◆ Girls are more likely to involve both boys and girls in their bullying pursuits against a victim.

◆ Boys identify their behaviors as bullying more often than girls.

HANDOUT/TRANSPARENCY 51
Normal Conflict vs. Bullying

Normal Conflict vs. Bullying	
Normal Conflict	**Bullying**
Equal power—friends	Imbalance of power; not friends
Happens occasionally	Repeated negative actions
Accidental	Purposeful
Not serious	Serious—threat of physical harm or emotional or psychological hurt
Equal emotional reaction	Strong emotional reaction on part of the victim
Not seeking power or attention	Seeking power, control
Not trying to get something	Trying to gain material things or power
Remorse—take responsibility	No remorse—blames victim
Effort to solve the problem	No effort to solve problem

HANDOUT/TRANSPARENCY 5J
Three Types of Victims

A Passive Victim:

♦ Is nonassertive and submissive

♦ Is cautious and quiet

♦ Cries easily and collapses quickly when bullied

♦ Has few friends and is not connected to a social network

♦ Is anxious and insecure

♦ Lacks humor and prosocial skills

♦ Is physically weak—boys especially

A Provocative Victim:

♦ Is aggressive and argumentative

♦ Displays disruptive and irritating behaviors

♦ Is easily emotionally aroused

♦ Prolongs the conflict even when losing

♦ May be diagnosed with Attention Deficit Hyperactivity Disorder (ADHD)

A Vicarious Victim:

♦ Feels vulnerable as a potential target

♦ Has a moderate to high degree of empathy and sensitivity

♦ Does not take a stand against bullying because of fear

♦ Experiences guilt about his/her failure to act

The Downward Spiral of Victimization

The Downward Spiral of Victimization

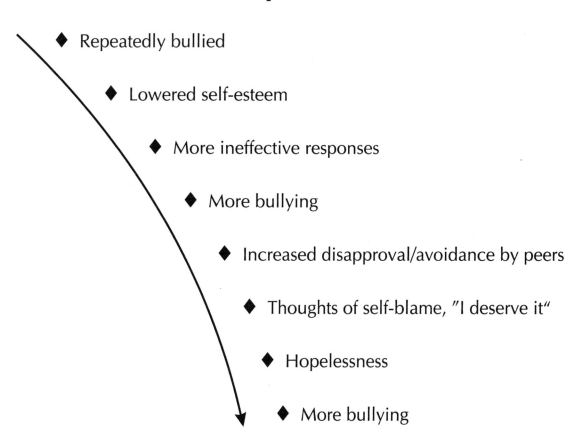

♦ Repeatedly bullied

    ♦ Lowered self-esteem

       ♦ More ineffective responses

          ♦ More bullying

             ♦ Increased disapproval/avoidance by peers

               ♦ Thoughts of self-blame, "I deserve it"

                 ♦ Hopelessness

                   ♦ More bullying

HANDOUT/TRANSPARENCY 5L
Effects of Bullying on Victims

Academic

School avoidance, truancy

Lowered grades and reduced learning

Lowered self-esteem

Diminished academic risk taking

Health Problems

Loss of appetite	Stomachaches, vomiting	Headaches
Nervousness	Depression	Loss of sleep
Frequent trips to the school nurse		

Adjustment Problems

Emotional distress	Lowered self-esteem	Loneliness
Anxiety	Homicidal ideation and attempts	
Depression	Suicidal ideation and attempts	

Bystanders

♦ Most ignored and underused resource in our schools

♦ 85% of a school population—the "silent majority"

♦ Become desensitized over time—diminished empathy

Why Don't They Get Involved?

1. Fear of retaliation

2. Don't know what to do

3. Afraid they'll make things worse

4. Worry about losing social status

5. Don't believe that adults will help

Silent Majority ♦ *Caring Majority* ♦ *Caring Community*

HANDOUT 5N
The Conflict Resolution Questionnaire

Teaching children to solve their own problems with peers is a difficult task. Some children seem to naturally do this better than others. We do know that those children who are not good at this skill can be taught strategies which assist them. There are no absolute right or wrong ways to solve problems, but there are techniques that work better at different ages and developmental levels.

The following questions will identify your primary approach to solving problems within your area of the school.

Directions:

Read the statements below. If a statement describes a response you typically make to conflict, write "3" in the space next to the question. If it is a response you occasionally make, write "2" in the space, and if you rarely or never make that response, write "1."

When there is a conflict, I:

1. Tell the children to stop it.   _____
2. Try to make everyone feel at ease.   _____
3. Help the children understand each others' point of view.   _____
4. Separate the children and keep them away from each other.   _____
5. Let the principal handle it.   _____
6. Decide who started it.   _____
7. Try to find out what the real problem is.   _____
8. Try to work out a compromise.   _____
9. Turn it into a joke.   _____
10. Tell the children to stop making such a fuss.   _____
11. Encourage one child to give in and apologize.   _____
12. Encourage the children to find an alternative solution.   _____
13. Help the children decide what they can compromise on.   _____
14. Try to divert attention away from the conflict.   _____
15. Let the children solve it, as long as no one is hurt.   _____
16. Threaten to send the children to the principal.   _____
17. Present some alternatives from which the children can choose.   _____
18. Help all the children to feel comfortable.   _____
19. Get all the children busy doing something else.   _____
20. Tell the children to try to settle it on their own.   _____

HANDOUT/5N (*continued*)

The Conflict Resolution Questionnaire Scoring Key

	I	II	III	IV	V
	1. _____	2. _____	3. _____	4. _____	5. _____
	6. _____	7. _____	8. _____	9. _____	10. _____
	11. _____	12. _____	13. _____	14. _____	15. _____
	16. _____	17. _____	18. _____	19. _____	20. _____
Totals	_____	_____	_____	_____	_____

Directions:

Add the numbers in each column, I–V. Each column reflects a particular approach and attitude toward conflict. Find the column with the highest score, and that will correspond to your predominant attitude and manner toward resolving conflict.

I   The No-Nonsense Approach.   I try to be fair and honest with the children but I believe that they need firm guidance in learning what's acceptable behavior and what isn't. If their behavior is unacceptable, I threaten with consequences or follow through with consequences.

II   The Problem Solving Approach.   If there's a conflict, I feel there is a problem. Instead of battling with the children, I try to set up a situation in which we can all solve the problem together. This produces creative ideas and stronger relationships.

III   The Compromising Approach.   I listen to the children and help them to listen to each other. Then I help them give a little. I believe that children need to learn that they can't always have everything they want when they want it.

IV   The Smoothing Approach.   I prefer that situations stay calm and peaceful whenever possible. Most of the conflicts the children get into are relatively minor, so I just divert their attention to other things.

V   The Ignoring Approach.   I point out the limits and let the children work things out for themselves. It is good for them to learn the consequences on their own for their behavior.

Strategies With Bullies

Strategies With Bullies

◆ A no-nonsense style

◆ Use prosocial consequences

◆ Give brief, clear descriptions of unacceptable behavior and consequences

◆ Do not have a long discussion of the situation

◆ Correct the bully's thinking errors

◆ Identify the victim's emotions

◆ Build empathy for the victim

◆ Re-channel power—do not try to suppress

◆ Set the culture for your school through the caring majority

H A N D O U T / T R A N S P A R E N C Y   5 P
Strategies With Victims

Strategies With Victims

◆ Use a supportive, fear-reducing style

◆ Reduce self-blame by clear identification of cruel behavior

◆ Demonstrate compassion and empathy

◆ Connect victim to helpful peers

◆ Mobilize caring majority in the classroom

◆ Remind of HA HA SO strategies

◆ Consider individual help with friendship skills

HANDOUT/TRANSPARENCY 5Q
Strategies for Bystanders

Strategies for Bystanders

◆ Normalize fears and worries

◆ Emphasize strength in numbers

◆ Communicate the expectation to take action

◆ Teach skills and strategies to take a stand

◆ Acknowledge and reward caring behaviors

HANDOUT/TRANSPARENCY 5R
Curriculum Overview

Curriculum Overview		
Sixth Grade: The Basics About Bullying		
Bullies	Bystanders	Empathy
Definition and Types of Bullying	Teasing	Taking a Stand
Normal Conflict vs. Bullying	Sexual Harassment	Inclusion
Victims	HA HA SO Strategies	
Seventh Grade: Creating the Caring Community		
Review of the Basics	Cliques	Flirting
Empathy	Taking a Stand	Levels of Risk-Taking
Inclusion	Sexual Harassment	Creative Problem Solving
Eighth Grade: Leadership		
Review of the Basics	Groups and Cliques	Empathy
Sexual Harassment	Characteristics and Styles of Positive Leadership	Taking a Stand
Flirting		Creative Problem Solving
Inclusion	Intention	
New Students: Establish a Connection with Their School		
New Students—Shared Experiences	Normal Conflict vs. Bullying	Empathy
Definition and Types of Bullying	Victims	Taking a Stand
No-bullying Expectations Stressed	Bystanders	Inclusion
Bullies	HA HA SO Strategies	Sexual Harassment

HA HA SO Strategies

Ha Ha So Strategies		
	STRATEGIES	**TIPS**
H Help:	Seek assistance from an adult, friend, or peer when a potentially threatening situation arises. Seek help also if other strategies aren't working.	1. Brainstorm all of the sources of help at your school—deans, counselors, teachers, nurse. 2. Stress the different ways to get help—anonymously, in a group, dean's hotline.
A Assert Yourself:	Make assertive statements to the bully addressing your feelings about the bully's *behavior*.	1. Should not be used with severe bullying. 2. Not as effective with group bullying. 3. Victim should look bully straight in the eye. 4. Use "I" statements. *Example:* "I don't like it when you pull on my backpack." 5. Make assertive statement and walk away. *Example:* "Stop talking about me behind my back."
H Humor:	Use humor to de-escalate a situation.	1. Use humor in a positive way. 2. Make the joke about what the bully said, not about the bully. 3. Make humorous statement and then leave the situation. 4. *Example:* When insulted about hairstyle, say "Gee, I didn't know you cared enough to notice."
A Avoid:	Walk away or avoid certain places in order to avoid a bullying situation.	1. Best for situations when victim is alone. 2. Avoid places where the bully hangs out. 3. Join with others rather than be alone.
S Self-Talk:	Use positive self-talk to maintain positive self-esteem during a bullying situation.	1. Use as a means to keep feeling good about self. 2. Think positive statements about self and accomplishments. 3. Rehearse mental statements to avoid being hooked by the bully. *Examples:* "It's his problem," "She doesn't know what she's talking about," "I know I'm smart." 4. Use positive self-talk when practicing all strategies.
O Own It:	"Own" the put-down or belittling comment in order to diffuse it.	1. Agree with the bully and leave the situation. 2. Combine with humor strategies such as, "Yeah, this **IS** a bad haircut. The lawn mower got out of control this weekend." 3. Combine with assertive strategies such as, "Yes, I did fail the test and I don't appreciate you looking at my paper."
Important Reminders:	1. Practice these strategies in any order, in any combination, or numerous times. 2. The Caring Community can remind each other of the strategies. 3. The Caring Community can help support the victim in using the strategies. 4. If the strategies aren't working, leave or disengage from the situation.	

HANDOUT/TRANSPARENCY 5T
HA HA SO STRATEGIES

Scenario: You are on the bus. As usual, the same kid is sitting behind you. He/She is kicking your seat, pulling your hair, and making rude comments about you. This has been happening every day for the past week.

Directions: Give an example of how you could use each of the strategies below to solve this problem.

Help _____

_____

Assert Yourself _____

_____

Humor _____

_____

Avoid _____

_____

Self-Talk_____

_____

Own It _____

_____

H A N D O U T / T R A N S P A R E N C Y   5 U
Sexual Harassment vs. Flirting

Sexual Harassment vs. Flirting	
Sexual Harassment makes the receiver feel:	**Flirting makes the receiver feel:**
Bad	Good
Angry/sad	Happy
Demeaned	Flattered
Ugly	Pretty/attractive
Powerless	In control
Sexual Harassment results in:	**Flirting results in:**
Negative self-esteem	Positive self-esteem
Sexual Harassment is perceived as:	**Flirting is perceived as:**
One-sided	Reciprocal
Demeaning	Flattering
Invading	Open
Degrading	A compliment
Sexual Harassment is:	**Flirting is:**
Unwanted	Wanted
Power-motivated	Equality-motivated
Illegal	Legal

Important reminders:
- Sexual harassment is against the law.
- The target decides whether the behaviors are harassing or flattering.
- Men and women often perceive sexual attention differently.
- "No" means "No."
- Sexual harassment is based on a need for power, **not** physical attraction.

Adapted with permission from authors. Copyright 1992 by Strauss & Espeland.

Sexual Harassment or Not Sexual Harassment
That is the question.

Group members: _____

Directions: Read each of the scenarios carefully. For each scenario write what would make the incident an example of flirting and what would make it an example of sexual harassment.

Scenario #1: A girl walks up to a guy in the hallway and hugs him.

What would make this incident flirting and what would make it sexual harassment?

Flirting: _____

_____

Sexual Harassment: _____

_____

Scenario #2: A student writes a note asking another student out.

What would make this incident flirting and what would make it sexual harassment?

Flirting: _____

_____

Sexual Harassment: _____

_____

Scenario—Creative Problem Solving

Scenario—Creative Problem Solving

The Faculty Lounge

Directions: Read the scenario below and discuss with your group creative ways to solve the problem. Write a low, medium, and high risk solution for the scenario.

Scenario: You're in the faculty lounge eating lunch. You overhear a staff member at another table making negative and sarcastic statements about a colleague who is not in the room. This has been happening periodically since the first of the year. You're worried that the statements he/she is making are starting to circulate throughout the building, and you have noticed that this kind of negative talk is spreading.

Solutions:

Low Risk

_____

_____

_____

Medium Risk

_____

_____

_____

High Risk

_____

_____

_____

Scenario—Creative Problem Solving

The Movie Theater

Directions: Read the scenario below and discuss with your group creative ways to solve the problem. Write a low, medium, and high risk solution for the scenario.

Scenario: You are sitting in the movie theater before the show begins. It is very crowded and almost all of the seats are taken. You are behind a woman who is sitting next to an empty seat that has a sweater draped over it. You watch as a large man sits in the empty seat with the sweater. The woman says, "This seat is saved," and the man replies in a very angry, intimidating, manner, "What do you mean. There are **no saved seats.**" The man settles into the seat and makes no effort to move even when the woman makes repeated requests. The woman looks very distressed. What could you do as a caring community member?

Solutions:

Low Risk

_____

_____

_____

Medium Risk

_____

_____

_____

High Risk

_____

_____

_____

Bully-Proofing Action Plan

Three things I learned which are most applicable to my school:

1. _____

2. _____

3. _____

Three action steps for utilization in my school:

1. _____

2. _____

3. _____

Barriers that may/do exist to carrying out these steps:

_____

_____

_____

_____

_____

_____

Solutions/strategies for dealing with barriers:

_____

_____

_____

_____

_____

_____

HANDOUT/TRANSPARENCY 5Z
What is Necessary for Bully-Proofing to Work

What is Necessary for Bully-Proofing to Work

1. The majority of teachers buy into it.

2. There is support from the administration.

3. There is an available facilitator to get the program started, to educate, to consult, and to handle logistics.

4. Patience. The greatest benefits will be seen starting in the middle of the second year.

5. Believe that ultimately your jobs as teachers and administrators will be easier. The children will keep the momentum going. Observe a tape of this or visit a school to see for yourself.

6. Not every child will change. Approximately 5% of the bullies and/or provocative victims will not benefit. Your job is not to change them; your job is to not allow them to disrupt.

7. Give up the notion that a power struggle with the bully is the only means of changing behavior.

8. "No" will mean "no" and consequences will happen.

9. The greatest control comes from the children themselves who eventually get tired of not having friends, and feeling left out. They will have the ultimate choice to join the caring majority or continue to be left out. You cannot change that choice. You can only show them the right way to get power.

10. Thinking of the big picture and where you want the climate of the school to be is more important than the day-to-day brush fires.

11. Think like the children do. They like the tools, the phrases, and the power of making and keeping their school safe.

12. Think about what you already have in place to enhance the climate of your school.

13. The broader the spectrum of character traits you can list, the better off things will be. Give every child value. Think of traits that enhance the classroom, playground, and school (i.e., a smile, a sense of humor, being tidy, being ready to work, being a good sport, sharing).

14. The caring majority is a positive peer culture group that most children will elect to join if given the means and opportunity. Those who elect not to may have that option; but they may not disrupt the rest of the group.

15. The most effective teacher, administrator, or dean combines two attributes: limit setting with relationship building.

16. The school is a community and, once that community is built into a safe and caring one, the children will work to keep it that way.

Section Two: Staff Issues

Though the problem of school bullying is finally getting the attention it deserves, most of the research and programming is directed towards students only, with very little consideration given to the important adult issues that are involved in any effort to combat bullying in the schools. In the implementation of a school-wide violence prevention effort, it is a mistake to focus only on the students and to forget that it is the adults in the school who truly set the tone for the school climate and who have the opportunity, daily, to model the caring behaviors that are expected of the students. For this reason, it is imperative that the adults in the school community take the time to examine and explore their specific roles in the bully-proofing effort as well as their relationships with students and each other.

In the three areas of staff involvement in the program, staff relationships with students, and relationships among staff members, there are adult issues and concerns that may develop and interfere with the program's successful implementation. An honest look at these potential problems and their solutions can help to prevent them from happening.

Staff Involvement

As stated in Chapter Four, the success of the *Bully-Proofing* program depends on each staff member in the school taking responsibility for dealing with bullying behaviors on a daily basis. Understanding that ignoring bullying is what allows it to prevail makes it clear that one of the staff's primary responsibilities is to get involved with bullying and deal with it when they see it occurring. To do this, they need to understand the seriousness of bullying and the effect it has on the school climate as well as the techniques available to help them handle bullying situations.

Unfortunately, studies show that school personnel often underestimate the amount of bullying that goes on in a school. When both students and staff are surveyed about the degree of safety in their schools, the adults generally rate the students as feeling safer in school than the students actually report. Smith and Sharp (1994) state that "most teachers are only aware of a fraction of the bullying which may be going on," and a study by O'Moore (Nash, 1989) reports that teachers grossly underestimated the amount of bullying in their schools and could not identify the majority of hard-core bullies in their schools.

There are many reasons why staff members may fail to intervene in bullying situations. They include:

1. Lack of understanding about the seriousness of bullying and its effect on school climate

2. Unawareness of the scope of the problem in the school

3. Lack of confidence in ability to handle bullying situations effectively

4. Fear or reluctance to challenge or discipline bullies because of potential consequences

5. Belief that other adults in the school should handle it

Since it is crucial that the adults intervene in bullying situations whether observed or reported to them by students, it is important to address with the staff the above listed issues around nonintervention as they arise. Some suggestions for addressing these (detailed in the following list) can be included in your school's staff development opportunities as well as in staff meetings.

Lack of understanding about the seriousness of bullying and its effect on school climate

◆ Educate staff with information and statistics about the prevalence and seriousness of bullying.

◆ Share with staff students' personal accounts of bullying by reading student essays and interview responses, by sharing audio or visual tapings of students' concerns and worries, or by sharing student poetry and drawings that illustrate their experiences with bullying.

◆ To give staff an opportunity to connect emotionally to the topic, conduct a visualization activity that invites them to remember a time when they experienced being bullied. (See Chapter Five on Faculty Training.)

Unawareness of the scope of the problem in the school

◆ Disseminate the results of the Colorado School Climate Survey which provide specific details about the present climate in the school. (See Chapter Four.)

◆ Provide staff with informal assessment results from student interviews, questionnaires, referral records, etc.

Lack of confidence in ability to handle bullying situations effectively

◆ Conduct the Conflict Resolution Questionnaire and facilitate a discussion about the value of different conflict management styles among staff members. (See Chapter Five.)

◆ Emphasize that the program's success is based on a team effort, and that the staff needs to work together to respect each others' styles and comfort levels in dealing with bullying issues.

◆ Make training and workshops available that teach the basic skills and strategies needed to deal with bullying problems.

◆ Provide continuous opportunities for staff to discuss their concerns, problems, and frustrations.

Fear or reluctance to challenge or discipline bullies because of potential consequences

◆ Emphasize the importance of not "looking the other way" and of the power created by adults supporting each other.

◆ Encourage teams to work together and share strengths in addressing particular problems. Examples: co-facilitate a parent conference, share responsibility for difficult phone calls, conduct student conferences with team members present.

◆ Invite a school administrator to speak with staff on a regular basis about administrative support. Facilitate staff and administration talking together about ways to support each other.

Belief that other adults in the school should handle it

◆ Reinforce the systemic and comprehensive nature of the program which requires all members of the school community to be involved.

◆ Remind staff that successful bullies count on loopholes in supervision and inconsistency among staff members in intervening in bullying situations.

◆ Ask the disciplinary team to talk with staff about appropriate behavior referrals to their office versus bullying problems that need to be addressed by staff members themselves.

Providing staff members with opportunities to learn about the dynamics of bullying and to practice the skills and strategies for successful interventions increases their confidence and their involvement in the program. Allowing the adults to talk freely and openly about their concerns and worries about the program is also an important part of the staff development process. The key to staff involvement is making sure that each individual staff member feels respected and accepted for his or her individual level of commitment, skills, and investment in the program as the implementation proceeds. Staff members who are more reticent or resistant to jumping on the bully-proofing bandwagon need to be given support and encouragement to join the effort.

Relationships Between Staff and Students

The foundation of the *Bully-Proofing Your School* program rests on the development of a caring community in the school where everyone feels cared for and safe. A key ingredient of this caring community is the strong and nurturing relationships staff members create with their students. By creating healthy and caring relationships with their students, educators meet the students' emotional needs as well as model for students the development of healthy relationships.

However, sometimes the adults can be part of the problem. As discussed in the previous section, one way adults can contribute to the problem is by not listening to students' reports of bullying and by avoiding the problem. By doing this adults are teaching students the behavior that is opposite of what is expected from the caring community. Consistent modeling by staff members of listening to students' reports of bullying, taking them seriously, and taking the appropriate action is the most effective way adults have of teaching students how to take responsibility in creating a bully-free school climate.

Another way staff members can contribute to the bullying problem is by acting like bullies toward their students. The fact is: there are "bully teachers"—usually at least one in every school. Bully teachers abuse their power by victimizing weaker students through the use of intimidation. Their bullying behaviors most commonly take the form of verbal, social, sexual, or racial harassment. For example, adults can use sarcasm or humor that singles out or ridicules a student as a form of bullying. This is particularly confusing and harmful both for the target of the ridicule and for the other students in the class. The bullying of students by staff members often goes unreported by students because of the natural imbalance of power between the student and the adult and their resulting fear of retaliation. Consequently, adults who are allowed to bully students are modeling bullying for their students, who in turn feel permission to imitate them. Bully teachers seriously sabotage the climate of a school and no curriculum or skill session can combat the negative message given by adults who themselves fail to model caring behaviors.

Since adults are the key players in teaching students about healthy and caring relationships, it is imperative that the staff address any issues that interfere with positive role modeling by the staff. The following are some suggestions for preventing and dealing with the problems that can occur in the area of staff and student relationships:

1. Adults must support each other and hold each other accountable for listening to students' reports of bullying and taking the appropriate action.

2. Adults must hold each other responsible for not "looking the other way."

3. Adults must listen to students who report being bullied by teachers or staff members and take the appropriate action rather than protecting the staff member.

4. Adults who are aware of staff members bullying students must take the appropriate action to make it stop.

Relationships Among Staff Members

Bullying is not just a phenomenon of childhood. It thrives in adulthood as well and exists in adult social groups in the same ways it does among children and adolescents. A typical school staff has members who sometimes display bullying behaviors as well as established cliques and groups that may use power inappropriately. And even though the adults may recognize and acknowledge that bullying exists among the students, they often don't see it among themselves. The bottom line is that adults need to address bullying issues among themselves if they expect students to do the same.

Bullying can be just as difficult for adults to handle as it is for students. Often a code of silence develops among the staff members with no one willing to confront the issues or the bad behaviors of certain individuals or groups. Just as students often feel afraid or hopeless and stuck in a situation over which they have no control, adults also have difficulty talking to a colleague or creating a situation which they fear may threaten their status or job. Walking away from a job that provides financial security is no easy task.

The knowledge and skills taught in the *Bully-Proofing Your School* program are as applicable to adults as they are to students. The strategies for avoiding victimization, taking a stand for others, and creating caring community are as important and useful for the adults to learn as they are for the students. And most importantly, if the staff expects the students to demonstrate these behaviors, then the adults must be willing and able to model the behaviors themselves.

The most valuable way to address the issue of bullying among the staff is to acknowledge that it exists and then focus on the goal of creating a caring community among the staff members. Being an educator in today's world is an incredibly challenging task and one that has the potential for creating stress and eventual burnout. Staff members must take the time to talk about ways to work together and solve problems among themselves if a true sense of collegiality is to develop. Though it may be necessary for individual interventions to occur to address specific bullying problems on the staff, an overall focus on how to consistently support and acknowledge each other as the adult members of the caring community is crucial to the creation of a safe school climate for all.

Since creating a safe school environment is a priority for the school, using staff meetings and staff development sessions to address these issues is necessary and appropriate. Listed below are some suggestions for preventing bullying issues among the staff by focusing on creating the adult caring community.

1. Provide numerous opportunities to talk about ways to develop the adult caring community in the school. Stress that adults cannot ask or expect students to do something that the adults themselves are not modeling.

2. Make the topic of the development of the adult caring community a consistent agenda item for staff meetings. Including it in this way gives is the status it requires.

3. Organize brainstorming and problem-solving sessions for the staff throughout the year during which members divide into groups to address issues such as handling conflict, reaching consensus, team decision making, and so forth.

4. Ask each staff member to make a personal commitment to being a member of the adult caring community. Ask them to write

their commitment on an index card and put in a sealed envelope addressed to themselves. A month later, send the envelopes to the staff to remind them of their commitment.

5. Conduct a staff activity in which groups brainstorm all the ways they can acknowledge and support each other. Type up these activities and give to the staff as a resource of caring ideas and behaviors.

6. Develop a written form for staff members to use to acknowledge each other. These can be delivered privately or read at faculty get-togethers or meetings.

7. Create spaces around your school where adults can write acknowledgments or thank you to each other to be seen by other staff members (i.e., dry-erase boards, laminated chart paper, etc.).

8. Design public displays such as bulletin boards to highlight staff members' families, talents, accomplishments, and so on.

It is a well-established fact that school staffs that display patterns of collegiality—staffs that are committed to working together cooperatively toward common goals—are more successful in implementing policy change and new programming. Adults who take the time to focus on their own professional relationships are giving a gift both to themselves and their students by modeling the importance of treating each other kindly and with respect.

Chapter Six

Notes And Sixth Grade Curriculum

Section One: Facilitator Notes

This curriculum is intended to be one part of a comprehensive, systemic, climate change program. As with all of the components of the *Bully-Proofing* program, it is important to tailor the curriculum to the needs and structure of your own school. The following ideas are offered as suggestions and have been found effective in a number of schools. You will, of course, need to assess your school resources including personnel available for training and class time for conducting the lessons, when designing this program for implementation in your school.

The middle school curriculum was written to cover the essential information as expediently as possible. However, the lessons could easily be slowed down, or enriched with additional lessons and activities. Each grade level curriculum is different and is designed to match the students' developmental needs and issues. Each year of the curriculum reviews and builds on the concepts discussed during the previous year's curriculum.

The curriculum consists of the following:

1. Five lessons for each grade level intended to be co-facilitated

2. Two classwork lessons intended to be conducted by the classroom teacher as follow-up between the co-facilitated sessions

3. Homework following each session

There are a number of ways to begin implementing this program. Some schools prefer to begin implementing the curriculum one grade level at a time. Other schools have chosen to train the entire school during one year. For these schools, a plan which allows for all students to get full exposure to the basic elements of the program as well as to their specific grade level material is as follows:

1. Sixth grade students follow the curriculum as outlined.

2. Seventh and eighth grade students first receive lessons 1 and 3 of the sixth grade curriculum. These lessons fully cover the essential concepts. Then lessons 2, 3, 4, and 5 as outlined for each grade level are delivered. This extends the total lessons to six each for both seventh and eighth grade levels.

3. In the second year of the program, the curriculum can be followed numerically for each grade level. However, you will need to be cognizant of the number of new students entering your school who may have never had the training.

Notes to Group Facilitators

Prior to Conducting Groups

Facilitators will benefit greatly from attending a daylong bully-proofing training session. This training provides important background information as well as strategies to assist with group delivery and program implementation. When facilitators have a solid base of conceptual knowledge, the classroom groups will flow effectively and can be more easily tailored to your school's needs and issues. Additionally, it will be very helpful to read the book, *Bully-Proofing Your School*.

The entire curriculum for each grade level should be reviewed by the facilitators prior to beginning the lessons. This will provide an overall idea of how the lessons fit together and allow for a more cohesive presentation to students.

Setting up Groups

It is strongly suggested that two facilitators conduct the groups. Two facilitators can work together to deliver the group activities expediently. More importantly, with two facilitators there is a rich background for answering questions and the facilitators can rely on each other for support. Additionally, facilitators can work together to maintain a psychologically safe, positive classroom atmosphere during the sessions.

One model of co-facilitation is to use two school support personnel, such as counselors, deans, administrators, and mental health personnel, as facilitators. If this model is used, it is very important for the classroom teacher to remain in the classroom during the lessons. This is one of the easiest ways for the teacher to learn the material. Remember, teachers will become the daily culture carriers of the concepts within the school. It will be the classroom teacher who reminds students of the caring community/bully-proofing expectations, uses the language in the classroom and hallways, and holds students accountable on a daily basis.

Another model of co-facilitation is for one trained facilitator to team with the classroom teacher for the sessions. This model engages the classroom teacher directly with the material and fewer trained facilitators can cover a greater number of classrooms. Keep in mind that teachers will have varying degrees of comfort and experience conducting classroom groups with affective content. Co-facilitators need to meet prior to conducting lessons so that they can discuss roles and responsibilities and so teachers will feel comfortable with the material.

It is recommended that classroom groups be scheduled one week apart for the following reasons:

1. Time between sessions increases the opportunity for the material to be integrated by students.

2. Homework is assigned after each classroom session and is to be completed by students prior to the next bully-proofing session.

3. Classwork is a follow-up lesson that is intended to be taught by the classroom teacher prior to the next co-facilitated session. There are two classwork lessons within each grade level curriculum. Facilitators need to inform classroom teachers of this requirement when groups are scheduled so that teachers can adapt their lesson plans.

Conducting Groups

Lessons are written in a format that clearly communicates the concept being taught. Included are questions which facilitate discussions with students. Additionally, transitional phrases and important statements that punctuate the key components of the program are presented in bold letters in script form. These scripts can be read verbatim by the facilitators or paraphrased to fit their own speaking style. In addition, handouts and transparencies are included at the end of each chapter to be used at the discretion of the facilitators. Suggestions for times to chart information on the blackboard or on chart paper are noted in the margin.

CHART

It is important to establish an open, trusting atmosphere in the classroom during Bully Proofing sessions. Lessons presented effectively provide opportunities for students to dialogue about important issues in a context that acknowledges and normalizes students' confusion as part of the self-discovery process. This open, safe environment creates a community within the classroom where students are free to express their ideas and disagree respectfully. As always it is imperative that group facilitators embrace and respect the students' cultural and racial differences as they express their ideas, strategies, and concerns during class discussions. Remembering and acknowledging that students have diverse backgrounds and experiences that influence their thoughts and concerns helps to establish the trusting atmosphere required for successful lessons.

It is important for facilitators who are, or have been, classroom teachers to spend some time reviewing the differences between a dynamic group process and structured classroom instruction. Some of the differences are summarized in the chart below.

At times, students will present some resistance and pose difficult questions during the group process. This type of dialogue and questioning is developmentally necessary for the adolescent to integrate the material. Adolescents no longer do what adults tell them or agree with our ideas just because we tell them to. They must learn to think and decide for themselves.

Another key factor when conducting classroom groups is to keep the primary focus on the caring majority of students. Classroom groups provide an important time to model dealing with bullies in a no-nonsense way. Be cautious regarding the possible domination of bullies within the groups. Students need to express their opinions and they won't always be positive, but bullies can be quite skilled at dominating and taking over the entire group process. Facilitators can easily fall into the trap of trying to convince the bully to buy into bully-proofing during the classroom groups. This leaves the majority of students watching and waiting and not getting the attention they deserve.

Use your school name in the delivery of the lessons. An important part of developing a sense of community is fostering school pride. In larger

Group Facilitation vs. Structured Classroom Instruction	
Differences	
Regular Classroom Instruction	Classroom Group Discussion
Information delivered by the teacher	Students encouraged to discover own knowledge
Teacher corrects student responses	Facilitator makes accepting comments and provokes further thought
Questions with definite right/wrong answers	Open-ended questions
Teacher remains primary focus of classroom throughout lesson	Students encouraged to comment on each others' thoughts and share information together
Often use closed questions to check for understanding. Burden of guiding talk remains on teacher. (Questions often start with Is . . . Are . . . Do . . .)	Often use open-ended questions to provoke thought and discussion. (Open-ended questions often start with What . . . How . . . Why . . . Could . . . What else . . .)
Similarities	
Teacher has clearly set behavioral expectations and consequences Intimidation and disrespect are dealt with swiftly by the teacher.	The facilitator has clearly set behavioral expectations and consequences. Intimidation and disrespect are dealt with swiftly by the facilitator.

schools a sense of community can be developed by building class unity. We have found that using the school name, class year of graduation (i.e., "You are the class of 2004. Look around, this is your community. These are your classmates.") helps build a sense of community and belonging.

General Information for School-Wide Implementation

It is important to have discussions among the support, administrative, disciplinary, and teaching personnel to develop consistent expectations and procedures in the following areas:

- ♦ **Methods and places for students to report bullying behaviors they observe**
  - ◇ Standard incident forms
  - ◇ Investigative procedures
- ♦ **Methods and parameters around students reporting incidences anonymously**
  - ◇ Can students report incidences anonymously?
  - ◇ What is the method for anonymous reporting?
- ♦ **Methods and consequences for retaliatory actions**
  - ◇ When students retaliate against students who report bullying, how is it handled?
- ♦ **Sexual harassment policies and investigative methods**
  - ◇ Can reports be kept confidential?
  - ◇ When do you involve police?
  - ◇ How do you support the victim during the investigation?
- ♦ **Support available for victims (school, parent, and community)**
  - ◇ Who is available for emotional support in your school or community?
  - ◇ Is privacy assured?

It is important to remember that this is a climate change program. At the onset of the program referrals initiated by both students and staff may actually increase. This is due to the heightened awareness of bullying and the consistent expectation that it will not be tolerated. Schools have found that behavioral referrals decrease after the expectations are consistently followed with consequences.

Remember, this program will not eliminate the bullies from your school. It is intended to minimize their impact by teaching students skills to avoid being victimized and by increasing student resiliency. The main goal of the *Bully-Proofing Your School* program is to mobilize the

85% of students who are interested in learning and being kind to others to take a stand to help peers and friends alike. By empowering this caring majority of our students, we can work collaboratively to create a school community where staff and students, friends and peers, feel cared for and safe.

SECTION TWO: Sixth Grade Curriculum

LESSON 1   The Basics of Bullying

Materials

- ◆ Chart paper
- ◆ Markers
- ◆ Overhead projector
- ◆ **Handout/Transparency 6A:** Types of Bullying Behaviors
- ◆ **Handout/Transparency 6B:** Normal Conflict versus Bullying
- ◆ **Handout/Transparency 6C:** Bully-Proofing Guidelines
- ◆ **Handout/Transparency 6D:** Bystander Scenarios

Objectives

- ◆ Establish rules and expectations for group discussions
- ◆ Understand Bully-Proofing Guidelines and program goals
- ◆ Develop understanding of the terms "bully," "victim," and "bystander"

Steps

1. Hook: Get students' attention by reading a short news article or story about a caring, life-changing experience. Suggestion: Read story titled, "Give Random Acts of Kindness a Try" from *Chicken Soup for the Teenage Soul II* by Canfield, Hansen, and Kirberger. Stress the importance of respect and caring for each other as illustrated in the story.

II. Establish rules for classroom meetings and conduct a discussion regarding reasons for the *Bully-Proofing* program.

    A. Rules and expectations for the group

        1. Respect for self and others—no put-downs, verbal or nonverbal

        2. Participate in your own way and style that is respectful of others

        3. While sharing stories or experiences, do not mention any particular names of individuals or groups. Instead, say, "I know someone who . . . "

    B. Discuss purpose of *Bully-Proofing* program

        1. Why do you think we are bully-proofing our school?

        2. What makes school a place where you want to be?

        3. How do you think the *Bully-Proofing* program can make our school a better place?

    Emphasize the point that this program is about developing a caring community in which each student is a valuable member and feels safe and respected. Use student responses to develop the idea that bullying behaviors cannot be tolerated in a caring community. Also assure students that the adults in the building have also been trained in bully-proofing and are committed to working with the students to make the school safe.

    C. Inquire about students' past training in bully-proofing. Poll students to find out how many had the bully-proofing training in elementary school. Let the experienced students know that we will be counting on them to use their bully-proofing skills to help their classmates and the new sixth graders who haven't learned the strategies.

III. Activity: Explore students' knowledge of the concepts of **bully, victim,** and **bystander.**

    A. Divide students into three groups. Give each group one large sheet of chart paper and a marking pen. Ask each group to select one member to be the recorder.

    B. Assign each group one of the three concepts—bully, victim, or bystander. Ask each group to generate a list of the characteristics of their assigned topic. For example, the *bully* group is responsible for writing down all the characteristics of a bully.

    C. Give the groups five minutes to create their lists. When completed, display the charts in front of the room.

IV. Explore and discuss the concept of "Bully."

    A. Ask a member of the *bully* group to read their list of characteristics. Students will often include physical characteristics such as

CHART

boy vs. girl, big vs. small. Reinforce the idea that bullies have no particular physical characteristics, but they do have some similar behaviors. Focus on bullying behaviors and use this discussion to dispel myths about bullies. Ask students:

1. Do all bullies look alike?

2. Are they all boys or girls?

3. What is the body language of a bully?

4. How do they walk and talk?

B. Generate a list of student ideas regarding examples of bullying behaviors (Handout/Transparency 6A). Students typically mention various kinds of bullying at this point. For example, when a student responds with "kicking or shoving," the facilitator categorizes this as physical aggression and continues to elicit student responses until all categories have been covered. The facilitator records the categories on chart paper which can be reposted in Lesson 2. (Note: We will go into

Handout/Transparency 6A

HANDOUT/TRANSPARENCY 6A
Types of Bullying Behaviors

Physical Aggression: Hitting, kicking, destroying property

Social Aggression: Spreading rumors, excluding from group, silent treatment

Verbal Aggression: Name calling, teasing, threatening, intimidating phone calls

Intimidation: Graffiti, a dirty trick, taking possession, coercion

Written Aggression: Note writing, graffiti, slam books

Sexual Harassment: Comments or actions of a sexual nature which are unwelcome and make the recipient uncomfortable. *Examples:* rumors of a sexual nature, inappropriate touching, grabbing, comments about someone's body

Racial and Ethnic Harassment: Comments or actions containing racial or ethnic content which are unwelcome and make the recipient uncomfortable. *Examples:* ethnic jokes, racial name calling, racial slurs

more detail about verbal aggression and sexual harassment in Lesson 2.)

1. What is bullying?

2. What are some typical bullying behaviors?

C. Explore reasons students bully. Ask:

1. Why do students bully?

Make sure the following reasons are included in the discussion. Emphasize that bullying is all about power—the bully wanting power over the victim.

CHART

Reasons Why Students Bully Others

1. To gain power

2. To gain popularity and attention

3. To act out problems from home

4. To copy what someone else does that they admire

5. They perceive it as fun

6. They have low self-esteem (sometimes)

D. Ask students to think about the differences between normal conflict and bullying. Encourage students' ideas. As students

We're Different
Drawn by
Alex Leonard

Just because you are different doesn't give the right for others to bully you.

share ideas, the facilitator writes them on chart paper with two colors—one for normal conflict and one for bullying. The facilitator can use Handout/Transparency 6B to summarize the ideas.

Focus on the question: What is the difference between normal conflict between friends and the more serious situation of bullying?

Emphasize the difference in power. This difference can be a red flag for students who may be experiencing more subtle types of bullying but do not recognize it.

V. Explore and develop the concept of "Victim."

   A. Ask a member of the *victim* group to read their list of characteristics. Students will often include physical characteristics such as boy vs. girl, big vs. small. Reinforce the idea that victims have no particular physical characteristics, but they do have some similar behaviors. Use this discussion to dispel myths about victims.

Handout/Transparency 6B

HANDOUT/TRANSPARENCY 6B
Normal Conflict versus Bullying

Normal Conflict	versus	Bullying
Equal power; friends	vs.	Imbalance of power; not friends
Happens occasionally	vs.	Repeated negative actions
Accidental	vs.	Purposeful
Not serious	vs.	Serious—threat of physical harm or emotional or psychological hurt
Equal emotional reaction	vs.	Strong emotional reaction on part of the victim
Not seeking power or attention	vs.	Seeking power, control
Not trying to get something	vs.	Trying to gain material things or power
Remorse—takes responsibility	vs.	No remorse—blames victim
Effort to solve the problem	vs.	No effort to solve problem

1. Do all victims look alike?

2. Are they all boys or girls?

3. What is the body language of a victim?

4. How do they walk and talk?

B. Generate a list of student ideas regarding the characteristics of a victim. The facilitator lists student responses on the board. Make sure the following starred (*) characteristics are included in the list which students generate. Briefly discuss each.

What are the characteristics of a victim?

♦ Alone and isolated*

♦ Trouble making friends*

♦ Small or weak—appears unsure of self*

♦ Cries easily and unable to stick up for self*

♦ May have suffered abuse at home

♦ May have difficulty learning

♦ Sometimes irritable and provokes other students*

♦ May try to fight back, but will still lose and get very upset

♦ Willing to keep quiet*

♦ New to school*

♦ Between friend groups*

C. Generate a list of the emotional consequences of being the victim.

How does a victim feel when he or she has been victimized?

What happens to a victim after a long period of victimization?

♦ Drop in self-esteem

♦ Fearful attitude

♦ Withdrawn or sad

♦ Headache, stomachache, fatigue, or other physical complaints

♦ Panic and irrational retaliation

♦ Fear of school

VI. Explore and develop the concept of "Bystander."

A. Ask a member of the *bystander* group to read their list of characteristics. Ask students for their definitions of the term "bystander." Accept different meanings, emphasizing that the one characteristic bystanders have in common is that they do not take action. Define bystander for students.

BYSTANDER: A person who stands near or looks on but does not take part; onlooker; spectator.

B. Ask students to think of a time they observed someone in the role of a bystander, or a time they were bystanders in a bullying situation. Invite students to talk about these experiences, making the point that all of us have been in this role because it's not always easy to know what to do when we see bullying taking place. Ask students:

Is a bystander who stands by and watches bullying take place without doing anything about it acting as a caring community member?

C. Guide the discussion to these important points:

1. If a person acts as a bystander and takes no action against bullying, then he or she is not acting as a member of the caring community.

2. Bullies like it when bystanders don't do anything. They count on the bystanders to remain silent so they can continue their bullying behaviors.

3. Bystanders make up the **most important** group in the school because once they learn how to take a stand against bullying, the bullies will lose their power.

D. Summarize the discussion about bystanders.

"We've all been bystanders at some time or another because sometimes it is difficult to know what to do when we see bullying taking place. But being a bystander means we are not acting like a caring community member because we are standing by and letting bullying continue.

"The *Bully-Proofing* program focuses on helping the silent majority of bystanders know what to do when they see bullying taking place so that they can help their school become a safe place. We are going to teach you some strategies to use so that you can work together to take the power away from the bullies and put it back in the hands of the caring majority where it belongs."

| Handout/Transparency 6C |

VII. Summarize program goals with Bully-Proofing Guidelines, Handout/Transparency 6C.

A. Present posted guidelines to class. Read through the guidelines with the class, emphasizing that these are the guidelines we will be using to bully-proof our school. Let the students know that we will be discussing the guidelines in more detail as we continue through the lessons.

HANDOUT/TRANSPARENCY 6C
Bully-Proofing Guidelines

1. **Respect yourself and others.**

2. **Contribute to a healthy and safe learning environment.**

3. **Use empathy and extra effort to include others.**

4. **Take a stand for what is right.**

5. **Encourage creative and peaceful problem solving.**

6. **Follow all school rules.**

Assure students of these things:

1. The adults in this school have as much interest in their school being safe as the students do. Remind them that we are all in this together and that adults are here to help them.

2. There is strength in numbers—that is the main idea behind the caring community. There are many more of us who want our school to be safe than there are bullies.

VIII. **Homework**

Ask students to write about a time when they were bullied either at school or on the way to or from school and how it made them feel. Encourage students to include details about their experiences. Some of these will be shared anonymously at the beginning of the next lesson.

IX. **Classwork**

To be completed during one class session by the classroom teacher prior to the next lesson.

CHART

A. Discuss and record ideas about how the students, faculty, and specifically your class can help to bully-proof your school.

B. Bystander Scenarios (Handout/Transparency 6D). Hand out worksheet to students. Read the scenarios aloud together and ask students to brainstorm ways that the bystander(s) in each scenario could act as caring community members by **Taking Action**.

What can bystanders do differently instead of looking the other way or allowing the bullying to continue?

Scenario #1: A student is purposefully shoved in the lunchroom and drops his tray. A bystander looks the other way and pretends to not notice.

Scenario #2: A group of guys are standing in the hall in a group. They begin to badmouth a girl they know who happens to be one of the group member's best friends.

Handout/Transparency 6D

HANDOUT/TRANSPARENCY 6D
Bystander Scenarios

Directions:

Read each scenario carefully. Think about all the different ways the bystanders in each scenario could act as caring community members by **TAKING ACTION**.

Scenario #1

A student is purposefully shoved in the cafeteria and drops his tray. A bystander looks the other way and pretends to not notice.

The bystander could take action by:

_____

_____

_____

Scenario #2

A group of guys are standing in the hall. They begin to bad-mouth a girl they know who happens to be one of the group member's best friends. A bystander doesn't say anything and allows the talk to continue.

The bystander could take action by:

_____

_____

_____

Scenario #3

A girl is yelling at another girl in the restroom and threatens to beat her up after school. A bystander hears it all but walks away and doesn't mention the incident to anyone.

The bystander could take action by:

_____

_____

_____

A bystander doesn't say anything and allows the talk to continue.

Scenario #3: A girl is yelling at another girl in the bathroom and threatens to beat her up after school. A bystander hears it all but walks away and doesn't mention the incident to anyone.

REMIND STUDENTS: By allowing the bullying to continue, bystanders are not acting as caring community members. Bystanders need to **Take Action** and take their power back from the bullies.

LESSON 2 Teasing and Sexual Harassment

Materials

- Charts from Lesson 1

- Overhead projector

- **Handout/Transparency 6E:** Friendly Teasing versus Hurtful Teasing

- **Worksheet 6F:** Check Your Understanding—Sexual Harassment and Teasing

Objectives

- Review Lesson 1 concepts

- Explore and understand the concept of teasing

- Develop understanding of sexual harassment as a type of bullying

Steps

I. Review Lesson 1 concepts.

A. Briefly review the classroom meeting rules.

1. Respect yourself and others—no put-downs, verbal or nonverbal

2. Participate—in your own way and style that is respectful of others

3. While sharing stories or experiences, do not mention any particular names of individuals or groups. Instead, say, "I know someone who. . ."

B. Briefly review the concepts of bully, victim, and bystander.

C. Students and/or facilitators read aloud students' homework assignments. Facilitators can read entries anonymously and need to be careful to screen out any names or potentially identifying information. Additionally, facilitators need to be careful not to glamorize any of the bullying events that are shared or to allow any inappropriate laughter. Use writing examples to reinforce concepts of bully, victim, and bystander.

D. State these important points about the *Bully-Proofing* program.

   1. The *Bully-Proofing* program will not eliminate all the bullies or all the bullying behavior in the school.

   2. The *Bully-Proofing* program will teach students the skills needed to avoid victimization.

   3. The main focus of the program is on teaching the silent majority, also called the bystanders, how to take a stand against bullying.

   4. The program challenges all the students to become members of the caring majority so that everyone will feel safe and respected.

II. Introduce concepts of teasing and sexual harassment.

A. Remind students that in Lesson 1 we talked about all the different kinds of bullying. Inform students that in middle school, two forms of bullying in particular—verbal aggression in the form of teasing and sexual harassment—get trickier and more complicated. Explain that during today's lesson we're going to go into more detail about these two kinds of bullying.

III. Explore and develop the concept of teasing as a form of verbal aggression.

A. Ask students to come up with examples of teasing. After they've thought of several examples, comment on the frequency and variety of teasing and ask the students their opinions about whether or not teasing is OK. Acknowledge that there is often confusion about teasing and when it crosses the line into bullying.

B. Facilitators role play the following teasing incident in front of the class.

Facilitator #1: You look really lame in that outfit today. Couldn't you find anything else to wear?

Facilitator #2: (in a sad, upset voice) Geez, you don't have to be so mean all the time.

Facilitator #1: What are you so upset about? I was just teasing. Can't you take a joke?

Facilitators ask students:

1. What just happened here?

2. Was this an example of verbal aggression? of teasing? of bullying?

3. She said she was just kidding or teasing, Does that make it OK?

4. Is teasing ever OK?

C. Generate a discussion with the students around the answers to the above questions. Introduce the idea that there are two kinds of teasing: friendly and hurtful. Friendly teasing happens among friends and can make people feel close and included. Hurtful teasing is done with the intent to make someone feel bad and excluded. Write the headings "Friendly Teasing" and "Hurtful Teasing" on the board and record students' ideas about the differences.

D. Summarize the above discussion by showing the chart Friendly Teasing vs. Hurtful Teasing, Handout/Transparency 6E. Discuss each point with the students.

Handout/Transparency 6E

HANDOUT/TRANSPARENCY 6E
Friendly Teasing versus Hurtful Teasing

Friendly Teasing	versus	Hurtful teasing
Equal power; friends	vs.	Imbalance of friends power; not friends
Neutral topic	vs.	Sensitive topic
Playful purpose	vs.	Purpose is to upset
Purpose is to include	vs.	Purpose is to exclude
Funny	vs.	Sarcastic

1. Teasing, just like bullying, is a power issue. Hurtful teasing usually doesn't happen between friends. Bullies use hurtful teasing to establish or maintain power over someone, or at the very least, to make the person feel bad.

2. All of us have personal topics and issues we are sensitive about, and it is never OK to tease people about these topics. Before you tease someone, think about whether this is a topic that may be off-limits.

3. The intention behind teasing behavior is what really makes the difference between friendly and hurtful teasing. Before you tease someone, ask yourself why you're doing it. If, for example, it's to have fun with your friends in a way that is playful and will make you all feel closer, then your intention is to include everyone, and your teasing may be friendly.

4. Again, your intention is what counts. If your teasing is intended to make someone feel left out, then you are involved in hurtful teasing.

5. There is a difference between funny humor and sarcastic humor. Comments made sarcastically are not always funny. Sarcasm is often "cutting," mean humor that is intended to put someone down. Sarcasm is often a put-down hidden in a joke.

Most Important—The person being teased makes the decision about whether the teasing is friendly or hurtful. Just because the teaser says he was "kidding" doesn't make it OK. The person being teased makes that decision. The person doing the teasing often thinks it's funnier than the person being teased. Bullies are especially good at convincing others that their put-downs and bully behaviors are only friendly teasing.

IV. Explore the topic of sexual harassment.

A. Define the term sexual harassment.

SEXUAL HARASSMENT: Any unwelcome comments or actions of a sexual nature that make the recipient uncomfortable.

B. Relate sexual harassment to both bullying and hurtful teasing. Sexual harassment is a form of bullying and also a form of hurtful teasing. In middle school, teasing sometimes has sexual content which makes people very uncomfortable. That's when teasing can become sexual harassment.

C. Examples of sexual harassment. Ask the students to think of examples of sexual harassment. Write student examples on the board. Guide the discussion carefully to avoid inappropriate comments and behaviors. If students have difficulty with this discussion, the facilitators can suggest some of the following examples:

1. Sexual or "dirty" jokes

2. Comments about body parts—male or female

3. Rating individuals on a scale of 1 to 10

4. Any inappropriate touching

5. Name-calling about sexual orientation

6. Rumors of a sexual nature—verbal, written

D. Important points about sexual harassment. Be sure to discuss each of these points with the students:

1. Just as in the case of teasing, the person who is the target of the harassing behavior gets to decide if the behavior constitutes sexual harassment. The target decides if he or she is uncomfortable with the harassment, and therefore decides if it is sexual harassment.

2. Sexual harassment is against school rules and can result in serious consequences.

3. Sexual harassment is against the law. Targets of the harassment can file charges with the police which can result in serious legal consequences.

4. Anyone who feels he or she is being sexually harassed needs to tell an adult immediately. Even though it can be embarrassing or scary, it is important to tell an adult anyway so that the harassment can be stopped.

5. Students can be assured that reporting sexual harassment is important and will be handled privately and sensitively by the adults in the building.

V. Activity: Check Your Understanding, Worksheet 6F.

Worksheet 6F

A. Hand out Worksheet 6F to students. They can work on it individually or in small groups. Go over answers together. Discuss any items that students have questions about.

VI. **Homework**

A. Write about teasing incidents. Ask students to write about their experiences with teasing, either friendly or hurtful, and how they felt.

B. Ask students to pay attention to their own teasing behaviors for the next few days. Remind them to think about their intention before they tease someone, and to notice the response of the person being teased.

Worksheet 6F

WORKSHEET 6F
Check Your Understanding—Sexual Harassment and Teasing

Directions:

Decide if each statement is True or False. Put a T or F in the line after each statement.

1. Teasing is OK if the person doing the teasing says, "I'm just teasing."   _____

2. It is alright to tease your best friend about anything.   _____

3. The person who is the target of sexual comments is the one who decides if it is sexual harassment.   _____

4. A purpose of playful teasing can be to make someone feel like he or she belongs.   _____

5. Sarcasm is a form of humor that can be hurtful and mean.   _____

6. Note writing can never be considered a form of sexual harassment.   _____

7. Teasing is never OK.   _____

8. A person who experiences sexual harassment should ask an adult for help.   _____

9. Bullies use teasing as a way of establishing power over their targeted victims.   _____

10. Hurtful teasing usually happens among people who are friends.   _____

11. Sexual harassment is against the law.   _____

12. Sexual harassment is a type of bullying.   _____

LESSON 3 Strategies To Avoid Victimization

Materials

◆ Overhead projector

◆ **Handout/Transparency 6G:** HA HA SO Strategies

◆ **Handout/Transparency 6H:** Tattling versus Telling

◆ **Worksheet 6I:** HA HA SO Scenario

Objectives

◆ Review Lesson 2 concepts

◆ Learn and practice the HA HA SO strategies

◆ Identify the difference between tattling and telling

◆ Apply HA HA SO strategies to bullying scenarios

Steps

I. Review Lesson 2 concepts and classroom group rules. Share and discuss homework assignments about times students felt teased. Use material in assignments to review concept of "friendly teasing" vs. "hurtful teasing." Briefly review topic of sexual harassment.

II. Introduce HA HA SO Strategies, Handout/Transparency 6G.

    A. Introduce HA HA SO as the strategies students can learn to help them and their friends avoid victimization. Remind students that even though they probably already use several of these ideas it is a good idea to review and practice them so they can be prepared to use them at the appropriate time.

    B. Using Handout/Transparency 6G, discuss and practice each of the strategies with the students. Share with students examples of each.

Handout/Transparency 6G

HA HA SO Strategies		
H - Help	H - Humor	S - Self-Talk
A - Assert Yourself	A - Avoid	O - Own It

HELP: Seek assistance from an adult, friend, or peer when a potentially threatening situation arises. Seek help when other strategies aren't working.

Discuss with the students when and how to get help from peers and adults. Create a list with the names of all adults in the building available to help students.

Tips:

1. Know all of the sources of help at your school: deans, counselors, teachers, nurse, etc.

2. Know the different ways to get help—anonymously, in a group, dean's hotline. As part of the **HELP** strategy, explore with students the differences between tattling and telling. Use Handout/Transparency 6H to cover the following points:

ASSERT YOURSELF: Make assertive statements to the bully addressing your feelings about the bully's behavior.

Teach the students when it is wise to use assertiveness and when it is not effective. Discuss with students the difference between being aggressive and assertive.

WORKSHEET 6F
Check Your Understanding—Sexual Harassment and Teasing

Directions:

Decide if each statement is True or False. Put a T or F in the line after each statement.

1. Teasing is OK if the person doing the teasing says, "I'm just teasing."   _____

2. It is alright to tease your best friend about anything.   _____

3. The person who is the target of sexual comments is the one who decides if it is sexual harassment.   _____

4. A purpose of playful teasing can be to make someone feel like he or she belongs.   _____

5. Sarcasm is a form of humor that can be hurtful and mean.   _____

6. Note writing can never be considered a form of sexual harassment.   _____

7. Teasing is never OK.   _____

8. A person who experiences sexual harassment should ask an adult for help.   _____

9. Bullies use teasing as a way of establishing power over their targeted victims.   _____

10. Hurtful teasing usually happens among people who are friends.   _____

11. Sexual harassment is against the law.   _____

12. Sexual harassment is a type of bullying.   _____

Tips:

1. Should not be used with severe bullying.

2. Not as effective with group bullying.

3. Victim should look bully straight in the eye.

4. Use "I" statements. *Example:* "I don't like it when you pull on my backpack."

5. Make assertive statement and walk away. *Example:* "Stop talking about me behind my back."

HUMOR: Use humor to de-escalate a situation.

Teach the students how to use humor to de-escalate a situation. Let them know that some people find the humor strategy easier than others.

Tips:

1. Use humor in a positive way.

2. Make sure the joke is about what the bully said, not about the bully.

Don't listen to bullies
Drawn by
Anthony Landrum

3. Make humorous statement and then leave the situation.

4. *Example:* When insulted about hairstyle, say "Gee, I didn't know you cared enough to notice."

AVOID: Walk away or avoid certain places in order to avoid a bullying situation.

Teach the students that it is appropriate and sometimes the best solution to walk away in order to avoid a bullying situation.

Tips:

1. Best for situations when victim is alone.

2. Avoid places where the bully hangs out.

3. Join with others rather than be alone.

SELF-TALK: Use positive self-talk to maintain positive self-esteem during a bullying situation.

Teach the students how to use their self-talk to maintain positive self-esteem during a bullying situation.

Tips:

1. Use as a means to keep feeling good about self.

2. Think positive statements about self and accomplishments.

3. Rehearse mental statements to avoid being hooked by the bully. *Examples:* "It's his problem," "She doesn't know what she's talking about," "I know I'm smart."

4. Use positive self-talk when practicing all strategies.

OWN IT: "Own" the put-down or belittling comment in order to defuse it.

Teach the students how to "own" the put-down instead of being defensive.

Tips:

1. Agree with the bully and leave the situation.

2. Combine with humor strategies such as, "Yeah, this **IS** a bad haircut. The lawn mower got out of control this weekend."

3. Combine with assertive strategies such as, "Yes, I did fail the test and I don't appreciate you looking at my paper."

Important Reminders:

1. Try these strategies in any order or numerous times.

2. It may take more than one strategy or more than one time to practice the strategies.

3. Caring community members can remind each other of the strategies.

4. Caring community members can help support the victim in using the strategies.

5. If the strategies aren't working, leave or disengage from the situation.

III. Assign activity to practice strategies.

A. Divide students into six groups.

B. Assign each group one of the HA HA SO strategies. Ask each group to design a scenario in which they use the assigned strategy to solve a typical bullying problem. Have students record their scenarios and solutions on paper.

C. Each group shares its scenario with the class. Encourage discussion about the creative use of the strategies.

IV. **Additional Activity:**   For further practice with strategies for dealing with bullies, see "What Should You Do?" in *The Bully-Free Classroom,* pp.42, 43 (Beane, 1999).

V.   **Homework**

Have students complete HA HA SO Strategies, Worksheet 6I.

Worksheet 6I

VI.   **Classwork** (Optional)

To be completed during one class session by classroom teacher prior to next lesson.

A. Invite students to design skits to model the HA HA SO strategies. Present to class and discuss.

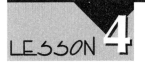

LESSON 4 · Creating Caring Communities: Empathy and Taking a Stand

Materials

◆ Chart paper

◆ Markers

◆ **Worksheet 6J:** Empathy and Taking a Stand

◆ VCR

◆ Video titled: "Don't Pick on Me," Sunburst Communications, Inc., 1993

◆ **Worksheet 6K:** Video Observations

Objectives

◆ Review the HA HA SO strategies

◆ Develop understanding of the concept of caring community

◆ Learn about and explore the concept of empathy

◆ Learn about and explore the concept of taking a stand

◆ Apply previously taught strategies to bullying scenarios

Steps

I.   Review HA HA SO strategies. Discuss homework—the HA HA SO Strategies worksheet.

II. Introduce the concept of building a caring community.

A. Ask students to generate ideas about how people behave in a caring community. Use the following questions to guide the discussion.

In a caring community:

1. How do people act toward each other?

2. How do people talk with each other?

3. What kinds of things do people do for each other?

4. What makes people feel safe and respected?

CHART

B. List students' ideas on chart paper and refer back to them during the lesson. Summarize their ideas of characteristics of caring communities and tell them that the last two lessons will focus on these and other ways to build caring communities.

III. Review the Bully-Proofing Guidelines posted in the classroom, Handout/Transparency 6C.

A. Review guidelines #1: **Respect yourself and others**, and #2: **Contribute to a healthy and safe learning environment**. Discuss how these guidelines state two of the key elements of creating a caring community at your school—respect and safety. Emphasize that these elements and the characteristics that students generated in the above class discussion about caring communities are what the *Bully-Proofing* program is all about.

IV. Introduce and explore the concept of empathy.

A. Review guideline #3: Use empathy and extra effort to include others. Ask students for their ideas about the meaning of empathy. The facilitator makes a list of their ideas on the chalkboard.

B. Define empathy for students. Discuss the difference between empathy and sympathy.

EMPATHY: The ability to participate in the feelings of another. Empathy is knowing how another person feels, and sympathy is feeling sorry for that person.

C. Ask students to share experiences they have had with empathy.

1. Do you remember a time when someone felt empathy for you?

2. Do you remember a time when you felt empathy for someone else?

D. Ask students why we need empathy in a caring community.

1. Why is empathy important in a caring community?

2. Is empathy something you can learn?

3. What are some ways to show empathy?

Stress that empathy is necessary in a caring community in order for people to take care of each other. You have to be able to understand how someone else might be feeling before you can reach out to help.

V. Introduce and explore the concept of taking a stand.

A. Refer to guideline #4 of the Bully-Proofing Guidelines: **Take a stand for what is right**. Ask students what they think the phrase "to take a stand " means. Listen to students' responses, then define the phrase.

Take a stand: Any positive behavior that supports the caring community.

Encourage students to share about times when they took a stand or when others took a stand to help them.

1. When is the last time you took a stand to do the right thing?

2. Can you remember a time when someone took a stand and did something that helped you?

B. Summarize students' comments and acknowledge them for the caring behaviors they shared. Emphasize that taking a stand can take all kinds of forms—it can be an action that is large or high profile and it can also take the form of an anonymous or low profile action. Taking a stand is any caring action that supports the caring community. Examples of taking a stand include ignoring or not passing on hurtful gossip and getting help from adults when there is a potentially dangerous situation.

CHART

C. Ask students to generate a list of different ways to take a stand. The facilitator writes the ideas on chart paper to remain on display in the classroom. Listed below are some examples:

Ways to Take A Stand

1. Stop rumors.

2. Don't pass on a hurtful note.

3. Speak up to a bully: "We don't do that here."

4. Ask someone new to join you at lunch.

5. Say "hi" to a new student or someone you don't know very well.

6. Include someone new in one of your activities.

7. Join up with someone who is being bothered and take he or her out of the situation.

8. Let adults know when someone needs help.

D. Review these important points with students:

1. When taking a stand, never put yourself in danger.

2. There are many ways to take a stand. Choose strategies that honor your own personality style, racial and cultural background, beliefs, and previous experiences.

3. Think creatively and share ideas with your friends and peers.

VI. Activity: Empathy and Taking a Stand, Worksheet 6J.

A. Hand out the worksheet. Go over directions with students. Remind them that caring behaviors can be high or low profile and that both are important in building a caring community. Give them a few minutes to fill out the worksheet. Invite students to share some of their experiences with the class.

Worksheet 6J

WORKSHEET 6J
Creating Caring Communities Through Empathy and Taking a Stand

Directions:
Think back to experiences you've had with empathy and taking a stand. Write down what you remember in the spaces below.

I remember . . .

A time I experienced empathy for someone else: _____

_____

_____

_____

A time someone showed empathy for me: _____

_____

_____

_____

A time I took a stand: _____

_____

_____

_____

A time someone took a stand for me: _____

_____

_____

_____

VII. **Homework**

Ask students to observe and record three examples each of empathy and taking a stand demonstrated by students in the caring community.

VIII. **Classwork**

To be completed during one class session by the classroom teacher prior to next lesson.

A. Introduce the video activity (Worksheet 6K). Say to students:

"We are coming to the end of our weekly bully-proofing lessons and we're impressed with your knowledge and willingness to share your ideas. We have covered some important concepts including:

1. Bullying

2. Victims

3. Bystanders

W O R K S H E E T   6 K
Bully-Proofing Video Observations

Name: _____

Directions:
Watch the video "Don't Pick on Me." Look for examples of the following concepts and write down the important points in each category.

1. **Bullying:** _____

_____

2. **Victim:** _____

_____

3. **Bystander:** _____

_____

4. **HA HA SO:** _____

_____

5. **Empathy:** _____

_____

6. **Taking a Stand:** _____

_____

7. **Caring Community:** _____

_____

4. **HA HA SO**

5. **Empathy**

6. **Taking a Stand**

7. **Caring Community**

Explain to students that these concepts will be demonstrated in various ways in the video they will be watching. Hand out the video worksheet. Ask students to watch the video carefully and write down the important points they notice in each of the categories.

B. Show the first scenario in the film, "Don't Pick on Me."

C. Discuss the scenario with students.

   1. Who was the victim?

   2. Who was the bully?

   3. Who were the bystanders?

   4. Who showed empathy?

   5. Who didn't show empathy? (Stress that bullies seldom show empathy.)

   6. Did the scenario show an example of a caring community?

D. If time allows, do the same exercises for the other scenarios on the video.

LESSON 5

Creating Caring Communities: Including Others

> I should have stood up when there was a fight outside in the morning, but I didn't. I just stood watching. When the two girls were in the dean's office, I felt very bad. I think if I would have stopped it they wouldn't have been there.

Materials

◆ Index cards

◆ **Worksheet 6L:** Putting It All Together

Objectives

◆ Review concepts of empathy and taking a stand

◆ Examine challenges of taking a stand

◆ Understand and examine inclusion of others as a characteristic of a caring community

Steps

I. Share and discuss homework. As students share their observations, review the concepts of empathy and taking a stand. Point out that these shared examples show that many students are already caring community members by virtue of their actions.

II. Activity: The challenges of taking a stand.

   A. Introduce the activity. Ask students to sit quietly and remember a time when they had the opportunity to take a stand and didn't. Ask them to write down a few sentences about this experience on an index card.

   "Think back to a time in your life when you wish you had taken a stand but you didn't. This could have happened at school, at home, or in your neighborhood. Where were you? Who were you with? What was happening? What were you thinking? How were you feeling? Were the other people involved friends of yours?"

   B. Collect and read some of the cards anonymously. Encourage discussion about what held them back—the concerns, worries, and fears that prevented them from taking any action. Generate with the students a list of reasons why students sometimes act like bystanders by not taking any action against bullying.

   What are some of the reasons bystanders don't take action when they see bullying taking place?

   1. Fear of retaliation

   2. Don't know what to do

   3. Afraid they'll make things worse

   4. Afraid of losing social status

   C. Acknowledge students' concerns and assure them that we all have times when it feels difficult to take a stand, because taking a stand isn't always the easiest thing to do. Remind them that throughout the *Bully-Proofing* program they have learned many skills and strategies about how to take a stand to avoid victimization of themselves and their peers. Encourage them to draw on each other and their "power in numbers" to do the right thing by standing up for themselves and others.

III. Introduce the concept of including others as a characteristic of caring communities.

   A. Review with students some of the characteristics of caring communities discussed in earlier lessons including:

   1. Respect for all

   2. Safe environment for all

   3. Empathy for others

   4. Willingness to take a stand

The time I should have taken a stand was back in fifth grade. There was a kid that always got picked on. One day he was on the monkey bars and some of the popular kids pulled him off. He fell and broke his arm. I walked away like I didn't see anything. I was afraid.

B. Introduce "including others" as another important characteristic of a caring community. Refer to guideline #3: Use empathy and extra effort **to include others.** Make a statement about the importance of inclusion.

C. Ask students for their ideas about the meaning of including others. Does including others mean:

1. You have to be best friends with everyone?

2. You have to include everyone in everything?

3. You have to invite everyone to your party?

4. You only include kids in your friend group or clique?

5. You only take a stand for students who are your friends?

Discuss with students their responses to the above questions. Encourage them to talk about the concerns they have about including and interacting with students who are not friends and are not in their friend group. Common concerns are:

1. Fear of being ostracized or made fun of by friends for including someone new

2. Worries about getting involved in something that is not "their business"

3. Fear that the person they reach out to might expect them to be friends

4. Worries that if they're seen helping out someone outside of their friend group they will lose social status

D. Acknowledge and normalize students' concerns. Remind them that they do have a responsibility as caring community members to include others, but that doesn't mean they have to be best friends with everyone. Including others means watching out for each other and taking a stand for each other when necessary so that everyone can feel like a valued community member.

Worksheet 6L

IV. Activity: Putting It All Together, Worksheet 6L.

A. Summarize with students the main characteristics of a caring community by reviewing the six Bully-Proofing Guidelines:

1. Respect yourself and others.

2. Contribute to a healthy and safe learning environment.

3. Use empathy and extra effort to include others.

4. Take a stand for what is right.

5. Encourage creative and peaceful problem solving.

6. Follow all school rules.

B. Divide the class into five groups. Hand out the worksheet and assign each group one of the five scenarios. For each scenario, the group is to write down how they think the person might be feeling and list several actions a caring community member could take to make this person feel included in the community. Allow from five to ten minutes for the groups to discuss their scenario and record their ideas.

C. Ask each group to share their solutions with the large group and discuss.

V. Summary and Acknowledgments.

A. Summary. Say to students:

"We are challenging you to be members of (your school's) caring community. This is a daily challenge, especially when it involves people you don't know or who aren't in your friend group. Look around the room. These are your fellow community members and your fellow sixth grade classmates. Many of you will be together here at (your school) for three years. You all deserve to feel safe and cared about here at school, and to make that happen you all have the responsibility of taking a stand for each other."

B. Closing acknowledgments. Say to students:

"We know many of you make choices every day to be positive members of this school's caring community, and we want you to know how much we appreciate you. We see sixth graders making good choices and using smart strategies to take care of each other daily. We hope that after we leave, you and your teacher will continue to talk about and practice all the ways to be caring community members. We look forward to hearing what a wonderful job the sixth graders are doing to continue bully-proofing our school."

HANDOUT/TRANSPARENCY 6A
Types of Bullying Behaviors

Physical Aggression: Hitting, kicking, destroying property

Social Aggression: Spreading rumors, excluding from group, silent treatment

Verbal Aggression: Name calling, teasing, threatening, intimidating phone calls

Intimidation: Graffiti, a dirty trick, taking possession, coercion

Written Aggression: Note writing, graffiti, slam books

Sexual Harassment: Comments or actions of a sexual nature which are unwelcome and make the recipient uncomfortable. *Examples:* rumors of a sexual nature, inappropriate touching, grabbing, comments about someone's body

Racial and Ethnic Harassment: Comments or actions containing racial or ethnic content which are unwelcome and make the recipient uncomfortable. *Examples:* ethnic jokes, racial name calling, racial slurs

Normal Conflict versus Bullying

Normal Conflict	versus	Bullying
Equal power; friends	vs.	Imbalance of power; not friends
Happens occasionally	vs.	Repeated negative actions
Accidental	vs.	Purposeful
Not serious	vs.	Serious—threat of physical harm or emotional or psychological hurt
Equal emotional reaction	vs.	Strong emotional reaction on part of the victim
Not seeking power or attention	vs.	Seeking power, control
Not trying to get something	vs.	Trying to gain material things or power
Remorse—takes responsibility	vs.	No remorse—blames victim
Effort to solve the problem	vs.	No effort to solve problem

HANDOUT/TRANSPARENCY 6C
Bully-Proofing Guidelines

1. Respect yourself and others.

2. Contribute to a healthy and safe learning environment.

3. Use empathy and extra effort to include others.

4. Take a stand for what is right.

5. Encourage creative and peaceful problem solving.

6. Follow all school rules.

Bystander Scenarios

Directions:

Read each scenario carefully. Think about all the different ways the bystanders in each scenario could act as caring community members by **TAKING ACTION**.

Scenario #1

A student is purposefully shoved in the cafeteria and drops his tray. A bystander looks the other way and pretends to not notice.

The bystander could take action by:

_____

_____

_____

Scenario #2

A group of guys are standing in the hall. They begin to bad-mouth a girl they know who happens to be one of the group member's best friends. A bystander doesn't say anything and allows the talk to continue.

The bystander could take action by:

_____

_____

_____

Scenario #3

A girl is yelling at another girl in the restroom and threatens to beat her up after school. A bystander hears it all but walks away and doesn't mention the incident to anyone.

The bystander could take action by:

_____

_____

_____

HANDOUT/TRANSPARENCY 6 E
Friendly Teasing versus Hurtful Teasing

Friendly Teasing	versus	Hurtful teasing
Equal power; friends	vs.	Imbalance of friends power; not friends
Neutral topic	vs.	Sensitive topic
Playful purpose	vs.	Purpose is to upset
Purpose is to include	vs.	Purpose is to exclude
Funny	vs.	Sarcastic

WORKSHEET 6F
Check Your Understanding—Sexual Harassment and Teasing

Directions:

Decide if each statement is True or False. Put a T or F in the line after each statement.

1. Teasing is OK if the person doing the teasing says, "I'm just teasing." _____

2. It is alright to tease your best friend about anything. _____

3. The person who is the target of sexual comments is the one who decides if it is sexual harassment. _____

4. A purpose of playful teasing can be to make someone feel like he or she belongs. _____

5. Sarcasm is a form of humor that can be hurtful and mean. _____

6. Note writing can never be considered a form of sexual harassment. _____

7. Teasing is never OK. _____

8. A person who experiences sexual harassment should ask an adult for help. _____

9. Bullies use teasing as a way of establishing power over their targeted victims. _____

10. Hurtful teasing usually happens among people who are friends. _____

11. Sexual harassment is against the law. _____

12. Sexual harassment is a type of bullying. _____

HANDOUT/TRANSPARENCY 6G
HA HA SO Strategies

Ha Ha So Strategies		
	STRATEGIES	**TIPS**
H **Help:**	Seek assistance from an adult, friend, or peer when a potentially threatening situation arises. Seek help also if other strategies aren't working.	1. Brainstorm all of the sources of help at your school—deans, counselors, teachers, nurse. 2. Stress the different ways to get help—anonymously, in a group, dean's hotline.
A **Assert Yourself:**	Make assertive statements to the bully addressing your feelings about the bully's *behavior.*	1. Should not be used with severe bullying. 2. Not as effective with group bullying. 3. Victim should look bully straight in the eye. 4. Use "I" statements. *Example:* "I don't like it when you pull on my backpack." 5. Make assertive statement and walk away. *Example:* "Stop talking about me behind my back."
H **Humor:**	Use humor to de-escalate a situation.	1. Use humor in a positive way. 2. Make the joke about what the bully said, not about the bully. 3. Make humorous statement and then leave the situation. 4. *Example:* When insulted about hairstyle, say "Gee, I didn't know you cared enough to notice."
A **Avoid:**	Walk away or avoid certain places in order to avoid a bullying situation.	1. Best for situations when victim is alone. 2. Avoid places where the bully hangs out. 3. Join with others rather than be alone.
S **Self-Talk:**	Use positive self-talk to maintain positive self-esteem during a bullying situation.	1. Use as a means to keep feeling good about self. 2. Think positive statements about self and accomplishments. 3. Rehearse mental statements to avoid being hooked by the bully. *Examples:* "It's his problem," "She doesn't know what she's talking about," "I know I'm smart." 4. Use positive self-talk when practicing all strategies.
O **Own It:**	"Own" the put-down or belittling comment in order to diffuse it.	1. Agree with the bully and leave the situation. 2. Combine with humor strategies such as, "Yeah, this **IS** a bad haircut. The lawn mower got out of control this weekend." 3. Combine with assertive strategies such as, "Yes, I did fail the test and I don't appreciate you looking at my paper."
Important Reminders:	1. Practice these strategies in any order, in any combination, or numerous times. 2. The Caring Community can remind each other of the strategies. 3. The Caring Community can help support the victim in using the strategies. 4. If the strategies aren't working, leave or disengage from the situation.	

HANDOUT/TRANSPARENCY 6H
Tattling versus Telling

Tattling	versus	Telling
Unimportant	vs.	Important
Harmless	vs.	Harmful or dangerous physically or psychologically
Can handle by self	vs.	Need help from an adult to solve
Purpose is to get someone in trouble	vs.	Purpose is to keep people safe
Behavior is accidental	vs.	Behavior is purposeful

WORKSHEET 61
HA HA SO Scenario

Student name: _____

Directions:

Give an example of how you could use each of the strategies below to solve this problem.

Scenario:

You are on the bus. As usual, the same kid is sitting behind you. He/She is kicking your seat, pulling your hair, and making rude comments about you. This has been happening every day for the past week.

Help _____

_____

_____

Assert Yourself _____

_____

_____

Humor _____

_____

_____

Avoid _____

_____

_____

Self-Talk _____

_____

_____

Own It _____

_____

_____

W O R K S H E E T   6 J
Creating Caring Communities Through Empathy and Taking a Stand

Directions:

Think back to experiences you've had with empathy and taking a stand. Write down what you remember in the spaces below.

I remember . . .

A time I experienced empathy for someone else: _____

_____

_____

_____

A time someone showed empathy for me: _____

_____

_____

_____

A time I took a stand: _____

_____

_____

_____

A time someone took a stand for me: _____

_____

_____

_____

W O R K S H E E T   6 K
Bully-Proofing Video Observations

Name: _____

Directions:

Watch the video "Don't Pick on Me." Look for examples of the following concepts and write down the important points in each category.

1. Bullying: _____

_____

2. Victim: _____

_____

3. Bystander: _____

_____

4. HA HA SO: _____

_____

5. Empathy: _____

_____

6. Taking a Stand: _____

_____

7. Caring Community:_____

_____

WORKSHEET 6L
Putting It All Together

Your group will be assigned one of the following scenarios. Read the scenario and write down your ideas about what the person might be feeling. Then list several things that members of the caring community could do to make this person feel included.

Scenario #1

You and your friends have been sitting at the same table every day in the cafeteria. You notice that a student at a table next to you has been sitting alone for a few days.

How do you think this person is feeling? _____

_____

_____

_____

What can the caring community members do to help? _____

_____

_____

_____

Scenario #2

One day in class the teacher asks you to divide into small groups for a class project. You notice that one of your classmates is not being asked to join anyone's group.

How do you think this person is feeling? _____

_____

_____

_____

What can the caring community members do to help? _____

_____

_____

_____

Scenario #3

You have heard that there is a new student on your team. You discover that this person is in one of your classes.

How do you think this person is feeling? _____

_____

_____

_____

What can the caring community members do to help? _____

_____

_____

_____

Scenario #4

You are walking down the hall and you notice that one of your classmates looks really sad.

How do you think this person is feeling? _____

_____

_____

_____

What can the caring community members do to help? _____

_____

_____

_____

Scenario #5

You're standing around with a group of friends. All of you have just received a party invitation except for one member of your group.

How do you think the person is feeling? _____

_____

_____

_____

What can the caring community members do to help? _____

_____

_____

_____

Chapter Seven

Seventh Grade Curriculum

LESSON 1 Review of Basic Concepts

Materials

- ◆ Chart paper
- ◆ Markers
- ◆ **Handout/Transparency 7A:** Normal Conflict vs. Bullying
- ◆ **Handout/Transparency 7B:** Bully-Proofing Guidelines
- ◆ **Handout/Transparency 7C:** HA HA SO Strategies
- ◆ **Worksheet 7D:** HA HA SO Scenario, one copy per student
- ◆ Overhead projector

Objectives

- ◆ Establish behavior expectations for sessions
- ◆ Review program concepts and definitions

◆ Introduce concept of caring community

◆ Generate ideas about caring community

STEPS

I. Hook: Get students' attention by reading a short news article or story about a caring, life-changing experience. *Suggestion:* Read the story titled, "Courage in Action" from *Chicken Soup for the Teenage Soul* by Canfield, Hansen, and Kirberger.

II. Introduce behavioral expectations for the groups

  A. Respect for self and others

  B. Participate—in your own way and style

  C. While sharing stories or experiences, do not mention any particular names of individuals or groups. Instead, say, "I know someone who . . ."

III. Establish purpose of sessions

  A. Ask students:

    1. Why are we doing this? To learn how to foster and create a caring community.

    2. Why seventh graders? Because you will be our leaders next year. We are counting on you to take care of others next year and to help make our school a caring place.

IV. Activity: Sharing previous school experiences

  A. Hand out an index card to each student. Have students write about a time when they felt unsafe or not cared about. Tell them to write their names on the cards. Tell them that while some of the cards will be read aloud, the authors will remain anonymous. Collect the cards.

  B. Facilitator reads a few examples and makes statements linking them to purpose.

    "This is why we're here . . . to help you foster your own caring community here at (your school). Everyone deserves to feel safe and respected at school. Unfortunately, we know that this is not always the case as we have heard about in your stories. Look around, there are many more of you students than there are of us adults. That is why we need you in order to build a caring community. This can't happen without you. (School name) is your community."

Handout/Transparency 6A

V. Review main concepts of bully-proofing (Handout/ Transparency 6A).

  A. Ask students, "What is bullying?" Students typically mention kinds of bullying at this point. For example, when a student responds with kicking or shoving, the facilitator categorizes that as physical aggression and continues to elicit student

HANDOUT/TRANSPARENCY 6A
Types of Bullying Behaviors

Physical Aggression: Hitting, kicking, destroying property

Social Aggression: Spreading rumors, excluding from group, silent treatment

Verbal Aggression: Name calling, teasing, threatening, intimidating phone calls

Intimidation: Graffiti, a dirty trick, taking possession, coercion

Written Aggression: Note writing, graffiti, slam books

Sexual Harassment: Comments or actions of a sexual nature which are unwelcome and make the recipient uncomfortable. *Examples:* rumors of a sexual nature, inappropriate touching, grabbing, comments about someone's body

Racial and Ethnic Harassment: Comments or actions containing racial or ethnic content which are unwelcome and make the recipient uncomfortable. *Examples:* ethnic jokes, racial name calling, racial slurs

responses until all categories have been covered. Record student responses on chart paper that can be reposted for review.

What is bullying? What are some typical bullying behaviors?

B. Display overhead of Normal Conflict vs. Bullying (Handout/ Transparency 7A). Review and discuss the differences between normal conflict and bullying.

How do we tell the difference between a conflict between friends and the more serious situation of bullying?

Make sure to emphasize with students the basic motivation of bullies: **POWER**.

C. Review the concept of "Bystander."

1. Review the definition of *bystander*.

   BYSTANDER: A person who stands near or looks on but does not take part; onlooker; spectator.

HANDOUT/TRANSPARENCY 7A
Normal Conflict versus Bullying

Normal Conflict	versus	Bullying
Equal power; friends	vs.	Imbalance of power; not friends
Happens occasionally	vs.	Repeated negative actions
Accidental	vs.	Purposeful
Not serious	vs.	Serious—threat of physical harm or emotional or psychological hurt
Equal emotional reaction	vs.	Strong emotional reaction on part of the victim
Not seeking power or attention	vs.	Seeking power, control
Not trying to get something	vs.	Trying to gain material things or power
Remorse—takes responsibility	vs.	No remorse—blames victim
Effort to solve the problem	vs.	No effort to solve problem

2. Review the following important points:

   a. If a person acts as a bystander and takes no action against bullying, then he or she is not acting as a member of the caring community.

   b. Bullies like it when bystanders don't do anything. They count on the bystanders to remain silent so they can continue their bullying behaviors.

   c. Bystanders make up the most important group in the school because once they learn how to take a stand against bullying, the bullies will lose their power.

VI. Review Bully-Proofing Guidelines with class (Handout/Transparency 7B).

   A. Explain that the concepts of empathy, taking a stand, and creative problem solving will be explored in depth throughout the bully-proofing lessons.

HANDOUT/TRANSPARENCY 7B
Bully-Proofing Guidelines

1. **Respect yourself and others.**

2. **Contribute to a healthy and safe learning environment.**

3. **Use empathy and extra effort to include others.**

4. **Take a stand for what is right.**

5. **Encourage creative and peaceful problem solving.**

6. **Follow all school rules.**

VII. **Homework**

A. Have students observe three caring behaviors in their school environment.

"During the next four sessions we will be talking about developing a caring community. There are a lot of caring actions that are already happening in your classes and our school every day. So, before our next meeting, observe and record at least three caring behaviors to share with the class."

VIII. **Classwork**

To be completed during one class session by the classroom teacher prior to the next lesson.

A. Use the overhead projector to review the HA HA SO Strategies (Handout/Transparency 7C). Discuss each strategy and have students generate examples of ways to use the strategies in situations at your school.

Handout/Transparency 7C

Handout/Transparency 7C

HANDOUT/TRANSPARENCY 7C
HA HA SO Strategies

Ha Ha So Strategies		
	STRATEGIES	**TIPS**
H Help:	Seek assistance from an adult, friend, or peer when a potentially threatening situation arises. Seek help also if other strategies aren't working.	1. Brainstorm all of the sources of help at your school—deans, counselors, teachers, nurse. 2. Stress the different ways to get help—anonymously, in a group, dean's hotline.
A Assert Yourself:	Make assertive statements to the bully addressing your feelings about the bully's *behavior*.	1. Should not be used with severe bullying. 2. Not as effective with group bullying. 3. Victim should look bully straight in the eye. 4. Use "I" statements. *Example:* "I don't like it when you pull on my backpack." 5. Make assertive statement and walk away. *Example:* "Stop talking about me behind my back."
H Humor:	Use humor to de-escalate a situation.	1. Use humor in a positive way. 2. Make the joke about what the bully said, not about the bully. 3. Make humorous statement and then leave the situation. 4. *Example:* When insulted about hairstyle, say "Gee, I didn't know you cared enough to notice."
A Avoid:	Walk away or avoid certain places in order to avoid a bullying situation.	1. Best for situations when victim is alone. 2. Avoid places where the bully hangs out. 3. Join with others rather than be alone.
S Self-Talk:	Use positive self-talk to maintain positive self-esteem during a bullying situation.	1. Use as a means to keep feeling good about self. 2. Think positive statements about self and accomplishments. 3. Rehearse mental statements to avoid being hooked by the bully. *Examples:* "It's his problem," "She doesn't know what she's talking about," "I know I'm smart." 4. Use positive self-talk when practicing all strategies.
O Own It:	"Own" the put-down or belittling comment in order to diffuse it.	1. Agree with the bully and leave the situation. 2. Combine with humor strategies such as, "Yeah, this **IS** a bad haircut. The lawn mower got out of control this weekend." 3. Combine with assertive strategies such as, "Yes, I did fail the test and I don't appreciate you looking at my paper."
Important Reminders:	1. Practice these strategies in any combination, or numerous times. 2. The Caring Community can remind each other of the strategies. 3. The Caring Community can help support the victim in using the strategies. 4. If the strategies aren't working, leave or disengage from the situation.	

Handout/Transparency 6H

B. Review with students the differences between tattling and telling when using the "Help" strategy. Record the differences on the chalkboard. Make sure to cover the point in Handout/Transparency 6H.

Worksheet 7D

C. Give students the HA HA SO Scenario Worksheet 7D, and ask them to design a way to use each of the strategies for the scene described. Have students share their answers with the class.

D. Discuss with students the seriousness of bullying. Ask what strategies students have remembered to use when they observe or are faced with a bullying situation.

HANDOUT/TRANSPARENCY 6H
Tattling versus Telling

Tattling	versus	Telling
Unimportant	vs.	Important
Harmless	vs.	Harmful or dangerous physically or psychologically
Can handle by self	vs.	Need help from an adult to solve
Purpose is to get someone in trouble	vs.	Purpose is to keep people safe
Behavior is accidental	vs.	Behavior is purposeful

 LESSON 2   Empathy and Inclusion

Materials

- ◆ Container (shoe box or coffee can)
- ◆ **Handout/Transparency 7E:** Role Play Skit
- ◆ **Handout 7F:** Acknowledgment Forms

Objectives

◆ Review HA HA SO strategies

◆ Introduce and explore concept of empathy

◆ Introduce inclusion and formation of cliques

Steps

I. Homework review and prepare for skit. *Facilitators ask for two volunteers to participate in a later skit. While the homework is being reviewed by one facilitator, the other facilitator coaches the student volunteers in the hallway.*

Handout/Transparency 7E

A. Skit preparation: Give students role play cards (Handout/ Transparency 7E). Tell them that on your cue they are to leave the classroom for approximately one minute. Both actors will then enter the room and walk to the front of the class. Actor #1 will enter the classroom carrying many books and papers in his/her arms. When they are approximately in front of the class, Actor #1 "accidentally" trips while standing close to Actor #2. The facilitator will say, "Freeze" and both actors freeze the action.

Have volunteer students rejoin the class and wait for your cue.

B. Review homework from lesson one.

Have students share the caring behaviors they observed during the past week.

II. Introduce acknowledgment activity.

A. Introduce a caring box. Ask students to decorate a container (shoe box or coffee can) which will remain in their classroom as a place where students can acknowledge classmates or teammates for caring acts.

Handout 7F

B. Tell students they can write acknowledgments and put them in the container during the next week (Handout 7F).

C. Additional Activity: For further ideas about generating caring behavior in the classroom, see the section called "Encourage Random Acts of Kindness" in *The Bully-Free Classroom*, pp. 50, 51 (Beane, 1999).

D. Explain to students that throughout our work with bully-proofing there will be a great deal of attention given to people doing caring things for others. This caring container will be the way the class can acknowledge peers who do caring things for each other.

III. Introduce the concept of empathy as a skill in building a caring community

A. Thank students for sharing their caring behaviors at beginning of class. Acknowledge them for already starting to build a caring community as evidenced by their behaviors. Explain to students that a caring community doesn't just happen automatically or magically—we have to create it ourselves by learning certain skills. We're not born knowing these skills, but we can learn them.

Cue skit actors to leave the classroom.

B. Introduce the first key skill: empathy. Ask for students' ideas regarding the meaning.

C. Define empathy for students.

EMPATHY: The ability to participate in the feelings or ideas of another. Not the same as sympathy; empathy is not feeling sorry for another person, but instead knowing HOW another person feels.

IV. Skit (See IA)

A. Actors #1 and #2 enter the room while the facilitator is discussing empathy. Actor #1 trips in front of the room sending books flying everywhere.

Helping Others
Drawn by
Ann Suchkov

"Should I help?"

B. One facilitator yells "FREEZE" and the actors freeze the motion. Ask the students how they think each of the actors is feeling. Generate a class discussion on empathy for the people in this situation.

   1. How do you think Actor #1 is feeling?

   2. How do you think Actor #2 is feeling?

   3. Have you had those feelings before?

C. Acknowledge the students for the empathy they demonstrated during the previous discussion. *Example:* "You are showing empathy now by sharing how you think the person is feeling. Being able to tune into how he/she is feeling is what empathy is all about."

D. Acknowledge students who participated in the role play.

V. Discuss empathy for students outside of students' friend groups or cliques.

A. Ask students about the limits of empathy.

   1. Can you feel empathy for someone:

   ♦ You don't know?

   ♦ Who is not like you?

   ♦ Who doesn't have anything in common with you?

   ♦ Who hangs out with an entirely different group?

   ♦ Who doesn't have anyone to hang out with?

   ♦ Who doesn't belong to any particular group?

   2. Why can we imagine what all of these people might be feeling?

B. Lead students to an understanding that we are all human and we all experience the same feelings, no matter what group, clique, neighborhood, or religious group we are involved with.

VI. Activity: Exploring formation of groups/cliques

A. Divide students into small groups (4–5 students each). Ask each group to appoint a recorder and a reporter. Instruct students to divide one piece of paper into two columns. In the column on the left have students write down the basic human needs—the things that all humans need for survival. They may need some guidance, particularly to think of the emotional needs. Make sure that students include the emotional needs related to belonging, love, and respect.

B. Ask students to brainstorm a list of peoples' various interests in the column on the right. They can list their own interests or those of others.

Example:

Needs	Interests
Oxygen	Sports
Shelter	Movies
Food	Computer games
Safety	TV
Love	Religious groups
Belonging	Shopping
Respect	

C. Students report answers to the class. Facilitator records their responses on the chalkboard.

D. Ask students to observe the two lists. The universal needs on the left are elements that all humans need in order to live. The interests on the right vary for each individual. Facilitator circles "belonging" on the left and uses it to explain why people form groups around their interests.

"The universal need that people have for belonging guides them to form groups. Groups can be small or large but people tend to form groups with other persons who they see as being similar to themselves. These similarities can be around racial and/or cultural background, interests, hobbies, and common experiences. But not everyone is the same. Some people are not interested in being in a school group, some people change groups, some people may not yet have decided which groups they want to spend time with, and some people may be a member of several groups such as a singing group, religious group, soccer group, or chess group."

E. Point out that often teenagers get so involved with their own group, they forget that we are all humans who need to feel that we belong and are respected.

"It is a normal part of life to belong to a group. However, oftentimes when people get into middle school they can become so involved with their own group that they forget the importance of empathy for people not in their group. Sometimes they even forget to have empathy for people within their own group. Group members can forget that we are all human with the same basic needs, regardless of our interests, our groups, or our personalities. We all have feelings.

We all want to belong, or feel accepted for who we are. We all want to be appreciated.

A caring community member has empathy for people in their group and for people not in their group. Everyone belongs in the caring community and we are all responsible for taking care of each other, even though we have different interests, tastes, friends, and talents."

VII. Discuss the ways different groups treat each other at your school.

A. Ask students to think of some examples they have observed of ways cliques/groups get so involved with their own interests that they forget to respect others. Prompt students not to use any group or individual names. *Example:* One group puts down the other group because of _____.

B. Emphasize with students that awareness and empathy can help groups be more respectful of each other. Encourage students to kindly remind each other to be respectful of students who have different interests, tastes, and skills.

VIII. **Homework**

Ask students to make three caring gestures during the next week to people they do not know or people outside their friend group (i.e., Saying "hi," loaning them supplies, giving them a compliment).

IX. **Classwork**

CHART

To be completed by the classroom teacher prior to the next co-facilitated bully-proofing lesson.

A. Divide students into groups of four or five. Choose one person in the group who will be the group's reporter.

1. Ask students, "How do people behave in a caring community?"

2. Instruct them to be specific: Not, "Be nice" but specific ways to be nice, such as, "Say hello to someone you don't know."

3. Elicit responses from groups and record ideas as reporters share them.

Write students' ideas on large chart paper which will be left hanging in the classroom as a reminder.

Handout 7F

B. Remind students to write acknowledgments and put them in the classroom container by next lesson (Handout 7F).

C. Remind students to decorate the caring box prior to the next bully-proofing session.

LESSON 3   Taking a Stand

Materials

- ◆ Chart paper
- ◆ Markers
- ◆ Reinforcers—optional (candy, food coupons, pencils, etc.)
- ◆ **Handout 7F:** Acknowledgment Forms
- ◆ **Handout 7G:** Taking a Stand

Objectives

- ◆ Review concepts of empathy and inclusion
- ◆ Develop understanding of concept of taking a stand
- ◆ Explore challenges of taking a stand

Steps

I.   Choose three acknowledgments from the classroom "I Caught You Caring" box. Reinforcers can be given to both the nominee and the student who wrote the acknowledgment.

II. Review the homework from the last session. Ask students to share their caring gestures. Emphasize the good examples of inclusion and the importance of inclusion in a caring community.

III. Activity: "Walk a mile in someone else's shoes" experiment.

   A. Ask for volunteers in the class who are willing to participate in an experiment which will involve taking off their shoes. Select six or eight students and have them switch one of their shoes with another person in the experiment.

   B. Direct volunteers to walk around the room in the other person's shoes. Ask the class if they can guess what is being acted out. Ask the volunteers questions such as: What does it feel like to be wearing someone else's shoes? Did it feel different from what you're used to?

   C. Ask if the class has heard the Native American proverb, "Walk a mile in my shoes." Ask about the meaning of the proverb and how it relates to the experiment. Facilitate a discussion with the students about how the proverb relates to empathy.

> I should have taken a stand when I saw a seventh grader pushing around a sixth grader. The seventh grader made him drop his books, but I didn't stand up for him.

IV. Introduce the concept of "Taking a Stand."

A. Acknowledge that students have experienced some great examples of empathy. Reinforce that empathy is one of the essential ingredients of a caring community. Provoke thought with the following questions:

1. Is empathy enough for this to be a caring community?

2. If we all had empathy for each other is that all it would take?

Lead students to the idea that positive **ACTION** is necessary in a caring community. Empathy helps you know how and when to act to help someone, but it is not enough on its own.

CHART

B. Ask students what it means to take a stand. Elicit some of their ideas and then define it for them. Write the definition on chart paper.

Taking a stand: Any positive behavior that supports the caring majority or caring community.

CHART

C. What are some examples of taking a stand? Chart these below the definition.

1. Speaking up for someone.

2. Asking someone "How are you?"

3. Including others in your group or activity.

4. Not participating in gossip.

5. Helping someone with his/her work.

D. Review these important points with students:

1. When taking a stand, never put yourself in danger.

2. There are many ways to take a stand. Choose strategies that honor your own personality style, racial and cultural background, beliefs, and previous experience.

3. Think creatively and share ideas with your friends and peers.

V. Explore the challenges of taking a stand.

A. Make a statement acknowledging that it is sometimes very difficult to take a stand. Give several examples of not taking a stand, such as going along with the crowd and excluding someone from your table in the lunch room or passing notes with negative gossip about someone. Explore with students the following questions:

1. Why don't people take a stand?

2. What makes it difficult?

B. Elicit ideas from students regarding why people often don't take a stand, such as:

1. Fear of retaliation

2. Don't know what to do

3. Afraid they'll make things worse

4. Fear of losing social status

Acknowledge the reasons students give during the discussion and empathetically address each of their primary concerns.

1. Retaliation: Even though we aren't in your shoes, we adults know this is a very real issue for you. And here's what we want you to know—We will do the best we can to keep any retaliation from happening.

   a. We have spoken to the deans. They have assured us that any threats of retaliation will be handled very seriously.

   b. In reality, retaliation doesn't often happen. It is what people threaten when they feel pushed into a corner or caught.

   c. When reporting things, you can request that your name not be used. Use the dean's hotline, if it is available, and if this is not an immediate concern or emergency situation.

   We are aware of your concerns and will do what is in our power to handle things gracefully and fairly.

2. Don't know what to do: We have already reviewed some strategies that can help. We will continue discussing ways to take a stand. It is important to keep an open mind and think creatively. There is ALWAYS more than one way to help someone.

3. Afraid of making things worse: We are usually unsure of ourselves when we take risks and try new behaviors. Remember, when someone is being hurt, doing *something* is always better than doing nothing. It may not be the perfect solution and we all make mistakes sometimes. Our good intentions and actions are what is important.

4. Fear of losing social status: It takes courage to take a stand. Remember, there is strength in numbers. You can ask a friend to go report with you or talk to friends and get their support when others from the group aren't around.

Note to Facilitators: The purpose of this discussion is to acknowledge students' fears and give them some realistic support. You will need to tailor the ideas surrounding adult support to what is available at your school (i.e., dean's hotline, reporting incidences anonymously). See Facilitator Notes for more discussion in this area.

VI. Courage to Care

"In spite of these difficulties, here at school people do take a stand and reach out to others. They take risks and let us know when dangerous or disrespectful things are happening."

A. Ask students: What gives people the courage to do caring things for others? *Examples:*

1. They care.

2. They want school to be safe.

3. They have empathy.

4. They are afraid it could happen to them.

B. Concluding statement:

"When you have the courage to take a stand you become part of the caring majority instead of being a silent member of the school. When you are silent, the bullies or people doing hurtful, negative things gain more power. Remember, there is strength in numbers and you aren't alone. If you think something isn't right, someone next to you is probably feeling the same way. This is your school. These are your fellow classmates. We are challenging you to be a member of the caring majority—not a silent member who stands back when they see negative, hurtful things happening. We are challenging you to stand up for each other, whether the person being bullied is your best friend or someone you hardly know."

VII. **Homework**

A. Have students continue "I Caught You Caring" acknowledgments. Note that this week's acknowledgments concern observing people who take a stand. Give example (Handout 7G).

Handout 7G

HANDOUT 7G
I Caught You Caring

I Caught You Caring
Taking a Stand

_____ acknowledges _____

for taking a stand by _____

_____

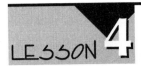 **LESSON 4** Sexual Harassment

Materials

- ◆ Reinforcers—optional (candy, food coupons, pencils, etc.)
- ◆ **Handout/Transparency 7H:** Sexual Harassment vs. Flirting
- ◆ **Handout 7I:** Sexual Harassment Scenarios
- ◆ Overhead projector

Objectives

- ◆ Review taking a stand
- ◆ Develop understanding of sexual harassment
- ◆ Differentiate flirting from sexual harassment

Notes for Facilitators:

- ◆ The topic of sexual harassment will undoubtedly be a sensitive topic for some students. Be aware of students' reactions and concerns. Resistant students may try to use humor or oppositionality to allay their anxieties. Be particularly vigilant of the tone and direction of discussions and/or side comments made by students.

- ◆ Some circumstances around sexual harassment can be ambiguous or confusing. Often males and females have differing views on what constitutes sexual harassment. Students may present either questions regarding the scenarios or experiences that have no definitive answer. It may be helpful to acknowledge the ambiguity and remind students to rely on their common sense and good judgment when making difficult interpersonal decisions.

- ◆ Throughout the discussions, remind students that it is the target of the action who decides whether the behavior is harassing or not.

- ◆ If a student brings up same gender issues, such as in scenario #2, reinforce that it could be sexual harassment in EITHER case.

- ◆ It is advisable to know your school's disciplinary policies regarding sexual harassment.

Steps

I. Review briefly the meaning of taking a stand. Read anonymously many of the students' homework assignments.

II. Draw three "Taking a Stand" acknowledgments from the classroom caring box and read aloud. (Rewards are optional.)

III. Introduce and explore the concept of sexual harassment.

A. Make an introductory statement explaining that sexual harassment is a particularly challenging type of bullying. Explain the following reasons for spending some extra time on this complicated form of bullying.

1. It can be tricky because some of the behaviors involved can be harassment in one case and not in another.

2. People's sexuality is a very personal and private topic which makes it a vulnerable area for people. Remind students that the bullies are looking for soft spots and places of vulnerability where they can upset others.

3. Young teenagers are starting to think about "going out" with others. Middle school people are figuring out how to get to know and develop relationships with other teens, which can be confusing.

B. Define sexual harassment.

Sexual harassment: Comments or actions of a sexual nature that are unwelcome and make the recipient uncomfortable.

C. Ask students to generate examples of behaviors they think are sexual harassment. This will illuminate their present understanding of the concept. Write student examples on the chalkboard. Students may be inhibited during this discussion in which case the facilitator can suggest some examples. Try to make sure that all of the following examples are covered in some fashion.

1. Graffiti of a sexual nature

2. Sexual remarks, teasing

3. Spreading rumors of a sexual nature about others

4. Rating other students in terms of their physical attractiveness

5. Sexual jokes

6. Accusations regarding sexual orientation

7. Pinching, brushing against, sexually suggestive touching

8. Underwear exposure or torment ("snuggies," "de-panting," bra snapping)

9. Verbal comments of a sexual nature about body parts

D. Ask students:

1. Are all of these always examples of sexual harassment?

2. What do they have in common?

E. Make the following points:

1. Explain that all of these behaviors could be sexual harassment if the target of the behavior is offended. Refer students back to the definition. Remind them that sexual harassment is in the eye of the beholder and that the person who is the target of the behavior gets to decide if it is harassment or not.

2. Many sexual or relating types of behaviors are against school rules whether the people involved feel harassed or not. They are against school rules because they distract students from learning and they might be offensive to others. Note that the two people involved may be comfortable with their behavior, but when they are doing it in a public place with lots of other people around, there is a good chance that their behaviors will be offensive to others. Reinforce that the school is the students' work environment. Sexual behaviors are not appropriate in the workplace just as they are not appropriate in school.

3. Any behavior determined to be sexual harassment is against the law. If the target of sexual harassment chooses, he or she can file charges with the police.

4. Sexual harassment should be reported to an adult. It can be embarrassing or scary, but encourage students to find a trusted adult and tell anyway. Reassure students that adults will handle the issues privately and sensitively.

IV. Explain the differences between flirting and sexual harassment.

A. Ask students about the differences between sexual harassment and flirting. Have them share their ideas.

B. Teach specific differences between sexual harassment and flirting using the Handout/Transparency 7H.

> **Handout/Transparency 7H**

> **CHART**

C. Read the following scenario in a neutral manner and discuss the questions. Discuss the variables that could make the difference between a normal flirting behavior and a harassing action in this circumstance. Make a chart of the differences on the chalkboard.

> **Scenario: A guy and a girl are standing together. The guy says, "You are really good looking."**

> *When could this be flirting and when could it be sexual harassment?*

Example:

Flirting	Sexual Harassment
Boyfriend/girlfriend	Don't like each other
OK voice	Sarcastic voice
Between friends	Not friends
Feels like a compliment	Feels scary or threatening
Safe distance	Too close physically
Agreed upon location	Uncomfortable location
Appropriate body language	Inappropriate body language

Handout/Transparency 7H

HANDOUT/TRANSPARENCY 7H
Sexual Harassment versus Flirting

Sexual Harassment versus Flirting	
Sexual Harassment makes the receiver feel:	**Flirting makes the receiver feel:**
Bad	Good
Angry/sad	Happy
Demeaned	Flattered
Ugly	Pretty/attractive
Powerless	In control
Sexual Harassment results in:	**Flirting results in:**
Negative self-esteem	Positive self-esteem
Sexual Harassment is perceived as:	**Flirting is perceived as:**
One-sided	Reciprocal
Demeaning	Flattering
Invading	Open
Degrading	A compliment
Sexual Harassment is:	**Flirting is:**
Unwanted	Wanted
Power-motivated	Equality-motivated
Illegal	Legal

Reprinted from *Sexual Harassment and Teens* by Strauss & Espeland, © 1992. Used with permission from Free Spirit Publishing, Minneapolis, MN; 1-800-735-7323; *www.freespirit.com.* ALL RIGHTS RESERVED.

Important Reminders:
♦ Sexual harassment is against the law.
♦ The target decides whether the behaviors are harassing or flattering.
♦ Men and women often perceive sexual attention differently.
♦ "No" means "No."
♦ Sexual harassment is based on a need for power, **not** physical attraction.

D. Divide students into groups of four or five. Have students
   read the two sexual harassment scenarios (Handout 7I), and
   answer the questions that follow. Ask a reporter from each
   group to share their answers and discuss as a class.

Handout 7I

HANDOUT 7I
Sexual Harassment or Not Sexual Harassment—That Is the Question

Group members: _____

Directions:

Read each of the scenarios carefully. For each scenario write what would make
the incident an example of flirting and what would make it an example of sexual
harassment.

Scenario #1:

A girl walks up to a guy in the hallway and hugs him.

What would make this incident flirting and what would make it sexual harassment?

Flirting: _____

_____

_____

Sexual Harassment: _____

_____

_____

Scenario #2:

A student writes a note asking another student out.

What would make this incident flirting and what would make it sexual harassment?

Flirting: _____

_____

_____

Sexual Harassment: _____

_____

_____

LESSON 5 — Creative Problem Solving

Materials

◆ Reinforcers—optional

◆ **Handout 7J:** Creative Problem Solving Scenarios, one copy of
   each scenario

Objectives

◆ Review concept of sexual harassment

◆ Develop understanding of the levels of risk in taking a stand

◆ Develop understanding and practice creative problem solving

◆ Make plan for being caring community members

Steps

I. Review sexual harassment. Ask students what they should do if they are being sexually harassed.

II. Draw three acknowledgments from caring box (reinforcers are optional).

III. Teach students the levels of risk involved in taking a stand.

A. *Low Risk:* Relating behaviors that don't upset anyone such as saying, "I'm sorry that happened," or "He shouldn't be saying that. It's rude and it's not OK." *Example:* Ignoring gossip or throwing a note away.

B. *Medium Risk:* Joining or other caring gestures that may pull some attention to the helper. *Example:* Asking others to join you if they are not included in an activity.

C. *High Risk:* Confronting behaviors. Assertive stances that may go against the group or the bully such as saying, "Stop that. We don't do that at our school," or "No, I won't give Margaret the silent treatment. I'm not angry with her. You are."

IV. Explain creative problem solving.

A. Remind students of the ingredients of a caring community discussed so far:

1. Empathy

2. Taking a stand

Introduce the next component:

3. Creative problem solving

B. Explain that there are many ways to creatively solve the problem of bullies. Every individual brings his or her own personality, style, racial and cultural background and previous experience to problem solving. For example, some people may be more comfortable with low risk caring behaviors and some may have more outgoing personalities and be comfortable with high risk helping behaviors.

C. Remind students that there are ways to take a stand that will not put individuals in danger. Encourage students to think creatively and use their friends and peers for help with ideas as well. There is always more than one way to help someone.

V. Activity: Empathy and creative problem solving.

A. Break students into six groups. Hand out Creative Problem Solving Scenarios, Handout 7J, giving one scenario to each group. Have students read scenarios and answer the questions. Give students about seven minutes to answer them. Have a spokesperson from each group present the answers. Stress that whether a response involves low, medium, or high levels of risk depends on the situation and the people involved.

Handout 7J

The scenarios from Handout 7J are printed below.

Creative Problem Solving Scenarios

Scenario #1

Marcus struggles in his seventh grade math class. Because of his difficulty understanding the lesson, he raises his hand often and it slows down the class. Today, when he raises his hand to ask a particular question, several students snicker and one student calls him a "retard." The teacher doesn't seem to hear the remarks. You are sitting close to Marcus and notice that he is visibly upset.

Scenario #2

This week a new girl joined your team. She's cute, dresses up a lot and the boys are giving her a lot of attention. Several girls who are friends of yours have started rumors about her. They have written a note that says really bad things about her including some crude pictures. You're sitting in class and the note is passed to you. Your friends expect you to read it and pass it on.

Scenario #3

You've known for a long time there is a tight clique on your team. The girls in this clique are rude and mean to others. They scare you a lot of the time and you've been avoiding them. They've never picked on you and you're thankful. One day, you are walking into class when you hear them making a racist comment to Leah, a new girl. You feel upset and sorry for Leah who seems pretty nice to you.

Scenario #4

You sit with the same group of friends every day at lunch in the cafeteria. You hear that Jason is mad at John. On this particular day before John comes to sit down, Jason tells everyone to save all of the seats so John won't have a seat at the table. Sure enough, when John comes to join the group you hear everyone at the table tell him that all of the seats are saved. As John wanders away, everyone at the table laughs.

Scenario #5

While in the hall between classes, Jessie hears about a fight between two seventh graders that is planned for today after school at the park. As the day progresses, Jessie hears about the fight from more and more people who all say that they are going to watch. Jessie has never seen a fight before and is curious. All of Jessie's friends say that they are going and are expecting Jessie to go, too.

Scenario #6

Janice is friends with both Samantha and Tanya and she knows that both girls like the same guy, Danzelle. She also knows there are rumors going around that Danzelle got together with Tanya the previous weekend. The next day Janice gets a note from Samantha that says all sorts of horrible things about Tanya and she also sees Samantha pass a note to at least five other people in class. Janice suspects that Samantha is writing the note because she is jealous. By the end of the day, Tanya is seen in the restroom crying.

VI. Conclusion

A. Ask students a question regarding integration of the *Bully-Proofing* program. Discuss and acknowledge students' ideas.

How are each of you going to keep this going in your classrooms?

B. Thank students for their active participation. Invite them to continue being a part of the caring majority.

"We are at the end of our structured bully-proofing sessions. But hopefully it doesn't end here. Whether each of you shows empathy or takes a stand for your classmates will be a decision you make every day. Every day you will be faced with the choices either to be a silent member of your school or a caring community member who takes an active part in establishing a school where people feel safe and cared about. All of you will soon be the eighth grade leaders of our school. The incoming sixth graders as well as the seventh graders will look to you for guidance. We are counting on you to continue establishing the (School name) caring community. This is your community. You can make it GREAT!"

HANDOUT/TRANSPARENCY 7A
Normal Conflict versus Bullying

Normal Conflict	versus	Bullying
Equal power; friends	vs.	Imbalance of power; not friends
Happens occasionally	vs.	Repeated negative actions
Accidental	vs.	Purposeful
Not serious	vs.	Serious—threat of physical harm or emotional or psychological hurt
Equal emotional reaction	vs.	Strong emotional reaction on part of the victim
Not seeking power or attention	vs.	Seeking power, control
Not trying to get something	vs.	Trying to gain material things or power
Remorse—takes responsibility	vs.	No remorse—blames victim
Effort to solve the problem	vs.	No effort to solve problem

HANDOUT/TRANSPARENCY 7B
Bully-Proofing Guidelines

1. **Respect yourself and others.**

2. **Contribute to a healthy and safe learning environment.**

3. **Use empathy and extra effort to include others.**

4. **Take a stand for what is right.**

5. **Encourage creative and peaceful problem solving.**

6. **Follow all school rules.**

HA HA SO Strategies

	STRATEGIES	TIPS
H Help:	Seek assistance from an adult, friend, or peer when a potentially threatening situation arises. Seek help also if other strategies aren't working.	1. Brainstorm all of the sources of help at your school—deans, counselors, teachers, nurse. 2. Stress the different ways to get help—anonymously, in a group, dean's hotline.
A Assert Yourself:	Make assertive statements to the bully addressing your feelings about the bully's *behavior*.	1. Should not be used with severe bullying. 2. Not as effective with group bullying. 3. Victim should look bully straight in the eye. 4. Use "I" statements. *Example:* "I don't like it when you pull on my backpack." 5. Make assertive statement and walk away. *Example:* "Stop talking about me behind my back."
H Humor:	Use humor to de-escalate a situation.	1. Use humor in a positive way. 2. Make the joke about what the bully said, not about the bully. 3. Make humorous statement and then leave the situation. 4. *Example:* When insulted about hairstyle, say "Gee, I didn't know you cared enough to notice."
A Avoid:	Walk away or avoid certain places in order to avoid a bullying situation.	1. Best for situations when victim is alone. 2. Avoid places where the bully hangs out. 3. Join with others rather than be alone.
S Self-Talk:	Use positive self-talk to maintain positive self-esteem during a bullying situation.	1. Use as a means to keep feeling good about self. 2. Think positive statements about self and accomplishments. 3. Rehearse mental statements to avoid being hooked by the bully. *Examples:* "It's his problem," "She doesn't know what she's talking about," "I know I'm smart." 4. Use positive self-talk when practicing all strategies.
O Own It:	"Own" the put-down or belittling comment in order to diffuse it.	1. Agree with the bully and leave the situation. 2. Combine with humor strategies such as, "Yeah, this **IS** a bad haircut. The lawn mower got out of control this weekend." 3. Combine with assertive strategies such as, "Yes, I did fail the test and I don't appreciate you looking at my paper."
Important Reminders:	1. Practice these strategies in any order, in any combination, or numerous times. 2. The Caring Community can remind each other of the strategies. 3. The Caring Community can help support the victim in using the strategies. 4. If the strategies aren't working, leave or disengage from the situation.	

Table title: Ha Ha So Strategies

H A N D O U T / T R A N S P A R E N C Y   6 H
Tattling versus Telling

Tattling	versus	Telling
Unimportant	vs.	Important
Harmless	vs.	Harmful or dangerous physically or psychologically
Can handle by self	vs.	Need help from an adult to solve
Purpose is to get someone in trouble	vs.	Purpose is to keep people safe
Behavior is accidental	vs.	Behavior is purposeful

WORKSHEET 7D
HA HA SO Scenario

Student name: _____

Directions:

Give an example of how you could use each of the strategies below to solve this problem.

Scenario:

You are walking down the hall and notice the same group of students hanging out at the same group of lockers. During this last year, every time you've walked by them they've made a comment about you. You have to pass their lockers to get to your own locker.

Help _____

_____

_____

Assert Yourself _____

_____

_____

Humor _____

_____

_____

Avoid _____

_____

_____

Self-Talk _____

_____

_____

Own It _____

_____

_____

Role Play Skit

LESSON 2

Actor #1

1. Wait for the teacher to tell you when to leave the classroom.

2. Go into the hallway and pick up a stack of books and papers.

3. After about one minute go back into the classroom.

4. Walk with Actor #2 up to the front of the class.

5. "Accidentally" trip in front of the students. (Don't hurt yourself.)

6. Look embarrassed and confused.

Actor #2

1. Wait for the teacher to tell you when to leave the classroom.

2. Go into the hallway and wait for one minute.

3. Go back into the classroom with Actor #1.

4. Walk with Actor #1 to the front of the class.

5. When Actor #1 trips, look shocked.

H A N D O U T　7 F
Acknowledgment Forms

I Caught You Caring

_____ acknowledges _____

for _____

_____

I Caught You Caring

_____ acknowledges _____

for _____

_____

I Caught You Caring

_____ acknowledges _____

for _____

_____

I Caught You Caring

_____ acknowledges _____

for _____

_____

H A N D O U T   7 G
I Caught You Caring

I Caught You Caring
Taking a Stand

_____ acknowledges _____

for taking a stand by _____

_____

I Caught You Caring
Taking a Stand

_____ acknowledges _____

for taking a stand by _____

_____

I Caught You Caring
Taking a Stand

_____ acknowledges _____

for taking a stand by _____

_____

I Caught You Caring
Taking a Stand

_____ acknowledges _____

for taking a stand by _____

_____

H A N D O U T / T R A N S P A R E N C Y   7 H
Sexual Harassment versus Flirting

Sexual Harassment versus Flirting	
Sexual Harassment makes the receiver feel:	**Flirting makes the receiver feel:**
Bad	Good
Angry/sad	Happy
Demeaned	Flattered
Ugly	Pretty/attractive
Powerless	In control
Sexual Harassment results in:	**Flirting results in:**
Negative self-esteem	Positive self-esteem
Sexual Harassment is perceived as:	**Flirting is perceived as:**
One-sided	Reciprocal
Demeaning	Flattering
Invading	Open
Degrading	A compliment
Sexual Harassment is:	**Flirting is:**
Unwanted	Wanted
Power-motivated	Equality-motivated
Illegal	Legal

Reprinted from *Sexual Harassment and Teens* by Strauss & Espeland, © 1992. Used with permission from Free Spirit Publishing, Minneapolis, MN; 1-800-735-7323; *www.freespirit.com.* ALL RIGHTS RESERVED.

Important Reminders:
- ♦ Sexual harassment is against the law.
- ♦ The target decides whether the behaviors are harassing or flattering.
- ♦ Men and women often perceive sexual attention differently.
- ♦ "No" means "No."
- ♦ Sexual harassment is based on a need for power, **not** physical attraction.

H A N D O U T   7 1
Sexual Harassment or Not Sexual Harassment—That Is the Question

Group members: _____

Directions:

Read each of the scenarios carefully. For each scenario write what would make the incident an example of flirting and what would make it an example of sexual harassment.

Scenario #1:

A girl walks up to a guy in the hallway and hugs him.

What would make this incident flirting and what would make it sexual harassment?

Flirting: _____

_____

_____

Sexual Harassment: _____

_____

_____

Scenario #2:

A student writes a note asking another student out.

What would make this incident flirting and what would make it sexual harassment?

Flirting: _____

_____

_____

Sexual Harassment: _____

_____

_____

HANDOUT 7J
Creative Problem Solving: Scenario 1

Group names: _____

Scenario #1

Marcus struggles in his seventh grade math class. Because of his difficulty understanding the lesson, he raises his hand often and it slows down the class. Today, when he raises his hand to ask a particular question, several students snicker and one student calls him a "retard." The teacher doesn't seem to hear the remarks. You are sitting close to Marcus and notice that he is visibly upset.

1. How might Marcus be feeling?

    _____

    _____

    _____

    _____

2. List three specific caring behaviors that you and the other bystanders could do as members of the caring majority.

    a. _____

    _____

    _____

    b. _____

    _____

    _____

    c. _____

    _____

    _____

HANDOUT 7J (*continued*)

Group names: _____

Scenario #2

This week a new girl joined your team. She's cute, dresses up a lot and the boys are giving her a lot of attention. Several girls who are friends of yours have started rumors about her. They have written a note that says really bad things about her including some crude pictures. You're sitting in class and the note is passed to you. Your friends expect you to read it and pass it on.

1. How might the new girl be feeling?

    _____

    _____

    _____

    _____

2. List three specific caring behaviors that you and other students could do as caring community members.

    a. _____

    _____

    _____

    b. _____

    _____

    _____

    c. _____

    _____

    _____

HANDOUT 7J (*continued*)

Group names: _____

Scenario #3

You've known for a long time there is a tight clique on your team. The girls in this clique are rude and mean to others. They scare you a lot of the time and you've been avoiding them. They've never picked on you and you're thankful. One day, you are walking into class when you hear them making a racist comment to Leah, a new girl. You feel upset and sorry for Leah who seems pretty nice to you.

1. How do you think that Leah might be feeling?

_____

_____

_____

_____

2. What are four *creative* ways you could handle this as a caring majority member?

a. _____

_____

_____

b. _____

_____

_____

c. _____

_____

_____

d. _____

_____

_____

HANDOUT 7J (*continued*)

Group names: _____

Scenario #4

You sit with the same group of friends every day at lunch in the cafeteria. You hear that Jason is mad at John. On this particular day before John comes to sit down, Jason tells everyone to save all of the seats so John won't have a seat at the table. Sure enough, when John comes to join the group you hear everyone at the table tell him that all of the seats are saved. As John wanders away, everyone at the table laughs.

1. What might John be feeling?

_____

_____

_____

_____

2. What are three things you could do to creatively solve this problem as a caring community member?

a. _____

_____

_____

_____

b. _____

_____

_____

_____

c. _____

_____

_____

_____

HANDOUT 7J (*continued*)

Group names: _____

Scenario #5

While in the hall between classes, Jessie hears about a fight between two seventh graders that is planned for today after school at the park. As the day progresses, Jessie hears about the fight from more and more people who all say that they are going to watch. Jessie has never seen a fight before and is curious. All of Jessie's friends say that they are going and are expecting Jessie to go, too.

1. How might Jessie be feeling?

_____

_____

_____

_____

2. What are four *creative* ways Jessie could deal with this situation as a caring majority member?

   a. _____

   _____

   _____

   b. _____

   _____

   _____

   c. _____

   _____

   _____

   d. _____

   _____

   _____

HANDOUT 7J (*continued*)

Group names: _____

Scenario #6

Janice is friends with both Samantha and Tanya and she knows that both girls like the same guy, Danzelle. She also knows there are rumors going around that Danzelle got together with Tanya the previous weekend. The next day Janice gets a note from Samantha that says all sorts of horrible things about Tanya and she also sees Samantha pass a note to at least five other people in class. Janice suspects that Samantha is writing the note because she is jealous. By the end of the day, Tanya is seen in the restroom crying.

1. How might Tanya be feeling?

   _____

   _____

   _____

   _____

2. List five caring behaviors that Janice and her classmates might do as part of the caring community.

   a. _____

   _____

   b. _____

   _____

   c. _____

   _____

   d. _____

   _____

   e. _____

   _____

Chapter Eight

Eighth Grade Curriculum

LESSON 1   Review of the Basic Concepts

Materials

- ◆ Short news article or story about a caring, life-changing experience
- ◆ **Poster or Handout/Transparency 8A:** Bully-Proofing Guidelines
- ◆ **Handout/Transparency 8B:** Types of Bullying Behaviors
- ◆ **Handout/Transparency 8C:** Normal Conflict vs. Bullying
- ◆ **Handout/Transparency 8D:** HA HA SO Strategies
- ◆ **Worksheet 8E:** Creative Problem Solving
- ◆ Overhead projector
- ◆ Chart paper/markers

Objectives

♦ Review the basic concepts of bullying

♦ Understand leadership role of eighth graders as members of caring community

♦ Review and practice different levels of risk in taking a stand

Steps

I. Hook: Get students' attention by reading a short news article or story about a caring, life-changing experience.

   A. *Suggestion:* Read the story titled, "The Most Mature Thing I've Ever Seen" from *Chicken Soup for the Teenage Soul* by Canfield, Hansen, and Kirberger.

      1. Can you imagine having that much courage?

      2. Do you think the boy who helped her knew his action would cause that much change?

      3. What do you think we will be talking about today?

II. Remind students of our expectations for eighth graders

   A. Reinforce with students that as the eighth graders at (your school), the school is counting on them to be the leaders of the caring community. Stress that a leader is someone who takes a stand for what is right. Briefly discuss their special leadership roles and responsibilities (student council, sports, knowledge of the school) as eighth graders.

   B. Review Session guidelines

      1. Respect self and others—no put-downs, verbal or nonverbal

      2. Participate—in your own way and style that is respectful of others

      3. While sharing stories or experiences, do not mention any particular names of individuals or groups. Instead, say "I know someone who . . ."

Handout/Transparency 8A

III. Review concepts involved in creating a caring community. Refer to poster or transparency of Bully-Proofing Guidelines (Handout/Transparency 8A). Read each guideline individually and connect them to building a caring community.

   A. Read and discuss rule #1: **Respect yourself and others.**

      1. What are some other words for respect?

2. What are some examples of respectful behaviors?

3. How does it feel to be respected?

B. Read and discuss rule #2: **Contribute to a healthy and safe learning environment.**

1. What does this mean to you?

2. What specific actions or behaviors does this involve?

C. Read rule #3: **Use empathy and extra effort to include others.**

1. Do you remember talking about empathy last year?

2. What does empathy mean?

3. What does inclusion mean?

4. Why do you think inclusion is important in a caring community?

D. Read rule #4: **Take a stand for what is right.**

Remind students of the definition of a bystander.

BYSTANDER: A person who stands near or looks on but does not take part; onlooker; spectator.

♦ If a person acts as a bystander and takes no action against bullying, then he or she is not acting as a member of the caring community.

♦ Bullies like it when bystanders don't do anything. They count on the bystanders to remain silent so they can continue their bullying behaviors.

♦ Bystanders make up the **most important** group in the school because once they learn how to take a stand against bullying, the bullies will lose their power.

1. What does taking a stand mean?

2. What are some different ways to take a stand?

E. Read rule #5: **Encourage creative and peaceful problem solving.**

1. What does it mean to think creatively when solving conflicts?

2. What ways can you think of to solve problems peacefully?

IV. Activity: Review of Bully-Proofing Concepts

A. Divide students into three groups. Make sure that students who are new to the school are grouped with students who have been involved with bully-proofing in previous years.

1. Give each group chart paper and markers and have them appoint a recorder and a reporter.

2. Assign each group one of the three bully-proofing concepts listed below and tell them that they are responsible for writing down all the facts they know and remember about that concept. Tell them that they will be responsible for teaching the information about their assigned concept to the rest of the class.

Group 1: Types of Bullying Behaviors—List the categories of bullying behaviors. Give two or three examples of each. *Hint:* There are six categories and one is physical aggression.

Group 2: Normal Conflict vs. Bullying—List the differences between normal conflict and bullying behavior.

Group 3: HA HA SO Strategies—Write down what each of the letters in HA HA SO stands for. Give an example of each strategy.

Handout/Transparency 8B
Handout/Transparency 8C
Handout/Transparency 8D

B. Give each group a few minutes to record on chart paper the facts they know about their assigned topic. When groups are ready, allow at least 15 minutes for the groups to present their information to the rest of the class. Following the group presentations, facilitators can assist groups by reviewing and reteaching any important points that were omitted. (Use Handout/Transparencies 8B, 8C, and 8D. See pages 307–309.)

C. Make a summarative statement regarding the important role of eighth graders in creating the caring community.

"You play a crucial role in creating a safe, caring community here at (your school). Remember, this program isn't about the bullies. It's about people like you who care about others and want (your school) to be a fun, safe school. We adults know that we aren't going to get everyone to buy into this. We know there are bullies in your class who are going to want to continue being bullies. But remember, there are more of you who care about (your school) and each other than there are bullies who enjoy and get power from hurting others. When you all get together and take a stand to help others and do what is right, you take the power away from the bullies. When that happens, then you—the caring majority—have the power and the recognition that comes with that power. In the end, each of you will need to make your own decision, moment by moment and day by day, about your role as a leader here at (your school). This class has already shown great leadership and we are excited for the legacy of kindness and caring that you will leave as your mark at (your school)."

V. **Homework**

A. Ask students to write a paragraph about the special role that eighth graders play in creating a caring community.

HANDOUT/TRANSPARENCY 8B
Types of Bullying Behaviors

Physical Aggression: Hitting, kicking, destroying property

Social Aggression: Spreading rumors, excluding from group, silent treatment

Verbal Aggression: Name calling, teasing, threatening, intimidating phone calls

Intimidation: Graffiti, a dirty trick, taking possession, coercion

Written Aggression: Note writing, graffiti, slam books

Sexual Harassment: Comments or actions of a sexual nature which are unwelcome and make the recipient uncomfortable. *Examples:* rumors of a sexual nature, inappropriate touching, grabbing, comments about someone's body

Racial and Ethnic Harassment: Comments or actions containing racial or ethnic content which are unwelcome and make the recipient uncomfortable. *Examples:* ethnic jokes, racial name calling, racial slurs

B. An optional homework assignment is to ask students to track bullying on TV. See "Track Bullying on TV" in *The Bully-Free Classroom,* pp. 63, 64 (Beane, 1999).

VI. **Classwork**

To be completed by the classroom teacher prior to the next bully-proofing session. (Worksheet 8E)

Worksheet 8E

A. Review the concept of low, medium, and high risk levels of taking a stand in creative problem solving.

1. *Low Risk:* Relating behaviors such as saying, "I'm sorry that happened," or "He shouldn't be saying that. It's rude and it's not OK." *Examples:* Behaviors that won't upset anyone; ignoring gossip or throwing a note away.

2. *Medium Risk:* Joining or other caring gestures that may attract some attention to the helper. Asking others to join you if they are not included in an activity.

Handout/Transparency 8C

Group 2

HANDOUT/TRANSPARENCY 8C
Normal Conflict versus Bullying

Normal Conflict	versus	Bullying
Equal power; friends	vs.	Imbalance of power; not friends
Happens occasionally	vs.	Repeated negative actions
Accidental	vs.	Purposeful
Not serious	vs.	Serious—threat of physical harm or emotional or psychological hurt
Equal emotional reaction	vs.	Strong emotional reaction on part of the victim
Not seeking power or attention	vs.	Seeking power, control
Not trying to get something	vs.	Trying to gain material things or power
Remorse—takes responsibility	vs.	No remorse—blames victim
Effort to solve the problem	vs.	No effort to solve problem

3. *High Risk:* Confronting behaviors. Assertive stances that may go against the group or the bully such as saying "Stop that. We don't do that at our school," or "No, I won't give Margaret the silent treatment. I'm not angry with her. You are."

Worksheet 8E

B. Divide students into groups of four. Give each group a worksheet (Worksheet 8E). Direct each group of students to select a recorder and a reporter. The recorder will record the group's ideas on the worksheet and the reporter will report the group's ideas to the whole class.

C. Allow the students about 10–15 minutes to work in their groups and another 15 minutes to share in the large group. Encourage creativity in their solutions and remind students again that there are many ways to take a stand at different levels of risk.

HANDOUT/TRANSPARENCY 8D
HA HA SO Strategies

Ha Ha So Strategies

	STRATEGIES	TIPS
H Help:	Seek assistance from an adult, friend, or peer when a potentially threatening situation arises. Seek help also if other strategies aren't working.	1. Brainstorm all of the sources of help at your school—deans, counselors, teachers, nurse. 2. Stress the different ways to get help—anonymously, in a group, dean's hotline.
A Assert Yourself:	Make assertive statements to the bully addressing your feelings about the bully's *behavior*.	1. Should not be used with severe bullying. 2. Not as effective with group bullying. 3. Victim should look bully straight in the eye. 4. Use "I" statements. *Example:* "I don't like it when you pull on my backpack." 5. Make assertive statement and walk away. *Example:* "Stop talking about me behind my back."
H Humor:	Use humor to de-escalate a situation.	1. Use humor in a positive way. 2. Make the joke about what the bully said, not about the bully. 3. Make humorous statement and then leave the situation. 4. E*xample:* When insulted about hairstyle, say "Gee, I didn't know you cared enough to notice."
A Avoid:	Walk away or avoid certain places in order to avoid a bullying situation.	1. Best for situations when victim is alone. 2. Avoid places where the bully hangs out. 3. Join with others rather than be alone.
S Self-Talk:	Use positive self-talk to maintain positive self-esteem during a bullying situation.	1. Use as a means to keep feeling good about self. 2. Think positive statements about self and accomplishments. 3. Rehearse mental statements to avoid being hooked by the bully. *Examples:* "It's his problem," "She doesn't know what she's talking about," "I know I'm smart." 4. Use positive self-talk when practicing all strategies.
O Own It:	"Own" the put-down or belittling comment in order to diffuse it.	1. Agree with the bully and leave the situation. 2. Combine with humor strategies such as, "Yeah, this **IS** a bad haircut. The lawn mower got out of control this weekend." 3. Combine with assertive strategies such as, "Yes, I did fail the test and I don't appreciate you looking at my paper."
Important Reminders:	1. Practice these strategies in any order, in any combination, or numerous times. 2. The Caring Community can remind each other of the strategies. 3. The Caring Community can help support the victim in using the strategies. 4. If the strategies aren't working, leave or disengage from the situation.	

LESSON 2 Sexual Harassment

Materials

- **Handout/Transparency 8F:** Sexual Harassment vs. Flirting

- **Worksheet 8G:** Sexual Harassment—Check Your Understanding (one copy per student)

- **Worksheet 8H:** What Could You Do? (one copy per student)

- Overhead projector

- Chart paper/markers

Objectives

♦ Review and discuss the concept of sexual harassment

♦ Differentiate between flirting and sexual harassment

♦ Learn what to do about sexual harassment

♦ Explore reasons why sexual harassment is not reported

Notes for Facilitators:

1. The topic of sexual harassment will be a sensitive topic for some students, and it is important to be aware of the students' concerns and reactions to the material presented.

2. Some students may use humor or oppositional behavior to mask their anxiety. Be particularly vigilant of the tone and direction of discussions and monitor carefully any side comments made by students.

3. Some circumstances around sexual harassment can be ambiguous and confusing. It is common for males and females to have differing views on what constitutes sexual harassment. Students may ask questions or relate experiences that have no definitive answer. It may be helpful to acknowledge the ambiguity and remind students to rely on their common sense and good judgment when making difficult interpersonal decisions.

4. Throughout the discussions, remind students that it is the target of the action who decides whether the behavior is sexual harassment or not.

5. If a student brings up same gender issues, remind him or her that the rules about sexual harassment apply whether it is a same sex or an opposite sex situation.

6. Know your school's policies regarding sexual harassment.

Steps

I. Review homework. Ask students to read their paragraphs about the special role that eighth graders have in creating a caring community. Emphasize any points they made in their assignments about eighth graders as leaders to stress that we are counting on them as important leaders in the school. Chart their ideas on poster paper that can be kept on display in the classroom.

II. Review classwork from Lesson 1 about low, medium, and high risk behaviors. Emphasize that an action that might be low risk for one person, could be a high risk behavior for another person.

III. Review and discuss the concept of sexual harassment as a type of bullying. Acknowledge with students that this type of bullying can be particularly difficult for middle school students to understand and address because of the sensitivity of the topic.

A. Teach the definition of sexual harassment. Ask the students for their definitions, then define for them:

SEXUAL HARASSMENT: Comments or actions of a sexual nature that are unwelcome and make the recipient uncomfortable.

B. Generate examples of sexual harassment. Ask the students to generate a list of behaviors that they think are examples of sexual harassment. Listed below are some examples to guide the discussion:

◆ Graffiti of a sexual nature

◆ Sexual remarks, teasing

◆ Spreading rumors of a sexual nature about others

◆ Rating other students in terms of their physical attractiveness

◆ Sexual jokes

◆ Accusations regarding sexual orientation

◆ Pinching, brushing against, sexually suggestive touching

◆ Underwear exposure or torment ("snuggies," "de-panting," bra snapping)

◆ Verbal comments of a sexual nature about body parts

C. Who decides if a behavior is sexual harassment? Ask students this question. Remind them of the very important fact that sexual harassment is in the eye of the beholder and that the person who is the target of the behavior is the one who decides if it is harassment or not.

IV. Review and discuss the differences between sexual harassment and flirting.

A. Ask students for their ideas about the differences between sexual harassment and flirting. The facilitator records the student responses on the board under the two different headings.

B. Read the following scenario to the class and ask the students to discuss when this scenario could be an example of flirting and when could it be an example of sexual harassment. Add any new ideas to the previous ideas listed on the board.

Scenario: A student walks up to another student and says "You look really good today."

C. Use Handout/Transparency 8F to review the differences between sexual harassment and flirting.

Handout/Transparency 8F

Make the following important points in the discussion:

1. The target of the behavior has the right to decide if it constitutes flirting or harassment.

HANDOUT/TRANSPARENCY 8F
Sexual Harassment versus Flirting

Sexual Harassment versus Flirting	
Sexual Harassment makes the receiver feel:	**Flirting makes the receiver feel:**
Bad	Good
Angry/sad	Happy
Demeaned	Flattered
Ugly	Pretty/attractive
Powerless	In control
Sexual Harassment results in:	**Flirting results in:**
Negative self-esteem	Positive self-esteem
Sexual Harassment is perceived as:	**Flirting is perceived as:**
One-sided	Reciprocal
Demeaning	Flattering
Invading	Open
Degrading	A compliment
Sexual Harassment is:	**Flirting is:**
Unwanted	Wanted
Power-motivated	Equality-motivated
Illegal	Legal

Reprinted from *Sexual Harassment and Teens* by Strauss & Espeland, © 1992. Used with permission from Free Spirit Publishing, Minneapolis, MN; 1-800-735-7323; *www.freespirit.com.* ALL RIGHTS RESERVED.

Important Reminders:
- Sexual harassment is against the law.
- The target decides whether the behaviors are harassing or flattering.
- Men and women often perceive sexual attention differently.
- "No" means "No."
- Sexual harassment is based on a need for power, **not** physical attraction.

2. Sexual harassment is against the law.

3. Sexual harassment violates school rules and policies. Even if the target does not find the behavior harassing, other people observing the behavior may find it offensive. *Example:* Students observing two people hugging in the hallway might be offended.

4. Sexual harassment is based on a need for power, just like bullying, and is **not** about physical attraction.

5. Consider school as your workplace. Sexual harassment is illegal in the workplace and is not appropriate or allowed.

6. Get help when you think you are being sexually harassed.

V. Teach what to do about sexual harassment. Tell students that there are two things they can do if they think they are being sexually harassed. They can try to handle it themselves, and they can get help from others.

A. Handle it yourself. You can decide to try to handle the situation yourself.

    1. Talk to the person harassing you. Tell him/her that you want them to stop the behavior—right now. Talk to them **assertively**, not **aggressively**, and use direct eye contact.

    2. Do not engage with them. Tell them to stop, then leave the situation.

    3. Ask a friend or friends to go with you for support.

B. Go to an adult for help.

    1. Choose an adult you trust and tell him/her about the harassment.

    2. If the first adult you go to does not respond appropriately, keep talking to adults until you find one who will help you and take the appropriate actions.

    3. Remember that you have the right to be heard and to be treated with respect and dignity.

VI. Discuss with students why victims don't report sexual harassment.

A. Ask students if they think most victims of sexual harassment report it when it happens. Let them know that the facts indicate that it usually goes unreported. Ask students for their ideas about why sexual harassment goes unreported and record on the chalkboard. Be sure that the following reasons are included in the list:

Why Victims Don't Report Sexual Harassment

1. They blame themselves; think they caused it to happen.

2. They feel powerless and afraid.

3. They feel embarrassed—the topic is very sensitive.

4. They fear retaliation.

5. They worry about losing social status and friends—its' not "cool" to complain.

6. They are afraid their complaint won't be taken seriously.

7. They are confused and don't trust their own experience.

B. Acknowledge that reporting can be difficult in the area of sexual harassment for all the reasons listed above and because it is such a sensitive topic. Draw a parallel between sexual harassment and other kinds of bullying by asking the students to think about what will happen if it goes unreported.

    1. What will happen if sexual harassment goes unreported? Will the harasser stop his or her behaviors? Will the target of the harassment feel safe?

2. Can our school be a caring community if sexual harassment is allowed to take place?

3. Do we have a responsibility to report sexual harassment if we know it is happening in our school?

C. To summarize, say to the students:

"Sexual harassment is a serious form of bullying that needs to be reported so that everyone can feel safe in our school community. Remember, sexual harassment will not stop unless we all take a stand against these types of behaviors. If you are being sexually harassed by someone, you can try to handle it yourself or you can ask your friends and the adults in the school for help. Sexual harassment is against the law, against school rules, and cannot be allowed in a caring community."

VII. Activity: Sexual Harassment—Check Your Understanding, Worksheet 8G

Worksheet 8G

WORKSHEET 8G
Sexual Harassment—Check Your Understanding

Directions:
Read each statement. Mark T or F to indicate whether the statement is true or false.

1. Hugging someone in the hallway could be an example of sexual harassment.   _____

2. The target gets to decide if the behavior is harassing or complimentary.   _____

3. Flirting usually makes a person feel good about himself or herself.   _____

4. Sexual harassment is not against school rules.   _____

5. Sexual harassment is not about power.   _____

6. Sexual harassment is against the law.   _____

7. If you think you're being sexually harassed, you should keep it to yourself.   _____

8. If the first adult you choose to talk to about being sexually harassed doesn't help you, you should find another adult to tell.   _____

9. It is the target's fault if he or she is being sexually harassed.   _____

10. A compliment that makes someone feel uncomfortable is considered sexual harassment.   _____

11. One way to put an end to sexual harassment is to tell the harasser to stop it.   _____

12. Students have a responsibility to take action against sexual harassment.   _____

A. Hand out worksheets to students to do individually. Allow 5–8 minutes for the activity.

B. Discuss answers together in class.

VIII. **Homework**

Assign "What Could You Do?" Worksheet 8H. Hand out a worksheet to each student. Go over the directions together and assign as homework.

Worksheet 8H

LESSON 3 Inclusion and Groups

Materials

♦ Chart paper/markers

♦ Index cards

♦ **Poster or Handout/Transparency 8A:** Bully-Proofing Guidelines

Objectives

♦ Review ways to take a stand against sexual harassment

♦ Explore and discuss the concept of inclusion in a caring community

♦ Examine the positive and negative aspects of being in a group

Steps

I. Check homework assignment, "What Could You Do?" Worksheet 8H. Ask students to share their answers with the group and discuss. Summarize the discussion by reminding students that: (1) they have a responsibility as caring community members to take a stand against sexual harassment, and (2) there are many different ways to take a stand.

Worksheet 8H

II. Generate a discussion about inclusion and friends.

A. Refer to the students' answers from the above homework assignment about the different ways they could take a stand for the students described in the scenarios. Ask the following questions to generate a discussion about inclusion and friends.

> In science when we were doing a lab, someone wanted to be in our group. The group would not let him in.

1. Should you demonstrate these caring behaviors only for people who are in your group or who are your friends?

2. If you observed Scenario #2 happening in the above homework assignment, would you be responsible for taking some kind of stand even if you didn't know the boy or the girl involved?

3. Does the idea of including others mean that we only have to include or take a stand for our friends or people we know?

B. Lead students to the understanding that inclusion is important in developing a caring community and that it means reaching out to others beyond just our own friends and our own friendship groups.

1. Refer to Bully-Proofing Guideline #3: **Use empathy and extra effort to include others.**

2. Explain: **"You do have the responsibility as caring community members to include others, but that doesn't mean that you have to be best friends with everyone. Including others means watching out for each other and taking a stand for each other when necessary so that everyone can feel like a valued community member."**

3. Acknowledge that it can feel difficult to reach out to others you may not know, but emphasize that it is important in a caring community because everyone has the right to feel that they are included and belong.

III. Discuss inclusion in the context of groups.

A. Begin the discussion by talking about how important it is for all of us to feel like we belong, and that one way people meet that need is by joining groups. Adolescents, especially, meet their needs for friendship and belonging by forming groups. Make these points:

1. There are many different kinds of groups. Ask students to name all the different groups that people can belong to: family, religious, community, sports, interest, club, and friendship groups.

2. Groups can be small or large, but people tend to form groups with other persons who they see as being similar to themselves. These similarities can be around racial and/or cultural background, interests, hobbies, and common experiences.

3. People can change groups or find themselves between groups at any given time.

4. A student may not be interested in joining a group at school, but may be in several groups outside of school.

B. Discuss with students both the positive and negative things that can result from being in a group. Remind them of these rules for the discussion:

♦ No names or labels of particular groups can be used

♦ No derogatory or disrespectful comments will be allowed

1. Ask students to think about all the positive things about being in a group. Put the following heading on the board and record their ideas. Make sure that the ideas below are included in the student list.

Positive Things About Being in a Group
Sense of belonging
Shared interests
Make friends
Feel accepted, liked

2. Ask students to think about some of the negative things about being in a group. What sometimes happens when people belong to a group? How do people sometimes act when they're in their group? Put the following heading on the board and record their ideas. Make sure that the ideas below are included in the student list.

Negative Things About Being in a Group
Act exclusive
Act snotty, better than, "all that"
Ignore others
Leave people out
Make fun of others; put others down

3. Acknowledge that groups provide good things but that *sometimes* people in a group can act in some of the negative ways listed above, especially by forgetting to include and respect others.

C. Explore reasons for negative group behaviors.

1. Ask students:

a. Why do you think the negative behaviors we listed above sometimes happen when people are in a group?

b. Why do people who are usually kind and caring community members as individuals sometimes act differently toward others when they're in a group?

2. Encourage discussion about these questions. Allow students time to talk about the reasons people sometimes behave badly in a group. Reasons may include:

a. Peer pressure

b. Pressure to conform

c. "Cliquish" nature of groups

3. Summarize and make these important points:

a. It is normal to want to belong to a group.

b. Being a member of a group makes us feel like we belong and are accepted.

c. Sometimes, we can get so involved in our own group that we forget to treat others who are not in our group with kindness and caring.

At lunch there is this kid that sits with us and we usually make fun of him and call him names. I think this makes him feel left out.

Say:

"It is a normal part of life to belong to a group. However, sometimes when people get into middle school they can become so involved with their own group that they forget to act in caring ways toward people they don't know or people who aren't in their friendship group. They can get so carried away with the sense of belonging and acceptance they get from their own group that they start to treat others badly by putting them down, making fun of them, leaving them out, and maybe even looking the other way when they're in trouble."

IV. Activity

A. Pass out index cards to each student. Have them put their names on the cards. Then ask them to write about either:

1. A time when a group's behavior toward you made you feel left out or uncared for.

2. A time when you were in a group and you or your group treated someone badly or made them feel left out or uncared for.

B. Give the students a few minutes to write, then collect cards. Read some of the stories anonymously to the class.

C. Ask the students to look back on the experiences they wrote about and think about how they wish they had been treated differently or how they wish they had acted differently. Discuss these ideas together.

D. As a class generate a list of ways groups should act in a caring community. Record on chart paper to be left in the classroom as a reminder.

CHART

1. Write the heading on the board and record students' ideas. Some suggested ideas are listed below.

Ways Groups Should Act in the Caring Community

Treat others with respect whether they're in your group or not.

Don't put down people you don't know or who aren't in your group.

Reach out to people whether they're in your group or not.

Get to know people outside of your group of friends.

2. Leave the chart posted in the classroom as a daily reminder to students of how to treat each other.

V. **Homework**

Record at least three caring gestures you make during the next week. These gestures need to be toward someone who is not in your friendship group or someone you don't know. Challenge yourself to reach outside of your comfort zone and do or say something nice for someone in the caring community you don't usually include in your everyday activities. Record the details of what you do as well as how it makes you feel. We will share these next week.

LESSON 4   Positive Leadership

Materials

♦ Chart paper/markers

Objectives

♦ Identify the characteristics of a positive leader

♦ Develop an understanding of intention and the role it plays in leadership

♦ Practice using the characteristics of a positive leader in a school situation

Steps

I. Review homework

    A. Ask students to share with the class some of the caring gestures they made during the past week to people outside of their friendship group. Use the examples to emphasize the importance of inclusion in the caring community. Remind students that inclusion doesn't necessarily mean friendship, but does involve reaching out and being kind to others, whether they're in your friendship group or not.

II. Identify and discuss the characteristics of a leader

    A. Begin a discussion with the students about leaders and their characteristics. Remind them that a leader is someone who takes a stand for what is right. Ask students to think of people who they think are leaders. Let them know that this can include famous people as well as people they know personally. Write these names on the chalkboard, accepting all ideas.

    B. Generate a list of the characteristics of the leaders previously named. Ask the following questions:

        1. What qualities and characteristics do these people have that make them leaders?

2. Do you think leaders have to have **all** these qualities in order to be a leader?

3. Do you think all leaders are positive?

4. Do you think there can be leaders who are both positive and negative?

Summarize students' answers to include the following characteristics: Leaders should (1) have empathy, (2) take a stand for others, (3) be creative problem solvers, and (4) make an effort to include others.

C. Generate a discussion of the difference between negative and positive leaders.

1. What makes negative leaders different from positive leaders?

2. Do negative leaders have some of the characteristics you listed under positive leaders?

3. Are bullies negative leaders?

D. Use the preceding answers to lead the students to a discussion about intention. Introduce the definition of intention.

Intention: The ultimate purpose, aim, or design.

Explain that the difference between positive and negative leadership is the intention behind the action. Use the contrasting words "help" and "hurt" to make the point.

1. Did the leader intend to help (positive) or hurt (negative) the person?

III. Activity: Helpful or hurtful action

A. Facilitator reads the following scenarios. Ask students to vote as to whether the person's intention is to be helpful or hurtful. Discuss briefly their responses and ideas.

1. You hear a rumor about a friend and pass it along to someone else. What is your intention?

2. You tell your friend something awful that was said about him/her. What is your intention?

3. You are friendly to someone who is being harassed in the cafeteria. What is your intention?

4. You don't report an incident where someone might be physically hurt. What is your intention?

Emphasize again that the intention of a positive leader is to help people, not hurt them or make them feel bad. Challenge students to examine their own intentions behind their daily actions.

IV. Discussion about different leadership styles

    A. Let students know that there are many different styles of leadership and many different ways to take action as a leader. A person can be one kind of leader one day and a different kind of leader another day. There are loud and quiet leaders, high risk and low risk leaders, daily leaders and occasional leaders.

    B. Encourage students to think about their own leadership styles. Discuss their answers to the following questions:

        1. What kind of positive leader are you?

        2. Do you have one style or lots of styles?

        3. Do you generally choose low, medium, or high risk leadership actions?

        4. What kinds of leaders are your friends?

        Summarize the discussion by stressing that it is important to honor your own leadership style. Encourage students to pay attention to their positive leadership behaviors during the next week and to experiment with different styles and behaviors.

V. Activity: Designing skits that demonstrate the characteristics of a positive leader

    A. Divide students into groups of five. Explain to students that each group is to write and perform a skit that demonstrates the characteristics of a positive leader. Give them the following guidelines:

        1. Write a two to three minute skit that demonstrates the elements of positive leadership listed below:
           a. Empathy
           b. Taking a stand
           c. Creative problem solving
           d. Inclusion

        2. The skit needs to depict a realistic scene that might appear here at (your school).

        3. The skit cannot involve any physical altercations—no physical fighting or physical contact.

        4. All people in your group need to have a part. One part can be that of narrator.

        5. The audience will be watching specifically for demonstrations of leadership that include examples of empathy, taking a stand, creative problem solving, and inclusion. When these characteristics appear in the skit the audience

Diversity

Drawn by
Nayla Pekarek

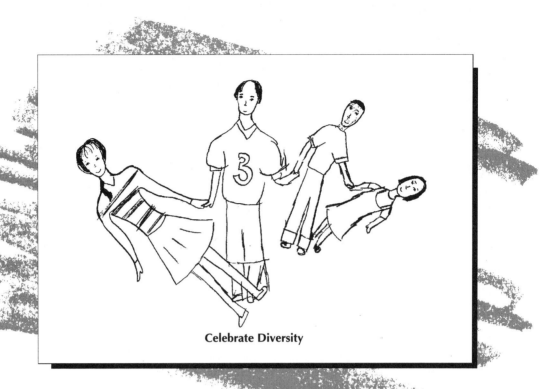

Celebrate Diversity

will hold up flashcards to acknowledge that they've been included in the skit.

6. Students will have one class before our next bully-proofing session to write and practice their skit.

7. Bonuses will be given for the use of props or costume items.

VI. **Classwork**

To be completed by the classroom teacher prior to the next bully-proofing session

A. Review the skit requirements with students.

B. Allow students time to write and practice their skits.

VII. **Homework**

Observe your classmates during the next week. Record three examples of classmates acting as positive leaders. Make special note of the ways they take a stand and categorize their actions as low, medium, or high risk behaviors.

LESSON 5   Characteristics of Leadership

Materials

- Flashcards for audience participants
- Rewards—candy, food coupons, etc.
- Chart paper/markers
- Index cards

Objectives

- Review the characteristics of a positive leader
- Presentation of skits
- Create personal leadership goals

Steps

I. Share homework assignments about observations of peers acting as positive leaders. Emphasize the many different styles of leadership as well as the different ways of taking a stand and being a leader.

II. Review the characteristics of a positive leader. Skit presentations.

  A. Review with students the four characteristics of positive leadership that are to be demonstrated in each group's skit. Write the following four characteristics on the board:

   1. **EMPATHY = E**

   2. **TAKING A STAND = T**

   3. **CREATIVE PROBLEM SOLVING = C**

   4. **INCLUSION = I**

  B. Explain the audience evaluation process. Hand out four sheets of paper to each student and ask them to write one of the four letters (E, T, C, I) on each of their pieces of paper. Explain to the students that as audience participants they are to use these "flashcards" during each performance to signal when one of the characteristics has been demonstrated. For example, when they observe an example of taking a stand in one of the skits, they are to raise their "T" flashcard.

C. Review appropriate audience behaviors. They include:

1. Show respect for self and others during the performances

2. Participate by listening and paying attention

3. Show appropriate appreciation by applauding at the end of each skit

D. Presentation of skits. Call on groups to present their skits to the class.

1. It is helpful for one of the facilitators to sit in the audience in order to model appropriate behavior and use of the flashcards.

2. The facilitators should briefly discuss and review the concepts presented at the end of each skit.

3. Rewards are given to groups that use props and/or costumes in their skits.

CHART

E. Summarize the leadership concepts presented in the skits. Discuss with students the important points about being a positive leader. Write the ideas on chart paper to remain on display in the classroom. Include these points in the discussion:

1. The four characteristics of positive leadership are: empathy, taking a stand, creative problem solving, and inclusion.

2. There are many different ways to be a positive leader.

3. Each person has his or her own leadership style and it can vary from day to day.

4. A leader can choose low, medium, or high risk actions in taking a stand.

5. The difference between being a positive and negative leader is in the person's intention.

III. Closing Activity: Acknowledgments and goal setting.

A. Say to students:

"We know many of you make excellent choices to be positive leaders in the (name of your school) Caring Community. We really appreciate all you are doing to make our school a safe, caring place. We know that each of you is capable of making the choice to be a positive leader and we count on you to keep making those choices in your very important role as the leaders of our school."

B. Pass out index cards to each student. Ask students to take a little time to think about their choices this year. Then ask them to write down two things they've already done this year as a positive leader at (your school). Remind them that it doesn't matter if their actions have been big or little, dramatic or ordinary. **Every caring gesture counts**. Then have them write down at least one leadership skill that they would like to strive for in the coming weeks.

C. Ask volunteers to read their goals to the class. Facilitators then collect cards and read some anonymously if there is time. Facilitators can hand back the cards to students at a later date to check on their progress toward their leadership goals.

IV. Conclusion of Sessions

A. Thank and acknowledge the group and encourage them to support each other to make their eighth grade year and everyone's year at (your school) successful and safe.

HANDOUT/TRANSPARENCY 8A
Bully-Proofing Guidelines

1. **Respect yourself and others.**

2. **Contribute to a healthy and safe learning environment.**

3. **Use empathy and extra effort to include others.**

4. **Take a stand for what is right.**

5. **Encourage creative and peaceful problem solving.**

6. **Follow all school rules.**

HANDOUT/TRANSPARENCY 8B
Types of Bullying Behaviors

Physical Aggression: Hitting, kicking, destroying property

Social Aggression: Spreading rumors, excluding from group, silent treatment

Verbal Aggression: Name calling, teasing, threatening, intimidating phone calls

Intimidation: Graffiti, a dirty trick, taking possession, coercion

Written Aggression: Note writing, graffiti, slam books

Sexual Harassment: Comments or actions of a sexual nature which are unwelcome and make the recipient uncomfortable. *Examples:* rumors of a sexual nature, inappropriate touching, grabbing, comments about someone's body

Racial and Ethnic Harassment: Comments or actions containing racial or ethnic content which are unwelcome and make the recipient uncomfortable. *Examples:* ethnic jokes, racial name calling, racial slurs

HANDOUT/TRANSPARENCY 8C
Normal Conflict versus Bullying

Normal Conflict	versus	Bullying
Equal power; friends	vs.	Imbalance of power; not friends
Happens occasionally	vs.	Repeated negative actions
Accidental	vs.	Purposeful
Not serious	vs.	Serious—threat of physical harm or emotional or psychological hurt
Equal emotional reaction	vs.	Strong emotional reaction on part of the victim
Not seeking power or attention	vs.	Seeking power, control
Not trying to get something	vs.	Trying to gain material things or power
Remorse—takes responsibility	vs.	No remorse—blames victim
Effort to solve the problem	vs.	No effort to solve problem

H A N D O U T / T R A N S P A R E N C Y   8 D
HA HA SO Strategies

Ha Ha So Strategies		
STRATEGIES		**TIPS**
H **Help:**	Seek assistance from an adult, friend, or peer when a potentially threatening situation arises. Seek help also if other strategies aren't working.	1. Brainstorm all of the sources of help at your school—deans, counselors, teachers, nurse. 2. Stress the different ways to get help—anonymously, in a group, dean's hotline.
A **Assert Yourself:**	Make assertive statements to the bully addressing your feelings about the bully's *behavior*.	1. Should not be used with severe bullying. 2. Not as effective with group bullying. 3. Victim should look bully straight in the eye. 4. Use "I" statements. *Example:* "I don't like it when you pull on my backpack." 5. Make assertive statement and walk away. *Example:* "Stop talking about me behind my back."
H **Humor:**	Use humor to de-escalate a situation.	1. Use humor in a positive way. 2. Make the joke about what the bully said, not about the bully. 3. Make humorous statement and then leave the situation. 4. *Example:* When insulted about hairstyle, say "Gee, I didn't know you cared enough to notice."
A **Avoid:**	Walk away or avoid certain places in order to avoid a bullying situation.	1. Best for situations when victim is alone. 2. Avoid places where the bully hangs out. 3. Join with others rather than be alone.
S **Self-Talk:**	Use positive self-talk to maintain positive self-esteem during a bullying situation.	1. Use as a means to keep feeling good about self. 2. Think positive statements about self and accomplishments. 3. Rehearse mental statements to avoid being hooked by the bully. *Examples:* "It's his problem," "She doesn't know what she's talking about," "I know I'm smart." 4. Use positive self-talk when practicing all strategies.
O **Own It:**	"Own" the put-down or belittling comment in order to diffuse it.	1. Agree with the bully and leave the situation. 2. Combine with humor strategies such as, "Yeah, this **IS** a bad haircut. The lawn mower got out of control this weekend." 3. Combine with assertive strategies such as, "Yes, I did fail the test and I don't appreciate you looking at my paper."
Important Reminders:	1. Practice these strategies in any order, in any combination, or numerous times. 2. The Caring Community can remind each other of the strategies. 3. The Caring Community can help support the victim in using the strategies. 4. If the strategies aren't working, leave or disengage from the situation.	

WORKSHEET 8E
Classroom Assignment—Creative Problem Solving

Group Names: _____

Directions:

1. Read each scenario and discuss with your group creative ways to solve the problem.

2. Be sure to write a low, medium, and high risk solution for each scenario.

Scenario #1:

You and your friend have just settled into your seats on the bus. A student comes up to your friend and says "Get out of my seat—NOW!" When your friend refuses to move, the student says: "I'll kick your butt at lunch!"

Low Risk:

_____

_____

_____

_____

Medium Risk:

_____

_____

_____

_____

High Risk:

_____

_____

_____

_____

WORKSHEET 8E (*continued*)

Scenario #2:

Monday morning when you get to school you hear a rumor about your friend Jennifer and her wild behavior at a weekend party. Throughout the day you are aware that many people are talking about Jennifer. Later in the day, a friend asks you what you've heard about the rumor.

Low Risk:

_____

_____

_____

_____

Medium Risk:

_____

_____

_____

_____

High Risk:

_____

_____

_____

_____

Sexual Harassment versus Flirting

Sexual Harassment versus Flirting	
Sexual Harassment makes the receiver feel:	**Flirting makes the receiver feel:**
Bad	Good
Angry/sad	Happy
Demeaned	Flattered
Ugly	Pretty/attractive
Powerless	In control
Sexual Harassment results in:	**Flirting results in:**
Negative self-esteem	Positive self-esteem
Sexual Harassment is perceived as:	**Flirting is perceived as:**
One-sided	Reciprocal
Demeaning	Flattering
Invading	Open
Degrading	A compliment
Sexual Harassment is:	**Flirting is:**
Unwanted	Wanted
Power-motivated	Equality-motivated
Illegal	Legal

Reprinted from *Sexual Harassment and Teens* by Strauss & Espeland, © 1992. Used with permission from Free Spirit Publishing, Minneapolis, MN; 1-800-735-7323; *www.freespirit.com.* ALL RIGHTS RESERVED.

Important Reminders:
- ◆ Sexual harassment is against the law.
- ◆ The target decides whether the behaviors are harassing or flattering.
- ◆ Men and women often perceive sexual attention differently.
- ◆ "No" means "No."
- ◆ Sexual harassment is based on a need for power, **not** physical attraction.

WORKSHEET 8G
Sexual Harassment—Check Your Understanding

Directions:

Read each statement. Mark T or F to indicate whether the statement is true or false.

1. Hugging someone in the hallway could be an example of sexual harassment.   _____

2. The target gets to decide if the behavior is harassing or complimentary.   _____

3. Flirting usually makes a person feel good about himself or herself.   _____

4. Sexual harassment is not against school rules.   _____

5. Sexual harassment is not about power.   _____

6. Sexual harassment is against the law.   _____

7. If you think you're being sexually harassed, you should keep it to yourself.   _____

8. If the first adult you choose to talk to about being sexually harassed doesn't help you, you should find another adult to tell.   _____

9. It is the target's fault if he or she is being sexually harassed.   _____

10. A compliment that makes someone feel uncomfortable is considered sexual harassment.   _____

11. One way to put an end to sexual harassment is to tell the harasser to stop it.   _____

12. Students have a responsibility to take action against sexual harassment.   _____

WORKSHEET 8H
What Could You Do?

Directions:

Described below are three sexual harassment scenarios. Read each scenario. Then write down your ideas about the ways a caring community member could take a stand in each situation.

Scenario #1

You observe a boy cornering a girl up against a locker. The girl looks frightened.

What could you do as a caring community member in this situation? _____

_____

_____

_____

Scenario #2

You overhear a girl calling a boy a "fag" in the hallway.

What could you do as a caring community member in this situation? _____

_____

_____

_____

Scenario #3

A friend shows you a note that someone gave him/her that includes sexual graffiti.

What could you do as a caring community member in this situation? _____

_____

_____

_____

Chapter Nine

Interventions

Section One: Interventions With Bullies

Children who repeatedly bully others present particularly difficult challenges to all those around them. By the time these children reach middle school, they have not only developed a pervasive pattern of aggressive behavior but have also acquired sophisticated methods that can make them more difficult to detect as well as discipline. And with these increasing cognitive and verbal capabilities, bullying students can more deeply entangle adults into their provocative game of excuses, blaming others, and never-ending power struggles. Students who intentionally hurt others understandably anger the adults around them. However, angry, aggressive responses to bullying students only ensure a longer power struggle, one which empowers the bully. It is no wonder that so many interventions are tried and so many interventions fail. The challenges are many but not insurmountable. This chapter will outline some strategies that are known to be effective with bullies.

Notably, there is a continuum of bullying behaviors and varying degrees of pervasiveness and chronicity for some children. The interventions presented are intended for students who have demonstrated the characteristics of bullies across settings. Bullies, in particular, need interventions that are driven first by behavior management and move toward relationship skills and interventions; whereas, with most students we begin with relationship-driven interventions. For this reason it can be beneficial to identify students who chronically bully. The intention is not to "label" certain students as "bullies" because it can significantly constrict our view of the person and the possibility for change. To effectively assist students who bully, we need to believe they are capable of change. Students who bully others need and deserve our compassion and caring just as other students do. They need some additional stern measures to affect change.

The following interventions have been found helpful and will be presented in Section One of this chapter:

- Consistent, predictable discipline structure
- No-nonsense interpersonal style
- Problem-solving approach
- Corrective social thinking and empathy development
- Prosocial consequences
- Caring majority

Consistent, Predictable Discipline Structure

Bullies need interventions that begin with behavior management where they are consistently held accountable for their behavior. It is paramount to have a well-defined, consistent system of discipline throughout the school. Aggressive, bullying students are often very good at finding and using loopholes, or weak links in very solid discipline structures.

Change for the chronically bullying student is a process that requires a great deal of valuable resource time with counselors, deans, mental health personnel, and/or administration. A well-planned and tightly coordinated individual behavior plan will be necessary when intervening with bullying teens so that all of the adults involved are working together. Behavior plans should include consequences, rewards, and goals for additional support resources. Engage the help of as many support personnel as possible—i.e., mental health workers, counseling staff, probation officers, community agencies, and favorite teachers. Each person involved with the student should delineate his or her role and responsibilities in the plan. Parents should be involved in formulating the plan, as well as identifying their responsibilities.

Group interventions with teenage bullies are not recommended. The struggle to be "top dog" can result in a group process whereby each of the members is trying to outdo the others' negative behaviors. Additionally, there are no positive role models except for the adult(s) facilitating the group. Given that bullies commonly see adults as adversarial, there is little likelihood they will see them as role models.

The first step in the discipline of bullying students most often begins with the classroom teacher. Teachers need to know the school's behavioral policies and carry them out. If teachers are fearful of retaliation from the bully or the bully's family, they may overlook harassing, aggressive behaviors to avoid involvement. Therefore, teachers need to be informed and reminded of the best strategies for managing the behavior of bullying students and parents. The Bully-Proofing Cadre can be used as support to remind teachers on a daily basis to keep their primary focus on the caring majority of students. During classroom instruction teachers need to use the matter-of-fact, no-nonsense approach and deliver direct warnings and consequences for misbehavior. Correcting social thinking errors or identifying the feelings of the victim should **not** happen in front of the classroom when the bully has engaged the teacher in a power struggle.

No-Nonsense Interpersonal Style

When intervening with bullies, a no-nonsense, directive, non-emotional approach is very important. Bullies naturally evoke strong emotions from the people around them and glean excitement from it. Therefore, it is necessary for the persons intervening to make directives in a matter-of-fact tone and not get into lengthy, detailed discussions with the bully.

Interventions with bullies will often occur during the disciplinary process. Following a behavioral infraction the bully is likely to be uncomfortable due to the pending consequences. This discomfort can provoke a desire for change and can be used as a "teachable moment." It is important to capitalize on the teachable moment and intervene with a number of strategies such as correcting his/her thinking errors and building empathy for the victim. During this counseling/disciplinary process it is important for the adult to maintain control of the meeting and avoid becoming emotional or being manipulated. As discussed in Chapter Four, students who bully are extremely good at blaming others, arguing, lying, and/or belaboring the smallest points. The following style of relating can be helpful:

- ♦ Use a no-nonsense, directive manner.
- ♦ Be confrontive without being provocative.
- ♦ Speak candidly.
- ♦ Avoid ridicule, anger, or sarcasm.
- ♦ Avoid becoming consumed with whether the student is telling the truth. Some listening and fact gathering is important. If overdone it can divert from your goal.
- ♦ Expect to have to repeat corrective social thinking points in different ways.
- ♦ If the student become overly angry or intimidating, end the meeting.
- ♦ Avoid wanting to get the student to "like" you. Respect will be earned through maintaining a polite and firm approach.

Problem-Solving Approach

A problem-solving, no-blame approach can be an effective intervening technique in the immediate handling of an incident as well as for developing long-term positive outcomes. Maines and Robinson advocate that blameful analysis does little to change the situation or alleviate the problem. The dynamics of the bullying student's life or childhood history are beyond the school's ability to affect, and teachers will inevitably gain more by problem solving than by an analysis of causation.

A summary of the steps in the problem-solving approach follows:

- ◆ State the incident in a no-blame manner.

- ◆ State the rule which was violated and the consequences.

- ◆ Remind the student of the school expectations regarding mutual respect.

- ◆ State the feelings of the victim.

- ◆ State the follow-up plan.

A no-blame, problem-solving approach first identifies the problem in a matter-of-fact manner. The details and issues of blame are not belabored. It is important for the intervening adult to label the emotions of the victim. In certain cases it may be appropriate to ask the student what he/she imagined the victim was feeling. However, with some bullies this can quickly become a point for debate and therefore be ineffective. Many teens who bully have little developed empathy and their responses to questions regarding the victims feelings can be insensitive, disturbing, or insincere. These types of responses may provoke an emotional reaction from the adult disciplinarian and a no-win power struggle may ensue. Following the statement of the victims feelings, a solution is sought. It is important for the adult disciplinarian to maintain a no-blame stance as well as model a great deal of empathy for the victim. Throughout the interaction it can be helpful for the adult to have a constructive expectation that the bully will eventually come to feel empathy.

Handout 9A

Schools have used incident follow-up forms to assist students with empathy development as well as leaning to monitor and control their own emotions. A sample form is included as Handout 9A. Follow-up forms can be used as part of a re-entry plan or completed during in-school detention if students are suspended from school. Copies of the completed forms should be kept in the student's behavior file to monitor the student's progress.

Corrective Social Thinking/Empathy Development

Everyone makes errors in their thinking occasionally. However, when children's thinking patterns contain serious errors, it is extremely maladaptive for them as well as difficult for the people surrounding them. Children who bully typically have a number of antisocial personality traits and an unrealistic view of the world that can never be realized. Their perceptions center around beliefs that they must always be right, the world must revolve around them, winning is everything, good grades and being on top should be easy, and that people's feelings are unimportant. Children with this pattern of thinking are perpetually angry because their expectations of themselves and others don't match the reality of the world. Stanton Samenow, Ph.D. (1989), an expert in the area of antisocial personality development and treatment, advocates that students with thinking errors such as this should be identified early just as we identify students with other problems such as learning deficits. As with other difficulties, the earlier children can receive interventions and begin to remediate their problems, the less habituated their behaviors will be and the greater likelihood that change will occur.

In Dr. Samenow's books, *Inside the Criminal Mind* (1984), and *Before It's Too Late* (1989), he stresses that school personnel and parents need to understand the incorrect thinking patterns of these children so that they can assist them in making corrections. The following chart gives a summary of the common thinking errors as well as the corrective responses.

Errors in Thinking	
Error	**Stance or Response**
Victim Stance	
In general, attempts to blame others. "He started it." "I couldn't help it." "She didn't give me a chance."	Accept no excuses. Bring the focus back to the individual.
"I Can't" Attitude	
A statement of inability which is really a statement of refusal.	Realize "I can't" means "I won't" and usually refers to doing that which he doesn't feel like doing.
Lack of Concept of Injury to Others	
Does not stop to think how her actions can harm others (except physically); no concept of hurting others' feelings.	Point out how she is injuring others. Ask her how she would like to be treated this way.
Failure to Put Himself in the Place of Others	
Little or no empathy unless it is to con someone.	Give him examples of how you do this with him.
Lack of Effort	
Unwilling to do anything which he/she finds boring, disagreeable. Engages in self-pity and looks for excuses.	Effort is doing what you don't want to do and sometimes not doing what you want to do.

Errors in Thinking *(continued)*	
Error	**Stance or Response**
Refusal to Accept Obligation	
Says she "forgot." Doesn't see things as a obligation to begin with.	Point out she remembers that which she wants. Consequences for not attending to obligations.
Attitude of Ownership	
"If you don't give it to me, I'll take it." Expecting you to do what he/she wants. Treating others' property as though it were already his/hers (theft, "borrowing" without permission).	Clear consequences for theft, or borrowing without permission. Reverse the circumstances and ask him/her how he/she would like it if you did specific things.
Trust (no concept of)	
He blames you for not trusting him. Tries to make you feel as though it is your fault. Says that he can't trust you.	Point out why you don't trust him; he has betrayed your trust. Never let his betrayal of your trust go. Insist that trust must be earned.
Unrealistic Expectations	
Because she thinks something will happen, it must (thinking makes it so).	Try to get her to spell out what she expects. Point out when she is expecting too much and what might in fact happen. Help her prepare herself for disappointment.
Irresponsible Decision Making	
Makes assumptions. Does not find facts. Does not suspend judgement. Blames others when things go wrong.	Help him examine assumptions. Help him find the facts. Teach him that sometimes decisions cannot be made immediately.
Pride	
Refuses to back down even on little points. Insists on his/her point of view to the exclusion of all others.	Show, be an example that we all make mistakes and that it is important to learn from them.
Failure to Plan Ahead or Think Long Range	
Future is not considered unless it is to accomplish something illicit or else a fantasy of tremendous success.	Help him/her think ahead at every step. Point out how thinking ahead could have avoided an unpleasant situation.

Errors in Thinking *(continued)*	
Error	**Stance or Response**
A Flawed Definition of Success and Failure	
Success—being #1 overnight. Failure—being anything less than #1. She considers herself a "zero."	Help her see things in stages. Point out again and again that one learns from mistakes.
Fear of Being Put Down	
Does not take criticism without flaring up, blaming others.	Help him/her see if criticism has is no merit, ignore it. Show him/her that his/her expectations were in error to begin with.
Refusal to Acknowledge Fear	
Denies being afraid. Sees fear as weakness. Fails to see fear can be constructive.	The best you can do is to reassure him about some fears, and help him examine others. Help see fear has value—fear of a ticket keeps us from speeding.
Anger	
Anger is used to try to control people. Anger may take the form of direct threat, intimidation, assault, sarcasm, annoyance. Anger may go underground: "I don't get mad, I get even." Anger grows and spreads; anyone or anything may be a target.	Realize that anger is produced by fear, e.g., fear that something won't turn out as he/she expects, fear of a put-down, fear of anyone not meeting his/her expectations. When you help him/her be more realistic about the world (expectations of self and others), less occasion for anger.
Power Tactics	
Attempt to overcome the authority in any struggle. Enjoys fighting for power for its own sake (the issue may be secondary).	Call attention to her attempt to use power over others, e.g., "I don't like you trying to manipulate me" and then show how she is doing it (i.e., how you are "on" to her). Help differentiate power that is legitimate through positive achievements vs. her struggle just to emerge as "top dog."

Adapted from Stanton E. Samenow, "Errors in Thinking," unpublished, from conference, Dover, Delaware, 1999.

Dr. Samenow emphasizes that feeling words is not generally helpful when intervening with these children. Bullying teens tend to use their feelings as excuses. Dr. Samenow suggests that delving into the bully's anger would not be helpful because, until the distorted thought processes are more accurately aligned with the world, the anger will persist.

Prosocial Consequences

It is important to use prosocial consequences for disciplining bullies whenever possible. Prosocial discipline involves the use of consequences that include positive actions such as helping behavior or a caring act. While the student is involved in the beneficial activity, adults can reinforce him/her for the positive behavior. Positive reinforcement is the strongest mechanism for changing behavior. Research has historically shown that fear and punishment do not change behavior; they only suppress behavior. When the bullies experience attention (power) for doing positive behaviors, there is an increase chance they will learn to channel their energy into more positive leadership roles. Because bullies can have many antisocial personality traits and the possibility of underlying attachment disorders, isolation, time-outs, and suspension will likely have little impact on changing their behavior. In fact, these consequences may reinforce their ideas that adults are the enemy, worthless to them, and to be avoided.

Caring Majority

Once a caring majority of students is mobilized within the school, they can be a powerful intervention with bullies. Bullies depend on the attention of others for their power, and in middle school the approval and acceptance of the group is extremely important. If the group rejects bullying behaviors and collectively takes a stand against bullying, the student who bullies will not have the power to influence others. When an expectation of caring behavior becomes integrated into the climate of the school, students will intervene and admonish others who bully or act aggressively. This positive social pressure is a very strong deterrent to bullying.

Parents Who Bully

Research has shown that many aggressive children have aggressive parents. It is important for parents, who may act aggressively when advocating for their child, to have structure and boundaries which align with the rules and expectations for the rest of the school. Intimidating behaviors or verbalizations, profanity, or insults are not allowed in the school environment and that expectation needs to be upheld for adults as well as students. Teachers may need special help and/or support from administration in establishing and maintaining these respectful boundaries. It can be helpful to spend time in a faculty meeting explaining these boundaries and role playing respectful ways to uphold them.

It is important to remember that all parents want the best for their sons and daughters and often the dreams they hold for them are not compatible with the behaviors we experience at school. This can create a great deal of confusion for the parent who may repeatedly tell the school, "My child couldn't have done that." Also, these parents are often frustrated, confused, and feeling hopeless. Consider assisting them with connections to community resources for support.

Section Two: Supporting the Victims

The most effective intervention that can be used to support the victims of bullying is to focus on changing the climate of the entire school to one that does not tolerate bullying behaviors and instead supports and encourages caring actions and behaviors. Ideally, with the caring majority of staff and students in power in the school, bullying behaviors will decrease and victims will feel safe and supported.

However, for some victimized students who need more training and support than is offered through the *Bully-Proofing* program and curriculum, it is necessary to design interventions as a supplement to the general skills learned in the classroom. These interventions can be provided on an individual or group basis, depending on the school's resources. Working with students individually, though not usually time efficient, can be helpful in diagnosing the factors that are contributing to the student's victim status. Including them in a group can be an effective next step in helping them learn how to change their victim status.

The focus of this section is on group work with students who consistently find themselves in the role of victims and who would benefit from the extra support and instruction provided by a group intervention.

Benefits of Group Work With Victims

There are many benefits to working with victims in small group settings. Research in England on the effectiveness of group skills training for victims of bullying found that group work was successful and resulted in victims having increased self-esteem, more self-confidence, and better response strategies. They also reported being bullied less after the group ended (Rigby, 1996).

The primary advantage of a group opportunity is the comfort and safety it provides its members. Groups offer victims a chance to experience, perhaps for the first time, that they are not alone with their problems and that support is available. Other benefits that support groups provide their members include:

♦ An opportunity to experience acceptance by a group

♦ A setting in which to experience a sense of belonging

♦ A safe place to experience feelings

♦ A chance to practice new skills

♦ An opportunity to feel similar to peers, rather than different

♦ A chance to make new friends

For the above reasons, using the group format to work with victims of bullying makes the most sense in a large middle school setting. Not only are groups both time and cost efficient, but the group format can be especially advantageous for adolescents because of their developmental need to experience a sense of belonging and social connection. Providing students the opportunity to practice social skills in a group setting can be beneficial for any middle school student who is struggling to find his or her way.

Setting Up the Groups

Some general guidelines for forming victim support groups are listed below. However, schools need to evaluate their own resources including time, energy, and personnel in order to design group interventions that fit the students' needs. Please note that it is advisable to not use the term "victim" when labeling the group. Instead facilitators might want to label it a support group, social skills group, or friendship group so that members are not further stigmatized.

1. Select group members carefully based on the observations of teachers, support personnel, and parents. Be aware that boys may have a more difficult time reporting being bullied because of cultural pressures and can be overlooked as candidates for a victim support group.

2. Both passive and provocative victims (see Chapter Three) are candidates for group work. Specific information about interventions with provocative victims is included at the end of this section.

3. Consider forming same gender groups. Since boys and girls experience different kinds of bullying, especially in middle school, it is valuable to form same gender groups where members can practice interventions specific to the type of bullying they most commonly experience.

4. Keep groups small, with the ideal number being between six and eight members. It is best to have two adult facilitators,

but groups can be facilitated by one skilled facilitator who understands the bullying dynamic and its effects on victims.

Handout/Transparency 9A

5. Groups are voluntary, and parental permission is required for students to participate. An example of a parent permission form is included at the end of this chapter. (Handout/ Transparency 9A)

6. Plan for six to eight sessions, with groups meeting once or twice a week. It is a good idea to rotate the period of the day during which the group is held so that students don't continuously miss the same class. A follow-up session two weeks after the group has ended is recommended to evaluate the progress of the members and the carryover of the skills.

Role of Group Facilitators

The facilitator of a support group for victims of bullying should be a skilled individual who has both compassion for the student victim and the expectation that the victim can assume responsibility for changing his or her situation. The facilitator can be a mental health professional, counselor, teacher, or staff member who has been trained in group dynamics and understands the specific dynamics of bullying. It is important for facilitators to demonstrate empathy for the group members and also assist them in seeing how their own behaviors may be contributing to the problem.

The most important responsibility of the group facilitator is to create an emotionally safe climate within the group so that students can develop the trust required to share and learn from each other. As we know, victims of bullying experience feelings of low self-worth and do not trust that people are available for support. In the safe environment of the support group, the student has the opportunity to work on his or her problems without the fear of being blamed or ignored.

An effective group facilitator:

◆ Creates a safe climate in the group

◆ Provides emotional support

◆ Communicates a belief that problems can be solved

◆ Encourages students to take responsibility for their own behaviors

◆ Listens carefully and demonstrates empathy

◆ Establishes trust

◆ Encourages risk-taking

◆ Acknowledges and rewards successes

Just as a teacher sets the tone for creating a caring community in the classroom, the support group facilitator sets the tone for a successful and productive group experience.

Group Topics

Two important topics need to be addressed during the first group session—establishing group norms and confidentiality:

1. Establishing group norms. Basic norms for group behavior should be established in the first session. Some suggestions are: each person agrees to participate to the best of his or her ability, put-ups only allowed, each person commits to being supportive of other group members, and members agree to help keep the group safe.

2. Establishing rules of confidentiality. The facilitator discusses the rules of confidentiality with group members and explains what group members may talk about outside of group.

Another important support group topic is developing trust among group members. This is an ongoing process, but taking some time to do group activities and games that help to develop a sense of community and teamwork among the members is a valuable part of the group process. Team games and activities can also help members develop valuable social skills that enable them to connect with others. A valuable resource for these kinds of activities is the book *Initiatives, Games & Activities* by MacIver and McCarroll, 1996.

There are three main categories of skills that need to be addressed in a support group for victims of bullying. Listed in the following chart are the three categories and some related topics that are found to be most effective in working with victims.

Categories of Effective Skills in Working with Victims		
Improved Self-Esteem	**Improved Social Skills**	**Protective Strategies**
Self-esteem inventory	Characteristics of good friends	HA HA SO strategies
Identification of strengths and weaknesses	Characteristics of bad friends	Assertiveness skills
Identification of talents	How to make friends	"I" messages
Acknowledgments	How to keep friends	Nonverbal communication
Positive self-talk	Joining groups	Reading social cues
Positive visualizations	Friendly behaviors	Understanding bullying behaviors
Affirmations	Conversational skills	Conflict resolution skills
Appreciation of differences	Social manners	Confidence building
Value of joining		Identification of thinking errors

There are numerous resources available to educators that include specific activities related to the topics listed in the chart above. An excellent
source of activities that directly relate to bullying prevention is found
in the book *The Bully Free Classroom* by Allan Beane (1999). This
user-friendly manual includes over 100 tips and strategies for teachers
K–8 and can be easily adapted for group work with the victims of
bullying. Handout 9B provides a sample consent form for support/skills
group.

Handout/Transparency 9B

Methods to Use in Groups

There are many effective methods and strategies the facilitator can use
when conducting student support groups. The success of the method
depends on the facilitator's knowledge about and comfort with the strategy involved. Most important, the facilitator needs to be familiar with a
variety of techniques and flexible enough to follow the energy of the
group. As in most support group experiences, the ability of the facilitator
to perceive the needs of the group and to design activities accordingly is
an important factor in the group's success.

Listed below are some commonly used group methods and techniques:

1. **Discussion**

   Many concepts and topics related to bullying and the prevention
   of bullying can be learned through group discussions where victims of bullying learn from each other as well as practice basic
   conversational skills.

2. **Sharing personal stories and experiences**

   It is beneficial for victims of bullying to share their stories and
   experiences with each other. This allows students the opportunity to hear about others' experiences and to realize that they
   are not alone. Being able to tell one's "story" can be a valuable
   intervention, particularly for students who have been either too
   afraid to talk about problems or who have been ignored in the
   past. Balancing this technique with other methods is important
   so that the group members do not over-identify with the victim
   role. It is also valuable to use the students' own experiences as
   material for practicing new behaviors.

3. **Role play**

   Role playing is a dynamic way for victims to learn about their
   role in the bullying dynamic and for practicing bully prevention
   strategies. Acting out a bullying episode can give participants
   new insights into both their own and the bully's behavior, which
   can then stimulate ideas for change. Reverse role playing in
   which the victim plays the role of the bully can provide victims
   with a different viewpoint and empower them to begin to think
   differently about the problem. Using role playing sessions to

practice and reinforce the HA HA SO strategies is also a valuable way to increase students' protective skills.

4. **Reenactments**

   Similar to role playing, a group member shares a personal experience of being bullied and the group acts out the incident and then problem solves effective solutions.

5. **Symbolic modeling**

   This technique consists of students reading or viewing videotaped stories or articles that illustrate right and wrong behaviors in bullying situations (Bandura, 1969). Reading or viewing stories of bullying and observing how the characters handle the situation can result, for some students, in new understandings and eventually new behaviors.

6. **Behavioral contracting**

   Behavior contracting consists of group members making agreements about certain defined behaviors and then contracting to work on them outside of group. For example, a student may agree to practice a certain number of assertive responses during the week, which are then recorded on some kind of contract or form. Built into most contracts is some form of reward for completing the contract successfully.

7. **Cognitive methods**

   These include thinking-based strategies to avoid victimization, such as teaching students to identify their own thinking mistakes, improve their internal dialogue, and learn effective coping skills (Hoover and Oliver, 1996). Allowing time for students to discuss and practice the HA HA SO strategies can also be a valuable intervention with victims of bullying.

Using a variety of methods can make the group sessions interesting and fun and gives the students a variety of opportunities to work through their problems.

Interventions with Provocative Victims

The group method discussed in this section is an effective and efficient way of working with the victims of bullying, and is especially designed with the passive victim in mind. Provocative victims can be included in these groups if their distracting behaviors are managed and if other group members can model appropriate behaviors and focus on accomplishing their goals.

Following is a summary of the characteristics of both passive and provocative victims:

Characteristics of Victims	
Passive Victims	**Provocative Victims**
Most common type; easy to identify	Difficult to recognize as victims
Lack social skills	Lack social skills
Cry easily	Restless; irritate and tease others
Lack ability to use humor to diffuse conflict	Ineffectual aggressors—fight back but lose
Yield easily to bullying	Easily emotionally aroused
Anxious and insecure	Anxious and reactive
Unable to defend themselves	Maintain conflict and lose with distress and frustration
	May be diagnosed with ADHD and/or ODD

Because of the characteristics of provocative victims, they may need individual guidance and support before they can work in a group successfully. There are some particular skills and interventions that may help these students change their inappropriate behaviors. Listed below are some specific topics for the facilitator to address when working with provocative victims:

1. Teach them to avoid picking fights and the provoking behaviors that get them into conflicts.

2. Encourage them to examine the reasons for their provoking behaviors. Why did they get involved in the situation? What were they trying to achieve? Help them trace their behaviors backward to the original triggering thought or event.

3. Brainstorm with them about ways to get their needs met that are more socially acceptable. *Example:* If they're wanting to gain recognition, they could help tutor younger children in the school, join a club, or help a teacher with a project.

4. Teach them how to develop better social skills and more socially acceptable ways to make friends and feel accepted.

Provocative victims are challenging to work with because of their impulsivity and lack of ability to understand or take responsibility for their own part in creating problems. However, it is very important that the facilitator who works with these students understands that underneath their irritating and attention-seeking behaviors is the same anxiety and unhappiness that all victims experience. They, too, need to feel like valued and respected members of the school community who deserve to feel safe in the school environment.

Section Three: **Interventions With Parents**

All parents want their children to be happy and successful in school. Finding out that their child is having problems in school, either because he she is behaving like a bully or being victimized by a bully, is an upsetting and disappointing experience for parents and one that usually motivates them to want to help their child. Though some parents may react inappropriately when they are informed of their child's problems, it is usually because they feel concerned about how to help and want to avoid the pain of admitting to themselves that their child is, indeed, having difficulties.

This section is divided into two parts. The first part is designed for school personnel and discusses how schools can collaborate with parents to effectively address the problem of bullying. Specific guidelines for working with parents of bullies and parents of victims are included.

The second part is designed for parents and offers ideas and suggestions for working with children to help them prevent the problems associated with bullying. General ideas for raising caring and kind children in today's violence-prone world are discussed, and specific suggestions are offered on how to help children who have been identified as either victims or bullies. The family dynamics that can contribute to children becoming either victims or bullies are discussed as well, so that parents can understand their potential for both contributing to and solving the problems associated with childhood bullying.

Working With Parents

Parents are a crucial factor in the success of the *Bully-Proofing Your School* program. As with any school-wide program, the support of the parent community can be the deciding factor in whether or not the program becomes an established and valued part of the school culture.

Successful collaboration with the parent community is the key to developing the cooperation and support of the community at large and to spreading the word about the creation of a bully-free school.

Collaboration With Parents

It is wise to include parents in the beginning stages of the plans to implement the *Bully-Proofing* program. In Chapter Four, "Establishing a School-Wide Program," suggested steps for involving parents in the development of the program are listed and include inviting parents to be members of the school's Bully-Proofing Committee. Their opinions and ideas can be invaluable in helping to design a program which is responsive to the needs of the families in the school community.

It is the school's primary responsibility to communicate clearly and consistently with the parents about the *Bully-Proofing* program and to make it clear to the entire parent community that making the school safe and bully-free is a school-wide priority. Using every opportunity to publicize the school's "no tolerance, no nonsense" policy toward bullying, as well as its commitment to the caring majority of students, is a key element to the success of the program. Ongoing communication and educational opportunities for parents are also necessary in order to keep the momentum going and to encourage continued involvement by the parents.

Meeting With Parents

It becomes easier to meet with parents to talk about individual situations and problems when the school has made a concerted effort to publicize and educate parents about the school's *Bully-Proofing* program. Using the language of bully-proofing as an umbrella for addressing behavior issues serves to keep everyone focused on the commitment of the school to create a caring climate where everyone feels safe.

The following points are important to consider when meeting with parents about bully/victim problems:

1. Be sensitive and respectful of the parents' concerns. Keep in mind that all parents feel protective of their children and are disappointed to know that their child is having problems. Parents feel emotional about their children's problems whether they are in the bully or the victim role, and sensitive listening on the part of school personnel can help diffuse their initial, upset feelings.

2. Inform your parent community about who they can contact with their concerns regarding bully/victim problems. For general questions about the *Bully-Proofing* program they can be directed to someone on the Bully-Proofing Committee. For specific concerns about bullying situations involving their children, they need to know how and with whom to make the initial contact. It may be one of their child's teachers or the counselor, but knowing that there is a designated person for them to contact can help alleviate their anxiety.

3. Meet with parents individually when there is a specific bullying problem. It is a mistake to intervene by arranging to get the parents of the bully together with the parents of the victim. This usually escalates the emotions and the problem, and very little is accomplished because of the conflicting needs of the parents. It is much more successful to meet with each set of parents separately.

4. Use meetings with parents as an opportunity to educate them about the bullying dynamic. Helping them to understand about bullying and how it affects everyone involved can assist parents in viewing the problem from a broader perspective. Refer them

to the information in this section titled "Suggestions for Parents," which includes specific ideas about how to work with children who are either bullies or victims.

Meeting With Parents of a Bully

When organizing a meeting with parents of a child who has been acting like a bully, plan the meeting with the following suggestions in mind:

1. **Decide who is the most appropriate person to contact the parents.** It is a good idea to choose a staff member who has a working relationship with the parents and whom the parents respect. Decide which staff members will attend the meeting as well as an effective number. Parents can feel outnumbered if too many people are involved, which is counterproductive to a successful outcome.

2. **Expect that the parents may be angry and defensive when contacted.** Parents of bullies often respond defensively when contacted about their child's bullying behaviors and they, like the child, tend to blame others for causing the problem or for picking on the child.

3. **Avoid getting hooked by parental anger or defensiveness.** Listen calmly, and do not argue with the parents about the details of the situation. Instead, restate the school's commitment to safety and a non-tolerance approach to bullying. Remind parents that regardless of the situation, the school takes the stand that it is **never** appropriate for a child to solve the problem by bullying or harassing another student.

4. **Use the no-nonsense approach when talking about the situation and the consequences.** Sometimes using phrases like, "I'm sure you understand that our commitment is to having a safe school environment" will help encourage parents to join with you in the problem solving. Do your best not to get engaged in processing or over-discussing the details of the situation.

5. **Design a plan together with the parents for ways to work with their child, both at school and at home.** Specific strategies for teaching the child how to use power appropriately can be designed, so that the parent leaves the meeting with some concrete ideas as well as a sense of collaboration with the school staff.

6. **If the parent becomes verbally abusive, or appears to be too angry to continue, politely and assertively state that the meeting cannot continue.** Suggest that he or she come back another time and that you would be happy to meet when the parent is calmer and able to problem solve with you. Discuss this with your administrator ahead of time to ensure support.

Meeting With the Parents of a Victim

Whether you call the parents or the parents contact you, understand that the parents of a child who has been victimized are often emotionally upset and concerned, as they have every right to be. If their child is being victimized, then their child is not safe at school, and it is the school's responsibility to take action.

The following are some suggestions for meeting with parents of children who are targets of bullying behaviors:

1. **Listen patiently and carefully.** Ask questions and talk with the parents to explore the details of the situation and to identify the contributing factors. It is helpful to ask about the child's history to determine if the child has been victimized previously and if so, how it was resolved.

2. **Assure the parents that the commitment of the school is to each child's safety and that something will be done to help their child.** Parents of students who are victimized are often very involved in their children's lives because they don't trust that the school can handle the situation. Assurance that the school will work together with them and their child can help to reduce their fears.

3. **Design a plan together of specific strategies to help the child both at school and at home.** Encourage the parent to let their child work with school personnel to alleviate the problem at school, while they concentrate their efforts on practicing strategies in the home environment. It is important that the parents communicate their trust in their child's problem-solving abilities and the school's ability to intervene successfully. Refer them to the section on "Suggestions for Parents" for ideas.

4. **Communicate with the parents frequently in the beginning of the process.** Have the child keep a weekly journal of strategies tried at school so he/she can share these with his/her parents. Parents who are anxious about their child's safety benefit from communication with the school about their child's progress.

Suggestions for Parents

Raising Caring Children

The most important factor in raising kind children whose caring acts contribute to a peaceful society is what one researcher calls "the indestructible link of caring between parent and child." (APA, What Makes Kids Care?) Children who feel loved and cared for by the adults who raise them are then able to turn around and demonstrate empathy and caring towards others in their daily lives. Children who experience this "link of caring" learn to feel confident in their own abilities to successfully navigate the world and are able to cope with the challenges of daily living.

Besides the establishment of this very important caring link between parent and child, there are several other things parents can do to raise children who are caring and responsible members of society (APA, What Makes Kids Care?; APA, Raising Children to Resist Violence).

1. **Model appropriate behaviors**

   Model caring and kind behaviors for your children. Be consistently caring and compassionate yourself and model kindness in your interactions with your own children and with the other people in your life. Use daily opportunities to model peaceful behaviors and nonviolent problem-solving strategies. Remember that your actions speak much louder than your words, and your actual behavior as a parent carries much more weight than anything you can say or tell your children to do.

2. **Appreciate and reward caring behaviors**

   Make sure to acknowledge and reward your children for their kind behaviors. Make it clear to them that you value behaviors and choices which contribute to peaceful and nonviolent problem solving and focus on "catching" them doing caring acts. Conversely, when they act inappropriately be clear that you do not approve of these kinds of behaviors and use the opportunity to remind them of your expectations about how to behave toward others.

3. **Use nonphysical methods of discipline**

   Use nonphysical methods of discipline with your children such as time-outs, loss of privileges, and groundings. Punishing them with physical force, such as hitting or slapping, teaches them violent, rather than peaceful problem solving and often results in feelings of humiliation and rage. Children who are disciplined with physical punishment may attempt to solve their own problems with their peers through the use of physical force, which can result in serious consequences for everyone involved. Parents who themselves experienced physical punishment when they were children need to be careful not to repeat inappropriate patterns with their own children.

4. **Teach about bullying and the importance of taking a stand against it**

   Teach your children about the dynamic of bullying so that they understand what it is and the different forms it can take. Knowledge is power, and children who have been taught about bullying and its characteristics can better avoid becoming victims of it. In addition to understanding bullying, teach your children the importance of both protecting themselves from violence and taking a stand against violence they witness. Make it clear to your children that you value their ability to stand up for both themselves and others.

5. **Be involved in your children's lives**

   Stay involved in your children's lives, in spite of their messages to you that they want you to leave them alone or supervise them less. It is important to gradually give your child more freedom with maturity, but be careful not to drop out of the parental role too early in your young adolescent's life, despite protests and complaints. Know where your children are and who they are with. Call parents of their friends and make yourself known as an involved parent who expects children to be supervised by adults at appropriate times. Encourage your children to be involved in clubs and activities and do as much as possible to prevent your child being faced with extended periods of unsupervised time with nothing to do. Despite their protests to the contrary, children want adults to be interested in and involved with their lives so that they know they are loved and cared for.

6. **Monitor your child's involvement with violence in the media**

   Monitor the amount of violence your children are exposed to through the media. There have been many studies done on the effects of TV violence on children. In general, the research (APA, Violence on Television) shows that the three main effects on children of watching violent TV are that they:

   ♦ Become less sensitive to the pain and suffering of others

   ♦ Become more fearful of the world

   ♦ Behave more aggressively towards others

   It makes sense that children who spend unsupervised time viewing violent television, movies, and video games can eventually become desensitized to violence in general. As a result, they can gradually lose their empathy for others, as well as increase their tendency to solve their own problems using forms of aggressive behavior.

   To combat these effects of media violence, parents can do the following things:

   ♦ Limit or ban particular TV shows, movies, and video games

   ♦ Watch the shows in question with your children so that you are aware of the content

   ♦ Discuss violent incidents in shows or movies with your children and talk about alternatives to the violence portrayed

   ♦ Encourage the viewing of TV shows and movies that depict caring and altruistic behaviors and characters

   ♦ Encourage the reading of books that include realistic story lines and characters who know right from wrong

Family Dynamics

Parents who are willing to look at their own family's dynamics to help understand their child's problems are not only courageous, but are truly demonstrating the "indestructible link of caring" discussed earlier. As difficult as it is for parents to learn that their child is having problems, either with aggression or victimization, it is important for them to neither overreact nor underreact, but to look at the problem realistically and try to understand the situation. It is important for parents to remember not to blame themselves for their children's problems, but to realize that there are many factors which contribute to a child acting as either a bully or a victim. Parents who truly want to help are willing to look at the ways they may have contributed or are contributing to the problem.

Research has been done to try to identify the family dynamics and patterns that may contribute to children who demonstrate problems associated with aggression or victimization. There is no clear-cut formula that can predict that one particular set of family dynamics leads to a child who bullies and another set leads to a child who is victimized. But there are several factors that have been consistently identified as contributing to each of the problems.

Bullies and Family Patterns

The following is a list of familial factors that have been shown to contribute to a child's aggressive and bullying behaviors:

- Rejection and negative attitudes toward child by one or both parents

- Lack of nurturing and emotional support for child; poor bonding between parent and child; emotional issues in family ignored or not addressed

- Parental disharmony and conflict

- Extensive physical punishment
    - Harsh, punitive punishments intended to control and coerce

- Inconsistent discipline
    - Failure to set consistent behavioral expectations—child's inappropriate aggressive acts are sometimes punished, sometimes condoned
    - Parents' discipline based on their mood at the moment rather than on the child's behavior

- Family is socially isolated; lacking outside support system

Identifying these contributing factors can assist parents in examining their own parenting styles and practices that may be contributing to the problem. Also, studies show that parents who themselves were bullies as children often tend to raise children who are bullies, making it even more important for adults to examine their own history and experiences to identify any factors that may be contributing to the problem.

Victims and Family Patterns

The following is a list of familial factors that have been shown to contribute to a child's becoming a victim. Though some of the characteristics are similar to those found in the families of bullies, others are unique to families of victimized children:

- Family members are entangled and family roles are not clearly defined

- Parents are overly emotionally involved in their child's problems

- Parents are overprotective; their eagerness to solve child's problems prevents child from developing age-appropriate problem solving and social skills

- Problems in parental relationship

- Problems with relationships outside the home

When parents are too eager to solve their child's problems rather than letting the child problem solve on his or her own, the child gradually becomes disempowered and starts to believe that he or she is incapable of handling difficult situations after all. It is easy to see how this can result in a child being victimized at school where parents are not available to rescue the child from the bullying situations that occur.

How Parents Can Help

As we have learned, bullying that is ignored by adults and therefore allowed to continue has serious consequences for both the bully and the victim. Adults who choose to deny that the problem exists or who avoid dealing with it in the hope that it will just go away are doing a grave disservice to all children who are forced to live in the climate of fear created by bullying.

The parents' primary responsibility is to model a healthy relationship and problem-solving skills for their children. If a child is behaving like a bully or a victim, there are things parents can do to change the child's unhealthy patterns and to encourage healthier and more successful choices.

If Your Child Is a Bully—Warning Signs

If your child is a bully, there are several warning signs you can look for that help to pinpoint the problem. A child who is acting like a bully can demonstrate the following behaviors:

- Often irritable and angry with others

- Believes it is OK to be mean to others if it means getting what he or she wants

- Blames others and takes no responsibility for the problem; i.e., "he made me do it"

♦ Shows little or no empathy for other people's problems or hardships; has difficulty showing remorse

♦ Demonstrates faulty thinking; i.e., "I am entitled to get my way no matter what"

In his book *Before It's Too Late* (Samenow, 1989), the author discusses the importance of early interventions with children who exhibit behavior problems: "Corrective measures must be taken as early as possible with the child who is already showing signs of heading in a direction that will bring him into repeated and increasingly serious conflict with the world around him" (p. 8). Parents who intervene early with their children who are exhibiting signs of being bullies can help to solve the problem before it becomes serious.

If Your Child Is a Bully—What You Can Do

1. **Take the problem seriously.** Resist a tendency to deny the problem or to discount the seriousness of it. Avoid denial thinking such as "Boys will be boys" or "Bullying is just a natural part of growing up."

2. **Listen carefully and check out the facts.** Do not believe everything your child tells you. Children who bully are good at manipulating adults and can be very artful at weaving a story that makes them look innocent.

3. **Resist the tendency to blame yourself.** Hold your child responsible for his or her own choices.

4. **Consequent your child appropriately for bullying behaviors.** Make it very clear that you will not tolerate mean or unkind actions and be consistent in your discipline as well as your expectations.

5. **Explore the reasons for your child's negative behaviors.** Get professional help if necessary for your child and/or your family.

6. **Teach and model appropriate, nonviolent problem-solving strategies and solutions.**

7. **Teach and model empathy.** Provide opportunities to talk with your child about his or her feelings as well as the feelings of others. Use media resources such as books, TV, and movies to develop empathy and compassion for others.

8. **Work to build a positive relationship with your child.** Encourage your child's realistic perceptions of self-worth and self-esteem.

9. **Reward your child for positive, caring actions and for peaceful problem solving.**

Children who are bullies need their parents' help and support in correcting their behaviors and negative interactions with people. A child bully who is now an adult and presently serving time in a federal prison was interviewed by researchers to help shed light on the problem of bullying and how children develop into bullies. When asked, as he looked back to his childhood, if there was anything anyone could have done to help him turn his life around he responded, "I believe the only thing that would have helped me then would have been teaching me about self-esteem and empathy and constant reinforcement of those ideals" (Fried, 1996, p. 94).

If Your Child Is a Victim—Warning Signs

There are several warning signs that indicate that your child is being bullied. Some are obvious physical signs or psychosomatic symptoms; others are behavioral and can be less obvious to parents. It is important to remember that a child who is being repeatedly victimized often feels shame and embarrassment about the situation. The resulting hopelessness can prevent the child from telling anyone about the problem.

If your child is being bullied, be aware of the following warning signs (Rigby, 1996):

- ◆ Unexplained marks or bruises
- ◆ Damaged or missing belongings
- ◆ Health complaints such as stomachaches, headaches
- ◆ Avoidance of school
- ◆ Drop in attendance or grades
- ◆ Change in eating or sleeping patterns
- ◆ Social isolation/withdrawal
- ◆ Increased anxiety and worry

These symptoms may indicate that your child is being bullied and may be a signal that your help is needed in solving the problem.

If Your Child Is a Victim—What You Can Do

One of the most dangerous consequences of being bullied is that the child who is the target of the bullying loses self-esteem and actually starts to believe that he or she deserves it. Caught in the cycle of low self-esteem and shame, the victim often remains silent. Parents who understand the dynamics of bullying and are observant of their child's moods and behaviors can intervene in several ways when their child does reach out for help.

1. **Listen carefully to your child's reports of being bullied.** Be sympathetic and take the problem seriously. Be careful not to overreact or underreact. Know the difference between normal conflict and bullying. (See Handout/Transparency 9I.)

2. **Do not blame the victim.** This is not the time to challenge your child about why he or she didn't "do something" or "try something different." When a child does get the courage to report

Handout/Transparency 9I

bullying it is not appropriate to criticize them about causing it or not handling it correctly.

3. **Get the necessary information—who, what, when, where, and how often.** This will help guide your discussion and problem-solving efforts.

4. **Educate your child about bullying and bullies.** Help your child put the problem in perspective and depersonalize it.

5. **Brainstorm and practice strategies with your child to avoid victimization.** Try the HA HA SO Strategies—Help, Assert, Humor, Avoid, Self-Talk, Own It. (See Chapter Six for a detailed description of these strategies.)

6. **Boost your child's self-esteem by praising him or her for confronting the problem.** Encourage your child to think of ways to solve the problem and acknowledge any successes and attempts at new responses and activities.

7. **Encourage your child to make friends in school and to get involved in school activities.** Since children who are victimized tend to be socially isolated, it is important for parents to teach and model effective social and joining skills.

8. **Determine the seriousness of the situation and contact appropriate people.** If the bullying is moderate to severe and happening at school, contact school personnel for assistance. Your child may resist your involvement, but moderate to severe bullying requires adult intervention.

Developing a Plan

Whether your child is experiencing problems because he or she is a bully or a victim, it is important to develop a plan together before serious problems occur. It is very important to communicate to your child that you are willing to support him/her in effective ways to solve the problem. The book *Bully-Proofing Your Child, A Parent's Guide* (Garrity, Baris, Porter, 2000) is an excellent source for parents and includes several strategies and interventions for bully-proofing your child. Developing a plan together gives you child the confidence to face the problem and begin taking action to deal with it.

If the plan involves contacting school personnel about your child being the target of bullying, it is important to remember that how you approach the school will often determine the successful outcome of the problem. An important first step is to ask your child what adults he or she has already gone to for help with their bullying problem. If your child hasn't talked to any adults in the school, help identify adults he or she can trust and go to for help.

One of your child's teachers is often a good initial contact to make. Remember, the more you can encourage and model for your child how to get help from the adults at school, the more confident your child will become in his or her abilities to handle the problem. If the problem is not resolved at this level, it may be necessary for you to go the next level and contact an administrator in the school. Just remember to remain level-headed and calm and to approach the situation with an intention to work together to resolve the problem in the best interests of your child. Sometimes parents are so upset and understandably angry about their child's situation that they forget to model rational and appropriate problem-solving strategies. Confronting school personnel in an angry and threatening way is much less successful than approaching the school assertively in the spirit of cooperation.

School districts are generally very responsive to parents' concerns and ideas. Parents play an important role in building school communities that provide safe environments for all children. Besides taking a stand for their own child, parents can be very effective in taking a stand for all the students in the school by educating and encouraging school personnel to adopt school-wide bully prevention programs such as *Bully-Proofing Your School.*

Section Four: Transportation—The Bus

The bus ride to and from school is a particularly precarious one for many middle school students. Most young teens are faced with a walk to the bus stop, where they wait, unsupervised, until the bus arrives. Once there, they board the bus only to jockey for a seat with up to 60 other middle schoolers sitting three to a seat while wearing coats and carrying backpacks or school projects. It is a wonder that they all even fit into the big yellow boat. And there they sit, with one adult to supervise, and that adult has his/her back to the group the entire trip to school. It is not surprising that many young teens feel very unsafe on the bus. This environment is ripe for harassment, intimidation, territoriality, and dangerous pranks. There are several strategies that can help make the bus ride a safer, kinder place for middle school students.

Include Drivers in the Caring Community

The school's bus drivers frequently feel as isolated from the school as the students do on their ride to and from home. It is highly recommended that ways be found to include them in the school community. Increasing the bus driver's sense of belonging to, and communication with the school will go a long way in connecting the students on the bus as well. The following ideas have been successful in accomplishing this. It is important for your school to evaluate the schedules of the drivers to establish a time that the Bully-Proofing Cadre or other school staff can meet with **all** the drivers. Frequently drivers arrive at schools in the morning prior to the start of their route or early in the afternoon before students are released from school.

Bus Driver Breakfasts/Afternoon Teas

Drivers are invited to a welcome breakfast or afternoon tea to get acquainted with school personnel. Each driver is acknowledged and thanked for the difficult job that he/she does. It is helpful to spend some time listening to their past experiences driving the school bus or in other areas of work, as well as any other interests they want to share. Breakfasts or afternoon teas are ideally scheduled each quarter to facilitate on-going communication and develop caring relationships. During the meetings, the following topics can be covered:

- An overview of the *Bully-Proofing* program is explained. The important role of the drivers in the development of the caring community is emphasized.

- Drivers are encouraged to learn each of the student's names. They are asked to introduce themselves to the students and to greet them as they board each day. Drivers are informed about the bullying dynamics and how anonymity breeds bullying.

- A laminated list of the Bully-Proofing Guidelines is given to each driver to post on his/her bus.

- The process for referring students with behavioral problems is reviewed.

- Group problem solving is done focusing specifically on the ways to improve communication between the driver, students, deans, or other disciplinarians, and the Bully-Proofing Cadre.

- Drivers are informed that students consistently report feeling safer on the bus when a seating chart is in place. School staff encourage the use of seating charts and offer their assistance in establishing them with the drivers, as well as working with drivers to maintain the seating charts.

- Drivers are asked to share successful strategies they have used in the past.

Disciplinary Strategies

Handout 9C

Parents need to be informed of the rules and expectations regarding bus behaviors. They can be instrumental in reinforcing the door-to-door caring community policies. An effective means for doing this is a parent letter, Handout 9C. Other ways to inform parents is to include articles in the school newspaper or student handbook.

Encourage the use of seating charts. Anonymity on the bus is a big problem. Students don't know each others' names, and when being harassed, many students have difficulty remembering details of the aggressor's appearance. Seating charts help tremendously in these circumstances. It is also recommended that the school keep a notebook of student pictures organized by bus number somewhere available for easy reference. This enables students to report incidents when they do not know the names of the students involved. Remember, you will be counting on the student and bus drivers to participate in establishing a safe and caring school.

The Bully-Proofing Guidelines should be posted on each bus (Handout/ Transparency 9F). It is important to empower the bus drivers and give them some leverage for dealing with students' behaviors, both positive and negative on a daily basis. A behavioral warning form (Handout 9D) gives bus drivers with a way to communicate with the student and school when behavioral expectations are not being met. This provides the opportunity for the bus driver and school to intervene with the student regarding his/her behavior before the behavior escalates into a referral with more severe consequences.

Handout 9F
Handout/Transparency 9D

Drivers are encouraged to use school personnel for behavior management strategies with particularly difficult students or situations.

Drivers are encouraged to attend a bully-proofing training session at the school. This session should be scheduled at a time the bus drivers can conveniently attend.

Bus Behavior and Driver Recognition

It is important to find ways to acknowledge students' positive and caring behaviors on the bus. One way to foster this is to keep track of behavior referrals. The bus with the least number of referrals (or those with no referrals) are rewarded and/or publicly acknowledged. The bus that makes the greatest improvement may also be recognized. Rewards for students can include:

- ♦ Gift certificates to the school store
- ♦ Small school supplies (pencils, pens, etc.)
- ♦ No homework pass for one night
- ♦ Extra credit in one class
- ♦ Tickets to a baseball game
- ♦ Tickets for one night of roller skating
- ♦ Tickets to a special dance
- ♦ Tickets to a special showing of a movie

Bus drivers should be included in any school-wide student acknowledgment programs. For example, drivers can be given "I Caught You Caring" acknowledgment forms to complete when they see students reaching out to help others. See Handout 9E. They turn the forms into the school's office and a weekly drawing is held whereby five students are given rewards. The other acknowledgment forms can be displayed in the school hallways on a Caring Wall or in a Caring Corner.

Handout 9E

Ask bus drivers for their ideas regarding ways to extend the caring community onto the buses. Your bus drivers should be included in rewards received by the bus, i.e., baseball tickets, movie tickets. Also include bus drivers in your school "Secret Santa" exchange, football pools, and picnics, and do special unexpected favors to acknowledge them throughout the year.

Section Five: New Students

The numbers of students changing schools has increased dramatically in the past ten years. Depending on geographical location and rental housing availability, some schools have as much as a 50% student mobility rate per year. No matter what the percentage, students who are new to a school can have a dramatic impact on the climate of the school.

Students who are new to a middle school are faced with issues such as which social group they will fit into and/or who will accept them, who can they trust and get help from, and where and/or who to avoid. Some mobile students become social chameleons and can easily size up the school's climate and find a place to fit in. Others may lack the social skills necessary to note the new school's cultural differences and/or assert themselves in ways to make new friends. These often timid students will commonly be slow to connect with adults as well as peers, which leaves them isolated and easy prey for bullies. Still another group of mobile students may lack the motivation to reach out and attach to others at school because indifference has settled in as they wait with trepidation for word of their next move. They may project an attitude of, "I'm tough so leave me alone," and "I don't need anyone." These students may resort to bullying to compete for their position in the social structure or as a means of establishing themselves as "tough" so as not to be bothered by others.

Becoming involved in the school culture is a primary factor in keeping a student from being "At-Risk." When students miss the introduction to the school year, they usually miss critical information needed to connect to the school community. Clubs, tutoring, peer mediation, sports teams, student government, all of these are usually explained those precious first days of school. It is no wonder that so many new students don't become involved in the school during their first year after a move. Equally important is the relationship building that occurs among students and adults during the first weeks of school. Additionally, students who enter during the school year may have missed the bully-proofing groups and will not have the information regarding the school's stance on bullying as well as critical strategies to avoid victimization.

Parents are another important consideration in intervening with new students. Parents who have recently moved are having to adjust to new school procedures, personnel, and resources which vary considerably from school district to school district. Just like the new students, new parents may not know where or whom to ask for help, or the resources that are available to them and their son or daughter.

This New Student section includes ideas to assist this population in three ways.

1. A welcome letter to parents.

2. Suggested methods for delivery of the lessons.

3. A four session curriculum which provides a brief overview of the Bully-Proofing concepts as well as activities to help students connect with each other and the school.

New Student Parent Letter

It is very helpful to send a letter to the parents of new students that outlines the *Bully-Proofing* program and the new student groups. This letter can reinforce the important role that parents play in establishing and maintaining a safe and caring school.

Additionally, the letter should communicate the expectation that bullying behaviors are not tolerated and that caring acts are rewarded. A sample letter is presented in Handout 9F.

Handout 9F

Delivery of the New Student Lessons

Lessons can be delivered in many ways depending on the number of new students within your school, your school resources, and your creativity. Below is a list of possible methods for meeting with these students with a minimum of coursework disruption.

♦ Hold groups every quarter. All of the "New Students" who began attending the previous quarter attend the next series of groups. Rotate group times through four different class periods so that students won't miss any class more than one time. Try to keep group size to fifteen.

♦ Hold groups every semester with the same parameters as above.

♦ Establish a "New Student" seminar which new students attend for one quarter during home room or guidance time.

♦ Establish a "New Student" seminar which is one elective and is mandatory for all new students. Course.material can include community building activities, bully-proofing lessons, review of school clubs and other activities, and entrance exams such as "levels" testing.

New Student Curriculum

The four new student lessons are designed to build a sense of connection and to provide a brief overview of the basic bully-proofing concepts. If time allows, it would be highly beneficial to integrate community building activities into the lessons. Books such as, *Initiatives, Games, & Activities* and *100 Ways to Increase Self-Esteem in the Classroom* are good, easy to use resources (See Resource section).

Helping new students and their parents feel included, valued, and comfortable in your school community will significantly improve their experience as well as the overall climate of your school.

Getting Acquainted

Materials

♦ Chart paper

♦ Markers

♦ Note cards

♦ **Handout/Transparency 9G:** Bully-Proofing Guidelines posted in classroom

♦ Overhead projector (optional)

Objectives

♦ Increase student comfort level and school connection

♦ Introduce basic concepts of *Bully-Proofing* program

Steps

I. Welcome Activities

    A. Welcome students to your school. Make summarative statements to students letting them know you are happy to have them as members of your school community. Let students know the details regarding the time, place, and number of your sessions. State the goals for the lessons. Emphasize that one of the goals is to inform new students about how your school works and where and how to get help. Invite each of them to be part of your school's caring community.

B. Geographical activity. Elicit information from students about where they lived before coming to your school. Record responses on chart paper, chalkboard or use a United States map, if available. Questions for discussion:

- ◆ How many of you are from (name of your state)?

- ◆ How many of you are from out of state?

- ◆ What other state ?

- ◆ How many of you are from out of the country?

- ◆ What other country are your from?

- ◆ Who has moved more than one time?

- ◆ How many times have you moved?

Summarize the information gathered about each student's background and acknowledge the variety of their experiences.

C. Discuss the new students' experiences

1. Ask students: "What is the one thing you all have in common?"

2. Elicit response that the one thing they have in common is that they are all new students at (your school).

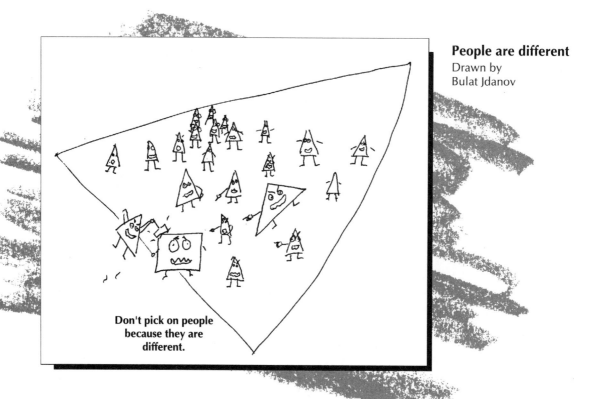

Don't pick on people because they are different.

People are different
Drawn by
Bulat Jdanov

3. Ask students to think back, visualize in their mind's eye what it has been like being a new student.

   ◆ How did you feel when you registered?

   ◆ How did you feel the first day you started school?

   ◆ Do you remember what it was like when you walked into your first class alone?

   ◆ How did others treat you?

   ◆ Were people welcoming or helpful?

   ◆ What has been the hardest part of starting school here?

   ◆ Do you think others know what it's like to be new here?

   ◆ Now that you have been through this experience, what would make it easier for other new students?

   ◆ What would you have liked to have happened?

   Discuss students' responses to the last question.

D. Introduce the *Bully-Proofing Your School* Program

   1. Relate the previous student responses to the important concepts of bully-proofing.

      "It sounds as if you want this to be a school where you feel welcome and respected. We agree. That is why we have adopted a program called Bully-Proofing. We want everyone to feel accepted, safe, and cared for here at school. This is your school now. And you are a very important part of making this the kind of community where people feel safe and cared for."

   2. Explain the following bully-proofing concepts:

      ◆ The power of the school is shared between students and adults to make the school a safe place.

      ◆ 85% of the students in your school are great, caring kids who are neither bullies nor victims—just strong young people willing to do the right thing. This is the caring majority. This 85% needs to have the power in the school. Not the bullies.

      ◆ Bullying is not tolerated at school, and there are swift and immediate consequences for bullying.

      ◆ No one deserves to be harassed or bullied.

Handout/Transparency 9G

II. Group leader reviews the Bully-Proofing Guidelines, Handout/Transparency 9G

III. Journal Activity

On note cards, have students write about a time they were bullied or felt uncared for, either at school or on the way to or from school. Encourage students to include details about **how** it made

HANDOUT/TRANSPARENCY 9G
Bully-Proofing Guidelines

1. **Respect yourself and others.**

2. **Contribute to a healthy and safe learning environment.**

3. **Use empathy and extra effort to include others.**

4. **Take a stand for what is right.**

5. **Encourage creative and peaceful problem solving.**

6. **Follow all school rules.**

them feel. Instruct students to write their names on their cards and put a star in the corner if they do not want the card read anonymously to the class at the beginning of your next session.

Bullies And Victims

Materials

♦ Chart paper

♦ Markers

♦ **Handout/Transparency 9H:** Types of Bullying Behaviors

♦ **Handout/Transparency 9I:** Normal Conflict vs. Bullying

♦ Overhead projector

> Much of my early life I simply felt on the outside looking in. Kids pointed and made racial digs. Other times I simply felt invisible.

Objectives

♦ Establish expectations for group participation

♦ Develop understanding of "bully" and "victim" concepts

♦ Develop understanding of normal conflict vs. bullying

Steps

I. Review Journal Assignment

  A. Read aloud note cards from Lesson One. Be careful to keep the student's name anonymous. Remember not to read any cards with a star in the corner. Make supportive statements that build empathy for the victims as well as emphasize that nearly **everyone** will be targeted by a bully at one time or another.

  B. Establish behavioral expectations for group meetings.

    1. Respect for self and others

    2. Participate—in your own way and style

    3. While sharing stories or experiences, do not mention any particular names of individuals or groups. Instead, say, "I know someone who . . . "

II. Explore and Categorize Bullying Behaviors

  A. Ask students to generate a list of bullying behaviors. Group student responses into the categories below. Use a transparency for review if desired. (Handout/Transparency 9H).

CHART
Handout/Transparency 9H

III. Explore and Discuss the Concept of "Bully"

  A. Elicit ideas from students about the characteristics of a bully. Students will mention **physical** characteristics such as boy vs. girl, big vs. small. Use this discussion to dispel myths about bullies. Reinforce the idea that bullies have **no particular physical characteristic**, but they **do have some similar behaviors**. Bring the focus to bullying behaviors. The facilitator makes a list of the student responses on chart paper which can be reported and reviewed in Lesson Three. Ask students:

    ♦ Do all bullies look alike?

    ♦ Are they all boys or girls?

    ♦ What is the body language of a bully?

    ♦ How do bullies walk and talk?

  B. Discuss the reasons students bully. Make sure the following reasons are included in the discussion. Students who bully:

    ♦ Gain power

    ♦ Gain popularity and attention

HANDOUT/TRANSPARENCY 9H
Types of Bullying Behaviors

Physical Aggression: Hitting, kicking, destroying property

Social Aggression: Spreading rumors, excluding from group, silent treatment

Verbal Aggression: Name calling, teasing, threatening, intimidating phone calls

Intimidation: Graffiti, a dirty trick, taking possessions, coercion

Written Aggression: Note writing, graffiti, slam books

Sexual Harassment: Comments or actions of a sexual nature which are unwelcome and make the recipient uncomfortable. *Examples:* rumors of a sexual nature, inappropriate touching, grabbing, comments about someone's body

Racial and Ethnic Harassment: Comments or actions containing racial or ethnic content which are unwelcome and make the recipient uncomfortable. *Examples:* ethnic jokes, racial name calling, racial slurs

◆ Act out problems from home

◆ Copy what someone else does that they admire

◆ Perceive it as fun

◆ Have low self-esteem (sometimes)

IV. Explore and Develop the Concept of "Victim"

A. Elicit ideas from students about the characteristics of a victim. Students will mention physical characteristics such as boy vs. girl, big vs. small. Ask students:

◆ Do all victims look alike?

◆ Are they all boys or girls?

◆ What is the body language of a victim?

◆ How do victims walk and talk?

Use this discussion to dispel myths about victims. Reinforce the idea that victims have **no particular physical characteristics**. But

CHART

they **do have some similar behaviors** that will make them more likely to be victimized. Bring the focus to behaviors that can lead to victimization. The facilitator makes a list of the student responses on chart paper. (Make sure that the starred categories are included in the student's list and briefly discuss each.)

What are the characteristics of a victim?

1. Alone and isolated

2. Trouble making friends

3. Small or weak or appear unsure of self

4. Cry easily and be unable to stick up for self

5. May have suffered abuse at home

6. May have difficulty learning

7. Sometimes be irritable and provoke other students

8. May try to fight back, still lose and get very upset

9. Willing to keep quiet

10. New to school

11. Between friend groups

B. Generate a list of the emotional consequences of the victim. *How do you think someone feels (initially and long term) when he or she has been the victim?*

1. Drop in self-esteem

2. Fearful attitude

3. Withdrawn or sad

4. Headache, stomachache, fatigue, or other physical complaints

5. Panic and react with irrational retaliation

6. Fear of school

V. Identify the Difference Between Normal Conflict and Bullying

A. Ask students if they know the difference between normal conflict and bullying. As students share ideas, the facilitator writes them on chart paper with two colors—one for normal conflict and one for bullying. This chart can be left in the room throughout the lessons. (Use Handout/Transparency 91 for review if desired.)

CHART

Handout/Transparency 91

Emphasize the difference in power. This difference can be a red flag for students who may be experiencing more subtle types of bullying and not recognizing it, i.e., groups of girls.

HANDOUT/TRANSPARENCY 91
Normal Conflict versus Bullying

Normal Conflict	versus	Bullying
Equal power; friends	vs.	Imbalance of power; not friends
Happens occasionally	vs.	Repeated negative actions
Accidental	vs.	Purposeful
Not serious	vs.	Serious—threat of physical harm or emotional or psychological hurt
Equal emotional reaction	vs.	Strong emotional reaction on part of the victim
Not seeking power or attention	vs.	Seeking power, control
Not trying to get something	vs.	Trying to gain material things or power
Remorse—takes responsibility	vs.	No remorse—blames victim
Effort to solve the problem	vs.	No effort to solve problem

B. Discuss when, where, and how to get adult help. Ask students:

♦ When do you seek adult help and in what situations is it appropriate for adults to intervene?

♦ Where or who could you go to at our school for help?

♦ What are some ways you can ask for help without your peers (or the bully) knowing about it?

1. Emphasize the need to get adult help with moderate to severe incidences of bullying—particularly if there is **any** chance of someone getting physically harmed or if the psychological harm is ongoing or serious.

2. Review with students the places to get adult help: dean, nurse, counselor, mental health worker, administrator, teacher, parent, bus driver, security, etc.

3. Stress the ways in your school to get help without others knowing. For example, students can give a note to

their counselor when no one is around, talk to a teacher alone after class or during lunch, get some friends to go report an incident in a group (strength in numbers), use an anonymous report phone line, report something and ask to not have their name used.

VI. Summarative Statement

"We've talked about bullies and victims today, but remember bully-proofing isn't about the bullies. It's about creating a Caring Community and supporting each other. Each one of you will make decisions every day, every hour about whether you are going to choose the kind of behaviors or actions that will make you a part of our school's caring community or whether you will be a bystander and stand back, just hoping it doesn't happen to you next. It is up to you."

VII. **Homework**

Have students notice three caring behaviors they observe at school during the next week.

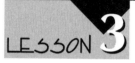

LESSON 3 Ha Ha So Strategies

Materials

♦ **Handout/Transparency 9J:** HA HA SO Strategies

♦ Overhead projector

Objectives

♦ Understand strategies to avoid victimization (HA HA SO)

♦ Understand differences between tattling and telling

Steps

I. Review Group Rules

   A. Ask student to review the group rules.

   1. Respect for self and others

   2. Participate—in your own way and style

   3. While sharing stories or experiences, do not mention any particular names of individuals or groups. Instead, say, "I know someone who . . . "

B. Remind students that bully-proofing will not eliminate the bullies or bullying behavior. The skills they are learning will help them stay out of the victim role and avoid being targeted by bullies. The *Bully-Proofing* program is intended to empower the majority of students who are not bullies. This majority is often silent and just watches while other peers or friends are picked on or hurt. Emphasize the challenge for students to help each other and not be silent bystanders. Stress that when enough people stand up for what is right, you will have a caring majority.

II. Present Strategies for the Victim. Use Handout/ Transparencies 9J and 9K if desired.

Handout/Transparency 9J
Handout/Transparency 9K

HA HA SO

H - Help	**H - Humor**	**S - Self-Talk**
A - Assert Yourself	**A - Avoid**	**O - Own It**

HELP

Discuss with the students when and how to get help from peers and adults. Explore with students the differences between tattling and telling. Make sure to cover the following points:

Tattling versus Telling		
Unimportant	vs.	Important
Harmless	vs.	Harmful or dangerous (physically or psychologically)
Can handle by self	vs.	Need help from an adult to solve
Mimicking someone else's business	vs.	Taking care of self
Accidental	vs	Getting help

Tips:

1. Brainstorm all of the sources of help: deans, counselors, teachers, nurse, etc.

2. Stress the different ways to get help—anonymously, in a group, dean's hotline.

ASSERT YOURSELF

Teach the students when it would be wise to use assertiveness and when it would not.

Tips:

1. Best strategy for a victim to start with.

2. Should not be used with severe bullying.

3. Victim should look bully straight in the eye.

4. Use "I" statements. (*Example:* "I don't like that.")

HUMOR

Teach the students how to use humor to de-escalate a situation.

Tips:

1. Have students practice using humor in a positive way.

2. Make sure the joke is about what the bully said, not about the bully.

AVOID

Teach the students how to walk away in order to avoid a bullying situation.

Tips:

1. Best for situations when victim is alone.

2. Avoid places where the bully hangs out.

3. Join with others rather than be alone.

SELF-TALK

Teach the students how to use their self-talk to maintain positive self-esteem during a bullying situation.

Tips:

1. Used as a means to keep feeling good about self.

2. Think positive statements about self and accomplishments.

3. Rehearse mental strategies to avoid being hooked by the bully.

OWN IT

Teach the students how to "own" the put-down or belittling comment in order to diffuse it.

Tips:

1. Agree with the bully and leave the situation.

2. Combine with humor strategies such as, "Yeah, this **IS** a bad haircut. The lawn mower got out of control this week-end."

3. Combine with assertive strategies such as, "Yes, I did fail

the test and I don't appreciate you looking at my paper."

Important Reminders:

1. Try these strategies in any order or numerous times.

2. It may take more than one strategy or more than one time to practice the strategies.

3. The Caring Community can remind each other of the strategies.

4. The Caring Community can help support the victim in using the strategies.

5. If the strategies aren't working, leave or disengage with the situation.

III. **Homework**

Ask students to practice using the HA HA SO strategies in their own life during the next week. Also have them observe strategies that their classmates and family members use and to come prepared to share one of their observations with the class.

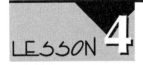

LESSON 4 Taking a Stand

Materials

♦ Chart paper

♦ Markers

♦ Note cards

Objectives

♦ Develop an understanding of empathy

♦ Understand the concept of "Taking a Stand"

Steps

I. Review HA HA SO Strategies

A. Ask students to share their homework observations about the use of the HA HA SO strategies.

II. Introduce and Explore the Concept of Empathy

A. Visualization: Ask students to get comfortable for a moment and imagine, with their eyes closed or open, the following scene:

You are walking into your first class. It is a fairly normal Monday morning. However, you see a new student walking down the hall, looking at each of the room numbers, then looking at locker numbers—looking rather desperate and confused while also trying to look cool. Later that day, you notice that he or she are struggling to figure out what line to get into at lunch. Because you have been new to a school, you may have experienced this. Take a moment to imagine how this person was feeling. Also imagine what the new student might be thinking.

Elicit feedback from students about the visualization. Make a strong statement connecting their imagined feelings to the word **empathy**.

B. Define empathy.

Empathy—the ability to participate in the feelings of another.

Discuss the difference between empathy and sympathy.

"Empathy is knowing how another person feels, and sympathy is feeling sorry for that person."

C. Ask students to share experiences they have had with empathy.

- Do you remember a time when someone felt empathy for you?

- Do you remember a time when you felt empathy for someone else?

D. Ask students why we need empathy in a caring community.

- Why is empathy important in a caring community?

- Is empathy something you can learn?

- What are some ways to show empathy?

III. Introduce and Explore the Concept of "Taking a Stand"

A. Ask students what they think the phrase "take a stand" means.

- What does it mean to take a stand?

- When is the last time you took a stand to do the right thing?

- Can you remember a time when someone took a stand and did something that helped you?

Define the phrase.

I should have stood up for Dustin when the whole math class was making a mockery of him. I felt really sorry for him.

Take a Stand: Any positive behaviors that support the caring community.

B. Have students generate a list of numerous ways to take a stand or to help others. Emphasize the small ways as well as large, risky, or very public ways of helping. It can be helpful to present students with incidences and have them generate all the ways to help that student. *Example:* "How could you take a stand to assist someone during his or her first day at a new school?"

C. Summarize students' comments and acknowledge them for the caring behaviors they shared.

IV. Activity: Make a Written Commitment to "Take a Stand"

A. Hand out an index card to each student. Have students put their name on one side. On the other side, ask them to write down at least one commitment they are willing to make to take a stand for what is right at school; one caring behavior which they are willing to concentrate or work on. *Examples*: be nice to sixth graders, help a friend who is being bullied, don't spread rumors.

B. Ask volunteers to read their commitments out loud. Facilitators collect cards and read some anonymously. Cards can be kept by the group facilitator and distributed at a later time to remind students of their commitment.

V. Summary: Remind Students of the Caring Community Concepts and Their Important Role in the School.

"Remember, bully-proofing isn't about the bullies. It's about people like you who care about others, and want (name of school) to be a fun, safe school. We know there are bullies in your classes who want to go on being bullies, but there are more of you who care about (name of school) and each other than there are of those who don't care for others. So, when you get together and take a stand to do the right thing, you move from being bystanders or a silent majority where the bullies have the power, to a caring community where <u>you</u> have the power. Don't be afraid to ask for help, to take a risk, and stand up for someone. At (school name) that's what people do for each other. We're glad you're a part of this great community."

CHART

H A N D O U T   9 A
Incident Report

Name: _____   Date: _____

Describe what happened: _____

_____

_____

_____

_____

_____

Your Feelings:

How did you feel during the incident? _____

_____

Why? _____

_____

What were the good choices and what were the bad choices in how you acted?

_____

_____

Controlling Yourself:

How much control did you feel you had over yourself during the incident?

_____

How do you usually calm yourself down? _____

_____

How are you calming yourself right now? _____

_____

Others' Feelings:

How do you think the other person was feeling during the incident? _____

_____

What things could you do now that would help them feel better? _____

_____

HANDOUT 9A (*continued*)

Planning:

What would you like to change about the way you handle these types of problems?

_____

_____

What would be some fair ways to solve this incident? _____

_____

_____

HANDOUT/TRANSPARENCY 9B
Sample Consent Form for Support/Skills Group

_____
Date

Dear Parent/Guardian:

I would like to invite your child to participate in a (Support/Skills) group at
_____ School. The purpose of the group is to help improve
your child's abilities in the areas of building self-esteem, social skills, assertive skills,
and communication.

The group will meet once a week for _____ weeks. The time of the sessions
will rotate weekly so that your student does not miss the same class continuously.
A permission slip is attached for you to sign and return so that your child can
participate. Please feel free to call me at _____ if you have any
questions.

Sincerely,

_____
Name and title of facilitator

Return to: _____   by _____

I/we the undersigned give my/our permission for my/our child

_____ to participate in a weekly skills group.

_____   _____
Signature of Parent(s) or Guardian   Date

Adapted with permission of authors. *Bully-Proofing Your School: A Comprehensive Approach for Elementary Schools (Second Editon),* Copyright, 2000.

HANDOUT 9C
Letter to Parents

_____
Date

To the parent(s) of _____:

Dear Parent(s):

The _____ School District want all children to feel safe while in the school environment. The bus ride to and from school is an important part of your child's school day. Everyone at _____ School is working toward safety on the bus and we would like you to join us in the effort.

This year we are planning several activities to extend the _____ Caring Community onto the buses. Bus drivers will be participating in our "I Caught You Caring" campaign and writing acknowledgments for students doing caring acts on the bus. There will be a weekly drawing of the acknowledgment forms and prizes for students who were recognized. The "I Caught You Caring" forms that are not chosen for prizes will be displayed on the "Caring Wall" outside the main office. Look for your son'/daughter's name on the wall next time you are in the school. Additionally, we will be rewarding the bus with the least referrals by giving **each** student on that bus a ticket to the _____ roller skating arena. We hope that students involved in positive behaviors on the bus will feel acknowledged for their positive leadership in our caring community.

Staff, students, parents, and community members will all need to participate in creating safer bus rides for _____ students. Please reinforce with your son/daughter that riding the bus is a privilege, and as an extension of the school day, it is important that the rules and behavioral expectations are the same. To get this conversation started, we have listed the existing bus rules below.

Bus Rules

Students must:
1. Follow the bus driver's directions the first time they are given.
2. Be seated whenever the bus door is closed.
3. Keep hands, feet, books, and objects to themselves.
4. Avoid getting involved in physical altercations or fights.
5. Refrain from bringing any weapons or facsimiles of weapons on the bus.
6. Avoid swearing, making rude gestures, teasing, or putting down other people.
7. Use classroom voices on the bus.
8. Avoid throwing anything off the bus or putting any part of your body outside the bus.
9. Refrain from smoking, chewing tobacco, eating, or drinking on the bus.
10. Avoid bringing anything alive or dangerous onto the bus.
11. Avoid bringing skateboards, roller skates, or roller blades onto the bus.

Thank You!

_____
Principal

H A N D O U T / T R A N S P A R E N C Y   9 D
Behavior Warning Form

_____
Name

_____
Bus Number

_____
Date

The problem that happened today was:

Disrespectful and rude behavior   _____

Not following the instructions of the driver   _____

Food on the bus   _____

Not in assigned seat   _____

Use of profanity   _____

Other: _____   _____

_____
Driver's Signature

_____
Student Signature

This section to be completed by the student

1. Describe the problem that happened today. _____

   _____

   _____

   _____

2. What could you have done differently? _____

   _____

   _____

   _____

Adapted with permission of authors. *Bully-Proofing Your School: A Comprehensive Approach for Elementary Schools (Second Edition),* Copyright, 2000.

H A N D O U T   9 E
I Caught You Caring

_____ **Caring Community**
Name of School

I, _____, would like to recognize the caring behavior

of _____. This person helped to make a safe and

caring school by: _____

_____

_____

_____

_____
Date

Thank you for being

a Caring Community Member!

HANDOUT 9F
New Student Parent Letter

_____
Date

Dear _____
Name of Parent/Guardian

We would like to take this opportunity to welcome you and your son/daughter into the _____ Caring Community. Our school has a strong
School Name
commitment to providing our students with a safe and caring environment in which to learn. We are currently implementing a school-wide program against bullying called "Bully-Proofing." It focuses on teaching students skills to avoid being victimized by bullying and empowers students to take a stand to help each other when they see friends or peers potentially being hurt by others.

This program will be most effective when the parental community, administration, staff, and students all share the belief that kindness and respect contribute to a positive environment which results in better academic success. Bullying and aggressive behaviors do not have a place at our school and will not be tolerated. On the other hand, acts of kindness will be recognized and rewarded.

Students and faculty have shown sincere efforts while participating in bully-proofing training sessions. These educational sessions have taught skills in how to deal with bullying situations, developing empathy for victims, ways to "Take a Stand," and creative problem solving. These learned skills help students take positive action when they see behaviors which are potentially harmful to others in our community.

Your child is invited to participate in some New Student Bully-Proofing Training Sessions to gain the knowledge and skills that have already been taught to other students in seventh and eighth grade. The sessions will begin in _____
Month
and meet four times during the _____. If you have any questions
Semester
or concerns about your child's participation in these groups, please contact

_____ at _____,
Contact Person   Phone Number

We appreciate your support. It is very important to us and to the success of the Caring Community at our school.

Sincerely,

_____
Name of Principal, Counselor, etc.

HANDOUT/TRANSPARENCY 9G
Bully-Proofing Guidelines

1. **Respect yourself and others.**

2. **Contribute to a healthy and safe learning environment.**

3. **Use empathy and extra effort to include others.**

4. **Take a stand for what is right.**

5. **Encourage creative and peaceful problem solving.**

6. **Follow all school rules.**

Types of Bullying Behaviors

Physical Aggression: Hitting, kicking, destroying property

Social Aggression: Spreading rumors, excluding from group, silent treatment

Verbal Aggression: Name calling, teasing, threatening, intimidating phone calls

Intimidation: Graffiti, a dirty trick, taking possessions, coercion

Written Aggression: Note writing, graffiti, slam books

Sexual Harassment: Comments or actions of a sexual nature which are unwelcome and make the recipient uncomfortable. *Examples:* rumors of a sexual nature, inappropriate touching, grabbing, comments about someone's body

Racial and Ethnic Harassment: Comments or actions containing racial or ethnic content which are unwelcome and make the recipient uncomfortable. *Examples:* ethnic jokes, racial name calling, racial slurs

HANDOUT/TRANSPARENCY 91
Normal Conflict versus Bullying

Normal Conflict	versus	Bullying
Equal power; friends	vs.	Imbalance of power; not friends
Happens occasionally	vs.	Repeated negative actions
Accidental	vs.	Purposeful
Not serious	vs.	Serious—threat of physical harm or emotional or psychological hurt
Equal emotional reaction	vs.	Strong emotional reaction on part of the victim
Not seeking power or attention	vs.	Seeking power, control
Not trying to get something	vs.	Trying to gain material things or power
Remorse—takes responsibility	vs.	No remorse—blames victim
Effort to solve the problem	vs.	No effort to solve problem

HA HA SO Strategies

Ha Ha So Strategies		
	STRATEGIES	**TIPS**
H **H**elp:	Seek assistance from an adult, friend, or peer when a potentially threatening situation arises. Seek help also if other strategies aren't working.	1. Brainstorm all of the sources of help at your school—deans, counselors, teachers, nurse. 2. Stress the different ways to get help—anonymously, in a group, dean's hotline.
A **A**ssert **Yourself:**	Make assertive statements to the bully addressing your feelings about the bully's *behavior.*	1. Should not be used with severe bullying. 2. Not as effective with group bullying. 3. Victim should look bully straight in the eye. 4. Use "I" statements. *Example:* "I don't like it when you pull on my backpack." 5. Make assertive statement and walk away. *Example:* "Stop talking about me behind my back."
H **H**umor:	Use humor to de-escalate a situation.	1. Use humor in a positive way. 2. Make the joke about what the bully said, not about the bully. 3. Make humorous statement and then leave the situation. 4. *Example:* When insulted about hairstyle, say "Gee, I didn't know you cared enough to notice."
A **A**void:	Walk away or avoid certain places in order to avoid a bullying situation.	1. Best for situations when victim is alone. 2. Avoid places where the bully hangs out. 3. Join with others rather than be alone.
S **S**elf-Talk:	Use positive self-talk to maintain positive self-esteem during a bullying situation.	1. Use as a means to keep feeling good about self. 2. Think positive statements about self and accomplishments. 3. Rehearse mental statements to avoid being hooked by the bully. *Examples:* "It's his problem," "She doesn't know what she's talking about," "I know I'm smart." 4. Use positive self-talk when practicing all strategies.
O **O**wn It:	"Own" the put-down or belittling comment in order to diffuse it.	1. Agree with the bully and leave the situation. 2. Combine with humor strategies such as, "Yeah, this **IS** a bad haircut. The lawn mower got out of control this weekend." 3. Combine with assertive strategies such as, "Yes, I did fail the test and I don't appreciate you looking at my paper."
Important Reminders:	1. Practice these strategies in any order, in any combination, or numerous times. 2. The Caring Community can remind each other of the strategies. 3. The Caring Community can help support the victim in using the strategies. 4. If the strategies aren't working, leave or disengage from the situation.	

HANDOUT/TRANSPARENCY 9K
Tattling versus Telling

Tattling	versus	Telling
Unimportant	vs.	Important
Harmless	vs.	Harmful or dangerous physically or psychologically
Can handle by self	vs.	Need help from an adult to solve
Purpose is to get someone in trouble	vs.	Purpose is to keep people safe
Behavior is accidental	vs.	Behavior is purposeful

Chapter
Ten

Conclusion

The Importance of the Caring Community

The concept of the caring majority is a powerful tool that has been ignored and underused in our schools. In a culture that values individuality and self-sufficiency, we must constantly remind ourselves and our students of the incredible power that is created when the majority of the people stand together for what is right.

Understanding the important shift that occurs when educators change their focus from the negative behaviors of a few to the positive, caring behaviors of the majority can create powerful change in our schools. The silent majority of students who have been standing by, watching, and waiting for an opportunity to make a difference is ready and able to become the true leaders of our schools. It is the responsibility of the adults to hold high expectations for these students and to share with them the power and skills necessary to make schools safe for everyone.

It is tempting to feel helpless in the face of the escalating violence that is taking place in our schools. By focusing our time, our energy, and our appreciation on the great majority of students who have a natural desire to be in a school where they feel safe and taken care of by each other, we unleash the incredible potential of the caring majority. Working together to maintain our schools as caring communities is crucial to ensuring that schools are the places they were meant to be—safe places where teachers can teach and students can learn.

References

AAUW Educational Foundation (1993). *Hostile Hallways: The AAUW survey on sexual harassment in America's schools.* Annapolis Junction, MD: Author.

APA Public Communications—Raising children to resist violence: What you can do (Electronic data tape). Available: Public Interest Directorate, American Psychological Association.

APA Public Communications—Violence on television (Electronic data tape). Available e-mail: public.affairs@apa.org

APA Public Communications—What makes kids care? (Electronic data tape). Available e-mail: public.affairs@apa.org

Bandura, A. (1969). *Principals of behavior modification.* New York: Holt, Rinehart.

Banks, R. (1997). *Bullying in schools.* (Report No. EDO-PS-97-17). Champaign, IL: Clearinghouse on Elementary and Early Childhood Education. (Eric Digest).

Batsche, G.M. & Knoff, H.M. (1994). Bullies and their victims: Understanding a pervasive problem in the schools. *School Psychology Review, 23 (2)*, 165–174.

Beane, A.L. (1999). *The bully-free classroom.* Minneapolis: Free Spirit Publishing.

Cotterell, J. (1996). *Social networks and social influences in adolescence.* New York: Routledge.

Craig, W.M. & Pepler, D.J. (1996). Peer processes in bullying and victimization: An observational study. *Exceptionality Education Canada, 5 (3,4), 81–95.*

Crick, N.R. & Bigbee, M.A. (1998). Relational and overt forms of peer victimization: A multi-informant approach. *Journal of Counseling and Clinical Psychology, 66 (2),* 337–347.

Crick, N.R. & Grotpeter, J.K. (1995). Relational aggression, gender, and social psychological adjustment. *Child Development, 66,* 710–722.

Eccles, J. S. (1991). Motivation and self-perceptions: Changes in adolescence. In R. M. Lerner, Peterson A. C. & J. Brooks-Gunn (Ed.), Encyclopedia of Adolescence (pp. 675–680). New York: Garland Publishing, Inc.

Elliott, D.S., Hamburg, B.A., & Williams, K.R. (eds.) (1998). *Violence in American schools.* Cambridge: Cambridge University Press.

Feminist Majority Foundation, (1997). What to do if you or someone you know is sexually harassed. www.feminist.org/911/harasswhattodo.html

Fried, P. & Fried, S. (1996). *Bullies & Victims.* New York: M. Evans and Company, Inc.

Garrity, C., Baris, M., & Porter, W. (2000). *Bully-proofing your child: A parent's guide.* Longmont, CO: Sopris West.

Greenbaum. S. (1989). *Set straight on bullies.* Malibu, CA: Pepperdine University Press.

Harris, L. & Associates (1993). *Violence in America's public schools: A survey of the American teacher.* New York: Metropolitan Life Insurance Company.

Hazler, R.J. (1996). Bystanders: An overlooked factor in peer on peer abuse. *The Journal for the Professional Counselor, 11 (2),* 11–22.

Hazler, R.J., Hoover, J.H., & Oliver, R. (1992). Student perceptions of victimization by bullies in school. *Journal of Humanistic Education and Development, 29,* 143–150.

Hoover, J.H. & Juul, K. (1993). Bullying in Europe and the U.S. *The Journal of Behavioral and Emotional Problems, 1 (2),* 25–29.

Hoover, J.H. & Oliver, R. (1996). *The Bullying Prevention Handbook.* Bloomington, IN: National Education Service.

Hoover, J.H., Oliver, R.L., & Hazler, R.J. (1992). Bullying: Perceptions of adolescent victims in the Midwestern USA. *School Psychology International, 13 (1),* 5–16.

Jaret, C. & Reitzes, D. (1999). The importance of racial-ethnic identity and social setting for blacks, whites, and multiracials. *Sociological Perspectives, 42,* (771–737).

Johnston, L.D., O'Malley, P.M. & Bachman, J.G. (1993). Monitoring the future study for goal 6 of the national education goals: A special report for the National Educational Goals Panel. Ann Arbor: University of Michigan's Institute for Social Research.

Keating, D.P. & Clark, L.V. (1980). Development of physical and social reasoning in adolescence. *Developmental Psychology, 16,* 23–30.

Kohlberg, L. (1984). *Essays on moral development: Vol: 2 The psychology of moral development.* San Francisco: Harper & Row.

Kohn, A. (1996). *Beyond discipline: From compliance to community.* Virginia: Association for Supervision and Curriculum Development.

Kuhn, D. (1991). Reasoning, higher-order in adolescence. In R.M. Lerner, A.C. Peterson & J. Brooks-Gunn (ed.), Encyclopedia of Adolescence (pp. 917–920). New York: Garland Publishing, Inc.

Lister, P. (1995, November). Bullies—the big new problem you must know about. *Redbook,* 117–119, 136, 138.

Miller, D. (1999). Racial socialization an racial identity: Can they promote resiliency for African American adolescents? *Adolescence, 34,* (403–501).

Nash, I. (1989, October 20). True extent of bullying hidden. *Times Educational Supplement,* p.5.

National Center for Education Statistics. (1995). *Student Victimization at school,* 1996 (National Household Education Survey: 93).

Nolin, M.J., Davies, E., Westat, Inc., Chandler, K., National Center for Educational Statistics, (1995). Student victimization at school http: nces.ed.gov/edstats/

Offer, D. & Boxer, A. M. (1991). Normal adolescent development: Empirical research findings. In M. Lewis (ed.), *Child and Adolecent Psychiatry* (pp. 266–275). Baltimore: Williams & Wilkins.

Olweus, D. (1991). Bully/victim problems among school children: Basic facts and effects of a school based intervention program. In D. Pepler & K. Rubin (eds.), *The development and treatment of childhood aggression.* Hillsdale, NJ: Erlbaum.

Olweus, D. (1992). Victimization by peers: Antecedents and long-term outcomes. In K.H. Rubin & J.B. Asendorf (Eds.), *Social withdrawal, inhibition, and shyness in childhood.* Hillsdale, NJ: Erlabaum.

Olweus, D. (1993a). *Bullying at school: what we know and what we can do.* Cambridge, MA: Blackwells.

Pepler, D.J. & Craig, W.M. (1995). Peer Processes in bullying and victimization: An observational study. *Exceptionality Education Canada, 5 (3,4),* 81–95.

Perry, D.G., Williard, J.C., & Perry, L.C. (1990). Peer's perceptions of the consequences that victimized children provide aggressors. *Child Development, 61,* 1310–1325.

Peterson, A.C., Silbereisen, R.K., & Sorensen, S. (1996). Adolescent development: A global perspective. In K. Hurrellmann & S.F. Hamilton (ed.), *Social Problems and Social Contexts in Adolescence* (pp. 3–39). New York: Walter de Gruyer, Inc.

Piaget, J. (1965). *The moral development of the child.* New York: Free Press.

Richards, M., Larson, R., & Casper, R. (1990). Weight and eating concerns among young adolescent boys and girls. *Journal of Adolescent Health Care, 11,* 203–209.

Rigby, K. (1996). *Bullying in schools & what to do about it.* Melborne, Australia: The Australian Council for Educational Research Ltd.

Rigby, K. (1998). Health effects of school bullying. *The Professional Reading Guide for Educational Administrators, 19 (2),* 35–38.

Ross, D.M., (1996). *Childhood bullying and teasing: what school personnel, other professionals and parents can do.* Alexandria, VA: American Counseling Association.

Samenow, S. (1989). *Before it's too late: why some kids get into trouble and what parents can do about it.* New York: Random House.

Shakesshaft, C., Barber, E., Hergenrother, Johnson, Y.M., Mandel, L.S., & Sawyer, J. (1995). Peer harassment in schools. *Journal for a Just and Caring Education, 1,* 30–44.

Simmons, R.G., Rosenberg, F., & Rosenberg M. (1973). Disturbance in the self-image at adolescence. *American Sociological Review, 38,* 553–568.

Smith, P.K. (1991). The silent nightmare: Bullying and victimization in school peer groups. *The Psychologist,* 4, 243–248.

Smith, P.K. & Sharp, S. (eds.) (1994). *School bullying: Insights and perspectives.* London: Routledge.

Stein, N., (1995). Sexual Harassment in School: The public performance of gendered violence. *Harvard Educational Review, 65 (2),* 145–162.

Stephens, R. (1998). Safe school planning. In D.S. Elliott, B.A. Hamburg, & K.R. Williams (eds.), *Violence in American Schools* (pp. 253–289). Cambridge, UK : Cambridge University Press.

Strauss, S. & Espeland, P., (1992). *Sexual harassment and teens.* Minneapolis, MN: Free Spirit Publishing Inc.

Tse, L. (1999). Finding a place to be: Ethnic identic exploration of Asian Americans. *Adolescence. 34,* (121–137).

Van Kammen, W.B. & Loeber, R. (1995). *Adolescents and their guns: Relationship to delinquency and victimization.* Presentation at the meeting of the American Society of Criminology, November 1995, Boston, MA.

Walker, H.M. & Grisham, F.M. (1997). Making schools safe and violence free. *Intervention in School and Clinic 32,* 199–204.

WGBY-TV, Stein, N., (1997). *Flirting or hurting?.* (Video-tape). (Available from GPN, Lincoln P.O. Box 80669, Lincoln, NE 68501.)

Whitney, I. & Smith, P.K. (1993). A survey of the nature and extent of bullying in junior/middle and secondary schools. *Educational Research, 35 (1),* 3–25.

Many books for children contain stories in which a character(s) is bullied. Much of the time the resolution includes aggressive retaliation. These stories may be humorous, but for purposes of teaching safe, non-aggressive responses to bullying behaviors, these stories lack efficacy. For this reason it is important to review books prior to having children read them. Search for books in which victims do not aggress against the bully, and/or bystanders take an active role in helping the targets of bullying. Another effective method is to read the stories with children and discuss the methods of intervention used by the victim(s) and bystander(s). The following books have been useful in teaching and reinforcing the bully-proofing concepts.

Books for Adolescents

Bosch, Carl. (1988). *Bully on the Bus*. Parenting Press.

> Several options are presented for handling a bullying situation on the bus. Readers choose an action, each of which is accompanied by an outcome. This provides readers with practice problem solving and seeing cause/effect relationships.

Canfield, Jack, Hansen, Mark Victor, and Kirberger, Kimberly. (1997). *Chicken Soup for the Teenage Soul*. Health Communications Inc.

> Inspirational, true stories and writings on family, friendship, difficult lessons, standing up for others, and other emotional lessons of adolescents. Helpful for day-starters, empathy development, and generating discussions regarding the caring school community concepts.

Canfield, Jack, Hansen, Mark Victor, and Kirberger, Kimberly. (1998). *Chicken Soup for the Teenage Soul II*. Health Communications Inc.

> See above.

Canfield, Jack, Hansen, Mark Victor, and Kirberger, Kimberly. (1998). *Chicken Soup for the Teenage Soul Journal*. Health Communications Inc.

> Journal starters intersperse with poems and inspirational writing on the topics of friendship, family, difficult lessons, standing up for others, and other emotional questions of adolescents.

Cohen-Posey, Kate. (1995). *How to Handle Bullies, Teasers and Other Meanies.* Rainbow Books

Excellent book with many strategies for dealing with bullying, prejudicial actions, and teasing.

Romain, Trevor. (1997). *Bullies are a Pain in the Brain.* Free Spirit.

Easy to read explanation of the bullying dynamics, dispels commons myths, and offers a number of non-aggressive strategies.

Romain, Trevor. (1998). *Cliques, Phonies and Other Baloney.* Free Spirit

A good, easy-to-read book describing cliques, "real" friends, popularity, and "Tips, Tricks and Helpful Hints" on friendship.

Zeier, Joan. (1993). *Stick Boy.* New York: Atheneum.

A sixth grade boy grows six inches and become the victim of bullying.

Books for Educators and Parents

Beane, Allan L. (1999). *The Bully-Free Classroom* Free Spirit.

A multitude of classroom activities for K–8 to assist classroom teachers with establishing a caring, safe classroom community. Lessons are practical, easy to implement, and effective for integrating the concepts of a caring school community.

Beland, K. *Second step.* Committee for Children, 2203 Airport Way South, Ste. 500, Seattle WA 92134, 1-800-634-4449.

A curriculum guide for teaching empathy problem solving and anger management from pre-school through eighth grade.

Borba, M. (1989). *Esteem builders.* Rolling Hills Estates, CA: Jalmar Press.

This self-esteem curriculum is designed for grades K–8, and presents specific ideas for improving student achievement and behavior as well as the overall school climate.

Canfield, Jack, and Wells, Harold. (1993). *100 Ways to Enhance Self-Concept in the Classroom.* Allyn & Bacon.

Easy to access activities and ideas for group or day starters, community or team building, and esteem-bolstering. Activities are fun, timeless reminders of ways to focus on positive assets in the classroom.

Freeman, Carol Goldberg. (1996). *Living with a Work in Progress: A Parents Guide to Surviving Adolescence.* National Middle School Association.

This is a humorous, easy-to-read book written by the mother of young teens. Included are specific ideas and strategies for limit-setting in both the social and schoolwork realms. Affectionate and humorous anecdotes and ideas are included in chapters such as "Schoolwork: Choosing Your Battles" and "Uncommon Traits: Snits, Zits, and Flammable Hair."

Garrity, Carla, Porter, William, Sager, Nancy, and Short-Camilli, Cam. (2000). *Bully-Proofing Your School: A Comprehensive Approach for Elementary Schools (Second Edition).* Sopris West.

A comprehensive, systemic climate change program for elementary school that is the forerunner to the middle school program. The book presents classroom sessions on the basics of the bullying dynamics, HA HA SO strategies to avoid victimization, caring majority concepts, and small group session outlines for children who bully or are chronically victimized.

Giannetti, Charlene C., and Sagarese, Margaret. (1997). *The Roller-Coaster Years: Raising Your Child through the Maddening Yet Magical Middle Years.* Broadway Books.

Written by two parents of middle school children, this book is a comprehensive resource for parents including ideas from experts as well as classroom teachers, parents, and adolescents themselves regarding ways to solve the common, often overwhelming, challenges of adolescence.

Goldstein, A. & Glick, B. (1987). *Aggression replacement training.* Champaign, IL: Research Press.

Presents a ten-week long training session for teachers or mental health staff to use for anger control with adolescents, specifically, but could be adapted for elementary age students. A guide to moral training is also included.

Goleman, D. (1995). *Emotional intelligence. New York: Bantam Books.*

Greenbaum, S., Turner, B., & Stephens, R. (1989). *Set straight on bullies.* Malibu, CA: Pepperdine University, National School Safety Foundation.

Presents statistics on bullying in the schools as well as guidelines for recognition of bullies and victims. Prevention strategies for changing the attitudes and actions of adults and students alike are provided.

Hoover, John H., and Oliver, Ronald. (1996). *The Bullying Prevention Handbook.* National Educational Service, 1996.

Kaufman, G. & Raphael, L. (1990). *Stick up for yourself: Teacher's guide.* Minneapolis, MN: Free Spirit Publishing.

A comprehensive guide to a ten-part course that correlates with the book by the same title. Blends self-esteem and assertiveness with activities for a full year in the classroom. Recommended for grades 4–8.

MacIver, Dan, and McCarroll, Les. (1996). *Initiatives, Games, and Activities—Middle School* Adventures in Education.

A thorough compilation of community and team building activities and initiatives.

McCoy, Elin. (1997). *What to Do When Kids are Mean to Your Child.* Readers Digest Parenting Guide Series.

An easy-to-read guide for parents including strategies for assisting children being victimized at school.

Peace Education Foundation, 1900 Biscayne Blvd., Miami, FL 33132-1025. (305) 576-5075.

An educational organization devoted to teaching children creative and nondestructive ways to handle conflicts. Curriculum guides, family support materials, and school-based training available.

Ross, Dorothea. (1996). *Childhood Bullying And Teasing.* American Counseling Association. Alexandria, Virginia.

A well researched book including information on the dynamics of bullying including in-depth chapters on sexual harassment and teasing. Ross includes prevention and intervention strategies for educators and parents.

Samenow, S. (1989). *Before it's too late: Why some kids get into trouble and what parents can do about it.* New York: Random House

This book describes the thinking patterns of antisocial children and shows parents how they might inadvertently be facilitating the antisocial behavior. Easy to read and understand, this book is full of good ideas for parents and professionals alike.

Schmidt, F. & Frideman, A. (1985). *Creative conflict solving for kids grades 4–9.* Miami, FL: Peaceworks.

Activities for use with the upper elementary grades.

Seligman, M. (1995). *The optimistic child.* New York: Harper Perennial.

Strauss, Susan, with Pamela Espeland. (1992). *Sexual Harassment and Teens.* Free Spirit, 1992.

A curriculum of many lessons designed to focus specifically on sexual harassment.

VIDEOS

Broken Toy. (1992). Summerhill Productions, 845 1/2 McIntire Avenue, Zanesville, OH 43701.

A 25-minute video that depicts a number of realistic scenarios in the life of a 12-year old boy who is ridiculed and physically assaulted at school. Not only is the home life of the victim portrayed, but the main bully's family is also depicted. While the story builds empathy for the victim, the content is dramatic. The ending, however, restores hope. The goal of this video is to build awareness and compassion in the bullies by showing them how much emotional damage their behavior can cause. For grades 5 and up. Preview before using.

Bully No More: Stopping the Abuse AIMS Multimedia. (1999) 26 minutes.

Discusses bullying with a wide variety of adolescents. Includes concepts regarding how to keep from being the target of a bully and what to do if you are a witness. Includes some fun animation.

Bullyproof. (1997). Future Wave, Inc., 105 Camino Teresa, Santa Fe, NM 87505. Fax: (505) 982-6460.

For younger children, a puppet show program is available that includes a portable stage, sound-track tape, curriculum, and supplies for creating a performance. For older children and teens, a rap and roll opera is available on video.

Don't Pick On Me! Sunburst. (1997). 20 minutes.

Video presents two well-acted vignettes of bullying incidences and the effective responses of the targets as well as bystanders. Bullying scenes include incidences of individual boy bullying and group intimidation by girls.

Flirting Not Hurting. WGBY-TV. (1997). 60 minutes.

Video presents segments defining sexual harassment, Title IX, and what to do if they are the target of sexual harassment. The final segment is suggestions for educators on the use of the program. Candid interviews of middle and high school students and a rapid pace makes this video interesting and real for students.

Hurting with Words: Understanding Emotional Violence and Abuse. Human Relations Media. (1997). 28 minutes.

Video describes emotional violence such as bullying, threats, intimidation, and their harmful effects. Concepts of emotional triggers, empathy, constructive criticism, and problem solving are presented. A teacher's guide is included.

Web Sites

www.pbs.org/seekingsolutions

www.teachingtolerance.org

www.sopriswest.com

www.education.unisa.edu.au/bullying/